The World of Thomas Wolfe

A SCRIBNER RESEARCH ANTHOLOGY

Martin Steinmann, Jr., GENERAL EDITOR

C. HUGH HOLMAN
University of North Carolina

The World of Thomas Wolfe

CHARLES SCRIBNER'S SONS
New York

Printed in the United States of America
Library of Congress Catalog Card Number 62-8483

Preface

Each Scribner Research Anthology is a collection of written sources upon a single historical, literary, or scientific topic—the Hungarian Revolt, Shakespeare's *Julius Caesar,* or extrasensory perception, for example. In addition to these sources, it contains (1) "Guide to Research," an account of the rationale and the methods of research and of research-paper writing, (2) an introduction to the topic of the anthology, (3) suggested topics for controlled research, and (4) suggested sources and topics for library research.

Each anthology is designed to serve two purposes. First, each gives the student access to important sources—texts, documents, letters, diaries, essays, for instance—on a given topic. Some of these sources are otherwise available in only a few libraries, some (manuscripts and historical documents) in only one. In any case, the collection as a whole is not otherwise available in one volume. Second, each anthology gives the student either all his sources for a controlled-research paper or some of them for a library-research paper. Each anthology can be valuable either for readings in courses in history, literature, science, or humanities or as the basis for a research paper in these or in other courses.

A controlled-research paper—a paper in which the student's search for sources is limited to, and in certain ways controlled by, those sources contained in one anthology—is not so noble an undertaking as a library-research paper. But it is often more successful—more rewarding for the student and easier for his instructor to teach effectively and judge fairly. Its advantages for both student and instructor are often considerable.

For the student, it sometimes provides sources unavailable in his school library. And it enables him to learn a good deal about research (selection, interpretation, and evaluation of sources; quotation and paraphrase; and documentation) without prior instruction in use of the library (and, incidentally, without overtaxing the facilities and the resources of his library and without loss of, or damage to, sources either irreplaceable or difficult and expensive to replace).

For the instructor, it permits focus of class discussion upon a limited set of topics. It enables him to track down the student's sources conveniently. And—perhaps the greatest advantage of all—it enables him to judge both conveniently and exactly how well the student has selected, interpreted, and evaluated his sources and how well he has quoted and paraphrased them.

In many schools, a controlled-research paper is either a preliminary to or a part of a library-research paper. A library-research paper is probably the most difficult paper that the student can be assigned to write. The problems that confront him are not simply those common to any paper—organization, paragraphing, and transitions, for instance—and those (already mentioned) common to all research papers. He has, in addition, the problem of using the library well—of, for example, using the card catalogue, periodical indexes, and other reference works. But, if the instructor assigns a controlled-research paper as a preliminary to or, as it were, an early part of a library-research paper, the student need not come to grips with all these problems at once.

Each Scribner Research Anthology is compiled according to the following editorial principles. Each source that is not anonymous is prefaced by a biographical note on its author. At the foot of the same page is a bibliographical note. Each source is reprinted exactly as it appears in the original except for (1) some typographical peculiarities, (2) explanatory notes, given in brackets, and (3) omissions, indicated by ellipses (". . ."). And, finally, for each source that has pagination in the original, page numbers are given in brackets within the source itself—thus: "**[320/321]**," where everything before the slash (and after the preceding slash, if any) is from page 320, and everything after the slash (and before the next slash, if any) is from page 321. For a source hitherto unpublished, no page numbers are given; and

the student who uses it should cite the page numbers of the Scribner Research Anthology. Footnotes to a source are given as in the original. Where the original pagination of a footnote is not evident, its page number precedes it in brackets.

MARTIN STEINMANN, JR.

Bingham Bay
Lake Gogebic
August, 1960

Guide to Research

THE IDEA OF RESEARCH

Research is the organized, disciplined search for truth; the aim of all research is to discover the truth about something. That thing may be a historical object like the Stonehenge monuments or a historical event like the Hungarian Revolt or the Battle of Waterloo. It may be a work of literature like Shakespeare's *Julius Caesar* or Miller's *Death of a Salesman*. It may be a recurring event like the motions of the planets or the circulation of the blood. Or it may be an experimentally repeatable phenomenon like behavior of rats in a maze or perception apparently unaccounted for by the five senses. Archeology, history, literary criticism and scholarship, astronomy, physiology, and psychology—these are some of the many divisions of research. Indeed, all the sciences—physical, biological, and social— and all other scholarly disciplines share this organized, disciplined search for truth.

The search for truth has often been confused with such aims as confirming prejudice, instilling patriotism, and praising friends and blaming enemies. The attempt to prove the preconceived conclusion *that* one college is superior to another, for example, is not research (though the attempt to discover *whether* one college is so superior is). Research is hostile to prejudice.

General Methods of Research. The best general method of research is first-hand observation. But this method is not always possible and, when it is possible, not always practical.

The best method to begin discovering the truth about something is to observe that thing and the circumstances surrounding it. To discover the truth about *Julius Caesar* or *Death of a Salesman*, get the play and read it, or go to the theatre and watch a performance. To discover the truth about the planets, observe them through your telescope. To discover the truth about the intelligence of rats, build a maze and run some rats through it.

This first-hand observation is not always possible, however. To discover the truth about the Battle of Waterloo, you can't observe the battle. The best that you or anyone else can do is to observe other persons' observations, the recorded observations of eye-witnesses: diaries, letters, and memoirs, for instance, of soldiers and generals who were in the battle. With more recent historical events—for example, the Hungarian Revolt—you are better off. You can watch films and listen to tape recordings. You may be able to interview people who were there. But these observations are still second-hand; and, on the whole, history can be observed only at second-hand. The sole exception is history that you have been part of. You may have fought in the Hungarian Revolt—though, if you did, you may be prejudiced.

Even when first-hand observation is possible, it is not always practical. You may have a copy of or tickets to *Julius Caesar* or *Death of a Salesman* but not know enough about the principles of dramatic criticism to interpret the play unaided. You may have a telescope but not know how to use it or, if you do, not know what to make of what you observe through it. You may have some rats but not know how to build a maze or, if you do, not know enough about animal psychology to run your rats through it properly. The best that *you* can do under these circumstances is to supplement whatever first-hand observations you can make with observations of the first-hand observations of other people better-trained or better-equipped than you. Read *Julius Caesar* or *Death of a Salesman* and also critics' interpretations of the play. Observe the planets, if you can, and read treatises on astronomy. Do what you can with your rats, and read reports of experiments with rats. After all, no one can master the special methods and come by the special equipment of all scholarly disciplines. Indeed, few people can do this with more than one discipline, and then not before they're thirty. But all people who want a liberal education should try to discover as much of the truth about as many scholarly disciplines as their abilities and their circumstances permit. Indeed, the achievement of this is what is meant by "a liberal education."

Primary and Secondary Sources. As the foregoing account of the general methods of research suggests, there is, ultimately, only one source of the truth about something—the thing, the event, or the phenomenon itself: the Stonehenge monuments, the Hungarian Revolt, or the Battle of Waterloo; the text of *Julius Caesar* or *Death of a Salesman;* the motions of the planets or the circulation of blood; extrasensory perceptions or rats running in a maze. Such a source is a *primary* source. And, in historical research, where the thing itself (the Hungarian Revolt or the Battle of Waterloo) cannot be observed at first hand, a report of an eyewitness or a film or a tape recording is also counted as a *primary* source. But any other second-hand source (an interpretation of *Julius Caesar* or *Death of a Salesman,* a treatise on astronomy, a report of an experiment with rats) is a *secondary* source.

A primary source is, of course, better. But, if a primary source is unavailable to you (if it is a book, perhaps your school library does not have it) or if you are not trained or equipped to use it (you don't know how to run rats through a maze or you have no telescope), then a secondary source must do. In any case, except for the most mature scientists and scholars, a good secondary source is useful and often indispensable.

It is worth noticing that being primary or being secondary is not an intrinsic characteristic of the source itself. It is, rather, a relationship that either exists or does not exist betweeen a given source and a given topic of research. Consequently, a given source may be primary in relation to one given topic but secondary in relation to another. Two examples may serve to make this important point clear. Edward Gibbon's *The Decline and Fall of the Roman Empire* (1776-1788) is a secondary source in relation to the topic of the Roman Empire but a primary source in relation to that of eighteenth-century English prose style or that of eighteenth-century historiography. Samuel Taylor Coleridge's *Lectures on Shakespeare* (1811-1812) is a secondary source in relation to the topic of Shakespeare's plays but a primary source in relation to that of nineteenth-century principles of dramatic criticism or that of Shakespeare's reputation.

It is worth noticing also that a given source may be primary or secondary in relationship to more than one topic. James Joyce's novel *A Portrait of the Artist as a Young Man* is a primary source in relation not only to the topic of the structure of *A Portrait of the Artist as a Young Man* (and dozens of other topics on the novel itself) but also to the topic of use of the stream-of-consciousness technique in twentieth-century fiction.

THE RESEARCH PAPER

A research paper is a paper giving the results of research, the methods by which they were reached, and the sources, primary or secondary, which were used. A research paper attempts to tell the truth about a topic, and also tells how and where this truth was discovered. As we have seen, the sources of a research paper may be either written sources (literary texts and historical documents, for example) or sources of other kinds (experiments, for example). Since a research paper written in school is almost always based upon written (printed) sources, we shall here discuss only that kind. A research paper based upon written sources may be either a library-research paper or a controlled-research paper. A library-research paper is a research paper for which your search for sources is limited to those sources contained in the libraries available to you; a controlled-research paper, to those sources contained in one anthology —to those contained in this volume, for example. Here we shall emphasize the latter kind.

Finding a Topic. The first step in writing a research paper based upon written sources, whether a library-research or a controlled-research paper, is finding a topic. We say "finding a topic" rather than "choosing a topic" because the process is more like finding a job than choosing a sandwich from a menu. Unless your instructor assigns you a topic, which he may do, you must look for one; and the one you find may not be just what you want but the best one that you can find. But, if you look long and carefully, you may find a topic that so well suits your interests, your capacities, and the time and the space at your disposal that your paper will almost surely be a success.

Finding a topic is the most important single step in writing a research paper, and the things that you should have in mind when looking for a topic are (1) your interests, (2) your capacities, and (3) the time and the space at your disposal. If you are interested in a topic, if you know something about the special methods of research that the topic requires, and if your topic is narrow enough to require no more time than you have for research and no greater development than you can give it in a paper of the length assigned you, then the paper that results will probably be satisfactory. For example, the topic of figures of speech in *Julius Caesar* may interest you greatly. But, if it does, you must ask yourself whether you know enough about figures of speech to do research on them and, if you do, whether this topic is narrow enough. Even the topic of metaphors in the play would be too broad for most

papers; metaphors in Brutus' soliloquies might be about right. In any case, before you take a topic for a paper, you should do some reading on that topic; otherwise, you won't know whether it is interesting, within your ability to handle, and within the scope of your assigned paper.

Once you think that you've found a topic, take great care in phrasing it. The best phrasing is a question or a series of closely related questions. Better than "The character of Brutus" is "To what extent is Brutus motivated by self-interest and to what extent by the public interest?" The latter is not only more narrow and more precise; it provides you with a criterion of relevance in selecting your sources. At the end of this volume, you will find a list of suggested topics, intended to call your attention to topics that might not occur to you. But these topics are suggestive rather than definitive or precise.

Finding Sources. Finding sources for a library-research paper and finding ones for a controlled-research paper, though different in several respects, are alike in certain others. Finding sources in the library requires knowledge of how to use the card catalogue, periodical indexes, special bibliographies, reserve shelves, and encyclopedias. Finding sources in this volume or a similar one does not. But, in either case, you must have a clear idea of what you are looking for; and you must be prepared to put up with a high ratio of looking to finding. In other words, you must have not only criteria of relevance but also a willingness to do a good deal of skimming and a good deal more of careful reading, some of it fruitless.

The basic criterion of relevance you provide by careful phrasing of your topic, a problem discussed in the preceding section. The other criteria you provide by making a preliminary or tentative outline —perhaps in the form of subtopics, perhaps in the form of questions. Such an outline is not to be used for your paper. The outline for your paper will probably be quite different and, in any event, cannot be made until after you find your sources and take your notes. This preliminary outline guides your research and, as we shall see, provides you with the subtopic headings necessary for your note-cards (see "Taking Notes," page *xi*).

Making Your Working Bibliography. Once you have found a promising source ("promising" because, though it seems to be relevant, it may turn out not to be) you want to make some record of it so that, once you have completed your search for sources, you can turn back to it, read it, and, if it turns out to be relevant, take notes on it. This record of promising sources is your *working* bibliography. It is so called for two reasons: first, because you work with it as you proceed with your research and the writing of your paper, adding promising sources to it and discarding irrelevant ones; and, second, because this designation distinguishes it from your final bibliography, which appears at the very end of your research paper and contains only sources actually used in the paper. For a controlled-research paper, your working bibliography may be nothing more elaborate than a series of check marks in the table of contents of your research anthology or a list of page numbers. For a library-research paper, however, you need something quite different.

A working bibliography for a library-research paper is a collection of three-by-five cards each representing a promising source and each containing full information about that source. Once you have completed your research, written your paper, and discarded all promising but (as they turned out) irrelevant sources, this bibliography is identical with your final bibliography. Having a separate card for each source enables you to add and to discard sources easily and to sort and arrange them easily in any order you please. Eventually, when this bibliography becomes identical with your final bibliography, you will arrange sources alphabetically by authors' last names. Having full information about each source on its card enables you

to turn back to it easily—to locate it in the library without first looking it up again. You find this information in the card catalogue, periodical indexes, or other bibliographical aids; or, when browsing through the shelves or the stacks of the library and coming upon a promising source, you find it in or on the source itself—for example, on the spine and the title page of a book.

If the source is a *book,* you should put the following information on the three-by-five working-bibliography card:

(1) the library call number,
(2) the author's (or authors') full name (or names), last name first for the first author,
(3) the title of the book,
(4) the name of the city of publication,
(5) the name of the publisher (*not* the printer), and
(6) the year of publication (often found on the other side of the title page).

See the example of such a card on the opposite page (note the punctuation carefully).

If the source is a *periodical article,* you should put the following information on the three-by-five working-bibliography card:

(1) the author's (or authors') full name (or names),
(2) the title of the article,
(3) the name of the periodical,
(4) the volume number,
(5) the week, the month, or the season of publication, together with the year, and
(6) the page numbers covered by the article.

See the example of such a card on the opposite page (note the punctuation carefully).

These two forms take care of the two standard cases. For special cases—such things as books with editors or translators as well as authors, books published in several editions or in several volumes, and daily newspapers—see any good handbook of composition.

860.3
J23
Jones, John A., and William C.
Brown. <u>A History of
Serbia</u>. New York: The
Rowland Press, Inc., 1934.

WORKING-BIBLIOGRAPHY CARD FOR A BOOK

Smith, Harold B. "Fishing
in Serbian Waters." <u>Journal
of Balkan Sports</u>, <u>VII</u>
(May, 1936), 26-32.

WORKING-BIBLIOGRAPHY CARD FOR A PERIODICAL ARTICLE

Taking Notes. Once you have found sources, entered them in your working bibliography, read them, and found them relevant, taking notes requires your exactly following a standard procedure if your notes are going to be useful to you when you come to write your paper. An extra five minutes given to taking a note correctly can save you a half hour in writing your paper. Here is the standard procedure:

(1) Take all notes on four-by-six cards. Never use notebooks, loose sheets of paper, or backs of old envelopes.

(2) Limit each note to information on a single subtopic of your preliminary outline *and* from a single source. It follows from this that you may have many cards on the same subtopic and many cards from the same source but that you may never have one card on more than one subtopic or from more than one source.

(3) On each card, in addition to the note itself, put

  (a) the appropriate subtopic heading in the upper left-hand corner.

  (b) the name of the source (usually the author's last name will do) in the upper right-hand corner, and

  (c) the page number (or numbers) of that part (or those parts) of the source that you have used in taking your note. If you have used more than one page, indicate your page numbers in such a way that, when you come to write your paper, you can tell what page each part of the note comes from, for you may not use the whole note.

(If you follow these first three rules, you will be able, when you come to outline and to organize your paper, to sort your notes in any way you please (by subtopic, for example) and to arrange them in any order you please. Such flexibility is impossible if you take your notes in a notebook. If you follow the third rule, you will also be able to document your paper—write footnotes, for example—without again referring to the sources themselves.)

(4) In taking the note itself, paraphrase or quote your source or do both; but do only one at a time, and use quotation very sparingly.

Paraphrase and quotation require special care. Anything between paraphrase and quotation is not acceptable to good writers: you either paraphrase or quote, but do nothing in between. To paraphrase a source (or part of a source) is to reproduce it in words and word orders substantially different from the original. When you paraphrase well, you keep the sense of the original but change the language,

retaining some key words, of course, but otherwise using your own words and your own sentence patterns. To quote a source (or part of a source) is to reproduce it exactly. When you quote well, you keep both the sense and the language of the original, retaining its punctuation, its capitalization, its type face (roman or italic), and its spelling (indeed, even its misspelling).

Omissions and additions require special care. If, when quoting, you wish to omit some of the original, you may do so only if the omission does not change the sense of the original (never leave out a "not," for example!) *and* if it is indicated by ellipses (three spaced periods: ". . ."). If you wish to add something to the original, you may do so only if the addition does not change the sense of the original (never add a "not"!) *and* it is indicated by square brackets. The most usual additions are explanations ("They [i.e., the people of Paris] were alarmed") and disclaimers of errors in the original, indicated by the Latin *"sic,"* meaning "thus" ("Colombis [*sic*] discovered America in 1592 [*sic*]"). You must, of course, carry these ellipses and square brackets from your note-cards to your paper. And, if you type your paper, brackets may be a problem, for most typewriter keyboards do not include them. If your keyboard does not, you may do one of two things—either use the slash ("/") and underlining ("___" and "‾‾") in such a way as to produce a bracket ("⌐" and "⌐") or draw brackets in with a pen. In any event, don't substitute parentheses for brackets.

In your paper, quotations no longer than three or four lines are to be enclosed within a set of quotation marks and run into your text; longer ones are to be set off from the text, without quotation marks, by indention from the left-hand margin and, especially in typewritten copy, by single-spacing. But never use either of these devices unless the language is exactly that of the original.

Your usual treatment of a source should be paraphrase; use quotation only if the

Fly-fishing   Smith

Smith says that fly-fishing is a method of fishing used chiefly by wealthy Serbians and foreign tourists, that the flies used are generally imported from Scotland, and that "Serbian trout are so snobbish that they won't glance [27/28] at a domestic fly."

[Query: How reliable is the information in this rather facetious article?]

NOTE-CARD

language of the original is striking (strikingly good or strikingly bad), if it is the very topic of your research (as in a paper on Shakespeare's style), or if it is so complex (as it might be in a legal document) that you don't want to risk paraphrasing it.

Let us look at the sample note-card on the opposite page. The topic of research is methods of fishing in Serbia; the subtopic that the note deals with is fly-fishing in Serbia; the source is Harold B. Smith's article "Fishing in Serbian Waters," from the *Journal of Balkan Sports* (see the second of the two working-bibliography cards on page *xi*).

Note the subtopic heading ("Fly-fishing") in the upper left-hand corner; the name of the source, abbreviated to the author's last name ("Smith"), in the upper right-hand corner; the page numbers ("[27/28]"), indicating that everything, both paraphrase and quotation, up through the word "glance" is from page 27 and that everything after that word is from page 28; the sparing and appropriate use of quotation; and the bracketed query, to remind the note-taker that he must use this source with caution.

Writing the Paper. Many of the problems of writing a research paper based upon written sources—organization, the outline, the thesis paragraph, topic sentences, transitions, and the like—are problems of expository writing generally. Here we shall discuss only those problems peculiar to such a paper. Two of these problems—paraphrase and quotation—we discussed in the preceding section. Two others remain: reaching conclusions and avoiding the scissors-and-paste organization.

When you come to make the outline for your paper and to write your paper, you will have before you three things: (1) your *preliminary* outline, containing ordered subtopics of your topic; (2) your working bibliography; and (3) your note-cards. These are the *immediate* results of your research; they are not the *final* results. They are only the raw material out of which you must fashion your paper. At best, they are an intermediate stage between finding your topic and making your final outline. The preliminary outline will not do for the final outline. The working bibliography will almost certainly require further pruning. And the note-cards will require sorting, evaluation, organization, pruning, and exercise of logic and common sense. All this needs to be done, preferably before you make your final outline and begin to write your paper, though almost inevitably some of it will remain to bedevil you while you are writing it. To put the matter in another way, you are, with these things before you, a Sherlock Holmes who has gathered all his clues but who has reached no conclusions from them, who has not come to the end of his search for truth. You must discard irrelevant clues, ones that have no bearing on the questions that you want answered. You must arbitrate the claims of conflicting or contradictory clues. You must decide which one of several probable conclusions is the most probable.

Once you have reached your conclusions, you must organize your paper and set forth this organization in your final outline. Organization and the outline are, of course, problems common to all expository writing. But a problem peculiar to the research paper is avoiding the scissors-and-paste organization—avoiding a paper that looks as though you had cut paraphrases and quotations out of your note-cards, pasted them in columns on paper, and connected them only with such phrases as "Jones says" and "On the other hand, Brown says." Such an organization is the result of a failure to reach conclusions (with the consequence that there is nothing but "Jones says" to put in between paraphrases and quotations); or it is a failure to see the necessity of giving the conclusions reached *and* the reasoning by

which they were reached (with the consequence that, though there is something to put between paraphrases and quotations, nothing is put there, and the reader is left to write the paper for himself).

Documenting Your Paper. To document your paper is to give the source of each paraphrase and quotation that it contains, so that your reader can, if he wishes to, check each of your sources and judge for himself what use you have made of it. To give the source is usually to give (1) either the information that you have about that source in your working bibliography (except that the name of the publisher of a book is usually not given) or the information that accompanies each source in a research anthology *and* (2) the information about page numbers that you have in your notes. This information you may give either formally or informally, as your instructor decides.

Formal documentation is given in footnotes. For a full discussion of footnotes, see any good handbook (one cheap and widely accepted one is *The MLA Style Sheet*). The form of footnotes is similar to, but not identical with, the form of bibliographical entries. With these three sample footnotes, compare the two sample working-bibliography cards on page *xi*:

[1] John A. Jones and William C. Brown, *A History of Serbia* (New York, 1934), p. 211.
[2] Harold B. Smith, "Fishing in Serbian Waters," *Journal of Balkan Sports*, VII (May, 1936), 27.
[3] Smith, pp. 27-28.

Informal documentation is given in the text of the paper, usually parenthetically, as in this example:

Fly-fishing in Serbia is chiefly a sport of wealthy Serbians and foreign tourists (Harold B. Smith, "Fishing in Serbian Waters," *Journal of Balkan Sports*, VII [May, 1936], 27), though in some mountain districts it is popular among the peasants (John A. Jones and William C. Brown. *A History of Serbia* [New York, 1934], p. 211). The flies used are generally imported from Scotland; indeed, Smith facetiously adds, "Serbian trout are so snobbish that they won't glance at a domestic fly" (pp. 27-28).

As this example suggests, however, informal documentation can be an annoying distraction. It probably works out best in papers that use only a few sources. In such papers, there are few occasions for long first-references to sources: for example, "(Harold B. Smith, "Fishing in Serbian Waters," *Journal of Balkan Sports,* VII [May, 1936], 27)." But there are many occasions for short succeeding-references: for example, "(Smith, pp. 27-28)" or "(pp. 27-28)." Occasionally, informal documentation may be profitably combined with formal, as in a paper about Shakespeare's *Julius Caesar.* In such a paper, references to the play might well be given informally —for example, "(III.ii.2-7)"—but references to critics formally.

How many footnotes (or parenthetical documentations) do you need in your paper? The answer is, of course, that you need as many footnotes as you have paraphrases or quotations of sources, unless you group several paraphrases or quotations *from the same page or consecutive pages of a given source* in such a way that one footnote will do for all. One way to do this grouping—almost the only way— is to introduce the group with such a sentence as "Smith's views on fly-fishing are quite different from Brown's" and to conclude it with the raised numeral referring to the footnote. Your reader will understand that everything between the introductory sentence and the numeral comes from the page or the successive pages of the source indicated in the footnote.

Making Your Final Bibliography. Your paper concludes with your final bibliography, which is simply a list of all the sources—and only those sources—that you actually paraphrase or quote in your paper. In other words, every source that you give in a footnote (or a parenthetical documentation) you include in your final bibliography; and you include no other sources (inclusion of others results in what is unfavorably known as "a padded bibliography"). The form for entries in your final bibliography is identical with that for ones in your working bibliography, given above. You should list these sources alphabetically by authors' last names or, if a source is anonymous, by the first word of its title, but not by "a," "an," or "the." For example:

BIBLIOGRAPHY

Jones, John A., and William C. Brown, *A History of Serbia.* New York: The Rowland Press, Inc., 1934.

"Serbian Pastimes." *Sports Gazette,* XCI (October 26, 1952), 18-19, 38, 40-42.

Smith, Harold B. "Fishing in Serbian Waters." *Journal of Balkan Sports,* VII (May, 1936), 26-32.

MARTIN STEINMANN, JR.

Contents

v   PREFACE

vii   GUIDE TO RESEARCH

1   INTRODUCTION

Part One: WOLFE SPEAKS

THOMAS WOLFE, from
6   Letter to His Mother, May, 1923

THOMAS WOLFE
9   *The Story of a Novel*

THOMAS WOLFE, from
33   No Door: A Story of Time and the Wanderer

CLIFTON FADIMAN
37   The Wolfe at the Door

Part Two: WOLFE'S WRITING METHODS

MAXWELL E. PERKINS, from
42   Thomas Wolfe

EDWARD C. ASWELL, from
45   A Note on Thomas Wolfe

FLOYD C. WATKINS, from
49   *Thomas Wolfe's Characters: Portraits from Life*

Part Three: REVIEWS OF *LOOK HOMEWARD, ANGEL*

BASIL DAVENPORT
54   C'est Maître François

C. HUGH HOLMAN, from
57   The Loneliness at the Core

PAMELA HANSFORD JOHNSON, from
60   Thomas Wolfe and the Kicking Season

Part Four: WOLFE'S STYLE

PAMELA HANSFORD JOHNSON, from
64   The Style

W. M. FROHOCK, from
69   Thomas Wolfe: Of Time and Neurosis

BERNARD DeVOTO, from
72 *The World of Fiction*

FLOYD C. WATKINS
75 Rhetoric in Southern Writing: Wolfe

MAURICE NATANSON
78 The Privileged Moment: A Study in the Rhetoric of Thomas Wolfe

Part Five: THE CRITICS SPEAK

BERNARD DeVOTO
86 Genius Is Not Enough

BERNARD DeVOTO
91 [Afterword]

JOHN PEALE BISHOP, from
92 The Sorrows of Thomas Wolfe

JOSEPH WARREN BEACH, from
96 Thomas Wolfe: Discovery of Brotherhood

BELLA KUSSY
101 The Vitalist Trend and Thomas Wolfe

EDGAR JOHNSON, from
112 Thomas Wolfe and the American Dream

EDWIN BERRY BURGUM, from
115 Thomas Wolfe's Discovery of America

HERBERT MULLER, from
120 *Thomas Wolfe*

PAMELA HANSFORD JOHNSON, from
130 *Hungry Gulliver: A Critical Study of Thomas Wolfe*

MAXWELL GEISMAR, from
133 A Cycle of Fiction

W. M. FROHOCK
136 [Wolfe and the National Neurosis]

HENRY STEELE COMMAGER, from
139 *The American Mind*

WALTER FULLER TAYLOR
141 Thomas Wolfe and the Middle-Class Tradition

WILLIAM F. KENNEDY, from
149 Economic Ideas in Contemporary Literature—The Novels of
      Thomas Wolfe

BLANCHE HOUSMAN GELFANT, from
153 The City as Symbol

LOUIS D. RUBIN, JR., from
157 The Time of Thomas Wolfe

ROBERT E. SPILLER, from
164   Full Circle

MALCOLM COWLEY
167   Thomas Wolfe

C. HUGH HOLMAN, from
175   *Thomas Wolfe*

J. B. PRIESTLEY, from
179   *Literature and Western Man*

181   SUGGESTED TOPICS FOR CONTROLLED RESEARCH

183   SUGGESTED TOPICS FOR LIBRARY RESEARCH

187   NOTE ON THE AVAILABILITY OF THE PRINCIPAL WORKS OF THOMAS WOLFE

Introduction

When the twenty-nine year old Thomas Wolfe published *Look Homeward, Angel,* he burst upon the literary scene with sudden and spectacular force. This first novel re-created the world of childhood and adolescence with great accuracy and intensity but often in sprawling profusion. Although questions were raised about Wolfe's intensely autobiographical subject matter, his verbose, rhetorical style, and his tendency toward formlessness, they were muted in the general expression of admiration for his obvious, unique, and highly personal talent. Sinclair Lewis, in accepting the Nobel Prize for Literature in 1930, saw Wolfe as a "Gargantuan creature with great gusto for life," and praised him as a young man of tremendous promise.

Then followed six years in which Wolfe groped agonizingly, striving for a form for his second novel. During these years he published in *Scribner's Magazine* a series of short novels that are among his most successful creations; but the "big book" on which he was struggling with the aid of his editor, Maxwell E. Perkins, of Charles Scribner's Sons, achieved publishable form as *Of Time and the River* only in 1935. Upon its publication came a series of critiques of Wolfe's methods and talent that raised serious issues about his accomplishments. In 1936 he published a long essay, *The Story of a Novel,* a remarkably frank and self-revealing account of the writing of *Of Time and the River* and of his artistic ideals and literary methods. To many, notable among them being Bernard DeVoto, this essay demonstrated what they had suspected: that Wolfe had genius but lacked the control and skill that could convert that genius into works of art. During the remaining two years of his short life, he published only a volume of short stories; but a new editor, Edward Aswell, of Harper and Brothers, extracted two posthumous novels and a second volume of short stories and sketches from the mass of manuscript that Wolfe left on his death.

All serious novelists attempt to represent in fiction their visions of reality, to make palpable to their readers some portion of their private worlds. In the case of a writer whose ostensible subject is as plainly himself as Wolfe's is, picturing that private world seems to be his major —indeed, almost sole—intent. But such a view of Wolfe's work is deceptively simple. His world, like almost everything about his life and his art, had two elements that were in opposition and a third that tended to reconcile the paradox.

On one level Wolfe's world was the very literal, immediate world of the 1920s and 1930s, a world presented in his fiction through objects, actions, persons, and events apparently so directly transcribed from life that their originals greeted them with angry recognition. This world is a social context usually described with great accuracy and directness but sometimes presented with satiric exaggeration. On the other hand, there was the world of his inner self, a world of consciousness, of impressions, of emotions, of nostalgic memories, brooded over by a sense of the inexorable passage of "dark time." This world of the self Wolfe articulated in ways that proved to be powerfully effective— and affective—to many readers, particularly the young. These two worlds were in conflict: the self in its insulated "dream of time" was surrounded by but found no door by which to enter the social context that constituted its milieu. In his early work Wolfe seemed content to let these two contradictory worlds co-exist, but by 1935 he began to attempt a reconciliation through a national vision, a kind of racial idealism realizing the democratic dream. In this larger world the self and the social world could be merged in an expression of the national ideal, as Whitman's self was: "One's self I sing, a simple separate person,/ Yet utter the word Democratic, the word En-Masse." Thus the world of Thomas Wolfe is actually three worlds— self, society, nation—and the problem of his art was that of successfully merging the three into a unity.

It is possible also to look at Wolfe's three worlds as being the actual, specific world of people, buildings, economic problems—the troubled world of the depression in the United States—in which he lived; the inner self, groping for meanings, trying to understand itself and to establish meaningful relations with others, the private world, what he called "the buried life"; and the world of the artist where, by various strategies and devices he attempted to fuse the two into a permanent expression of something significant about life.

Another way of approaching the problem of Wolfe's effort to realize his world in fiction is to distinguish three elements in a writer's work: his *talent*, which includes his technical skills, literary conventions, and linguistic aptitudes; his *subject*, which is the matter that his talent works upon as action, story, characters, structure of images, or pattern; and, finally, his *theme*, which is the end-product, the often nonconceptualized intention, which is realized through the play of *talent* upon *subject*. I am following—from afar off and with much variation—Robert Penn Warren's assertion that "the subject of *Paradise Lost* is the story of the Fall of Man, the story of what happened to Adam and Eve. But the theme is the nature of justice, the relation of human will to Divine Will, the relation of Good to Evil. . . . It is conceivable that Milton might have used another subject, though probably one not as effective, for the vehicle of his theme."* In a similar way we might say that Thomas Wolfe's *theme* is the expression of the national ideal or character, that his *subject* is himself and the imme-

diate world around him, and that his *talent* is the uniquely effective use of language by which he expressed this theme through this subject. On the other hand, Wolfe's theme might also be considered to be loneliness or time or death; and other views of his talent might be taken; but his subject, however, remains remarkably himself and his personal experiences.

With the publication of *The Story of a Novel* the chief critical issues about Wolfe's work were established—indeed, they are implicitly present in the essay itself. This controlled-research anthology is, therefore, built around that primary document. In an ideal sense, *Look Homeward, Angel*—the most satisfactory of his long novels—is equally a center for this anthology, for even an elementary understanding of Wolfe's work must rest upon this novel. In the suggested topics for research I have indicated several areas involving this novel. Also included are a selection from his short novel, *No Door*, to illustrate his rhetorical, "poetic" style, and Clifton Fadiman's delightful and startlingly accurate parody, which describes by exaggeration some very real characteristics of Wolfe's work.

I have let Perkins and Aswell speak directly on the question of how Wolfe worked—and how they worked with him —and I have added a factual segment by Floyd C. Watkins that shows Wolfe's use of material out of his immediate experience. I have also brought together three reviews of *Look Homeward, Angel* that cover thirty years of Wolfe criticism. This section is followed by a selection of comments on Wolfe's style, ranging from Watkins' high praise to DeVoto's assertion that it is no style at all. Finally in the largest section are assembled a number of critical statements on Wolfe's methods, his themes, his subject matter, his use of time, his social purposes, and other aspects of his work. Although several of these essays are given in full, in many cases I have selected

---

* "Literature as a Symptom," *Who Owns America?*, ed. Herbert Agar and Allen Tate (Boston, 1936), pp. 268-269. The idea of *talent* is my addition to Warren's dichotomy.

from general essays or books extracts on particular issues. Both in the section on his style and in the section of critical statements the arrangement has been chronological. I believe that significant critical judgments are passed in these two sections on the major issues that Wolfe raised in *The Story of a Novel,* but I have left it to the student to discover them for himself, for in the search and in the discovery I think the student will learn something about Wolfe and writing—and perhaps even about himself.

Much has been written about Wolfe. Some of it has been extravagant praise; some has been unreasonable attack. I have attempted to avoid these extremes. The people represented in this anthology have said significant things about Wolfe's work, I believe, and their judgments, however they may differ, have rested upon careful readings of the text and not merely upon an emotional response or a personal sympathy or antipathy. No attempt has been made to represent all the aspects and attitudes of the critics of Wolfe. In particular I have excluded biographical studies, studies identifying characters and events (with one notable exception), studies of

literary influences on Wolfe, and (with the exception of DeVoto's "Genius Is Not Enough") studies that have been frequently anthologized. I believe that the fresh and relatively long selections by Bella Kussy, Pamela Hansford Johnson, Herbert Muller, Walter Fuller Taylor, Louis D. Rubin, Jr., Maurice Natanson, and Malcolm Cowley represent a disciplined and lively criticism that takes Wolfe seriously as an artist.

In this introduction I have suggested some broad approaches to the problems of Wolfe's representations of his world; in the suggested topics for research I have given a number of specific topics for investigation. I would remind you, however, that Thomas Wolfe, when he was an undergraduate at the University of North Carolina, came under the influence of a philosophy teacher, Horace Williams (the "Vergil Weldon" of *Look Homeward, Angel*), who taught him that asking the right question was a door to the truth quite as important as knowing the right answer. It is my hope that Wolfe and these critics will lead you to ask some of the right questions about literature—as well as find some of the right answers.

PART ONE

WOLFE SPEAKS

Letter to His Mother, May, 1923*

THOMAS WOLFE (1900-1938) wrote this letter to his mother, Julia Elizabeth Wolfe, very near the end of his third year at Harvard, where he was studying playwriting in George Pierce Baker's "47 Workshop" drama course. The preceding year he had received a Master of Arts degree in English literature.

. . . .
. . . I know this now: I am inevitable. I sincerely believe the only thing that can stop me now is insanity, disease, or death. The plays I am going to write may not be suited to the tender bellies of old maids, sweet young girls, or Baptist Ministers but they will be true and honest and courageous, and the rest doesn't matter. If my play goes on I want you to be prepared for execrations upon my head. I have stepped on toes right and left—I spared Boston with its nigger-sentimentalists no more than the South, which I love, but which I am nevertheless pounding. I am not interested in writing what our pot-bellied members of the Rotary and Kiwanis call a "good show"—I want to know life and understand it and interpret it without fear or favor. This, I feel is a man's work and worthy of a man's dignity. For life is not made up of sugary, sticky, sickening Edgar A. Guest sentimentality, it is not made up of dishonest optimism, God is *not* always in his Heaven, all is *not* always right with the world. It is [49/50] not all bad, but it is not all good, it is not all ugly, but it is not all beautiful, it is life, life, life— the only thing that matters. It is savage, cruel, kind, noble, passionate, selfish, generous, stupid, ugly, beautiful, painful, joyous,—it is all these, and more, and it's all these I want to know and, by God, I shall, though they crucify me for it. I will go to the ends of the earth to find it, to understand it, I will know this country when I am through as I know the palm of my hand, and I will put it on paper, and make it true and beautiful.

I will step on toes, I will not hesitate to say what I think of those people who shout "Progress, Progress, Progress"—when what they mean is more Ford automobiles, more Rotary Clubs, more Baptist Ladies Social unions. I will say that "Greater Asheville" does not necessarily mean "100,000 by 1930," that we are not necessarily 4 times as civilized as our grandfathers because we go four times as fast in automobiles, because our buildings are four times as tall. What I shall try to get into their dusty little pint-measure minds is that a full belly, a good automobile, paved streets, and so on, do not make them one whit better or finer,—that there is beauty in this world,—beauty even in this wilderness of ugliness and provincialism that is at present our country, beauty and spirit which will make us men instead of cheap Board of Trade Boosters, and blatant pamphleteers. I shall try to impress upon their little craniums that one does not have to be a "highbrow" or "queer" or "impractical" to know these things, to love them, and to realize they are our common heritage, there for us all to possess and make a part of us. In the name of God, let us learn to be men, not monkies.

*Thomas Wolfe, from a letter to his mother, May, 1923, *Thomas Wolfe's Letters to His Mother Julia Elizabeth Wolfe*, ed. John Skally Terry (New York: Charles Scribner's Sons, 1943), pp. 48-53. Copyright 1943 Charles Scribner's Sons. Used by permission of the publisher.

When I speak of beauty I do not mean a movie close-up where Susie and Johnnie meet at the end and clinch and all the gum-chewing ladies go home thinking husband is not so good [50/51] a lover as Valentino. That's cheap and vulgar. I mean everything which is lovely, and noble, and true. It does not have to be sweet, it may be bitter, it does not have to be joyous, it may be sad.

When Spring comes I think of a cool, narrow back yard in North Carolina with green, damp earth, and cherry trees in blossom. I think of a skinny little boy at the top of one of those trees, with the fragrant blooms about him, with the tang of the sap in his nose, looking out on a world of back yards, and building his Castles in Spain. That's beauty, that's romance. I think of an old man[1] in the grip of a terrible disease, who thought he was afraid to die, but who died like a warrior in an epic poem. That's beauty. I think of a boy[2] of twenty-six years heaving his life away, and gasping to regain it, I think of the frightened glare in his eyes and the way he seizes my hands, and cries "What have you come home for." I think of the lie that trembles in my throat. I think of a woman who sits with a face as white and set as if cut from marble, and whose fingers can not be unclasped from his hand. And the boy of eighteen sees and knows for the first time that more than a son is dying, that part of a mother is being buried before her,—life in death, that something which she nursed and loved, something out of her blood, out of her life, is taken away. It's terrible but it's beautiful. I think of the devotion of a woman of frail physique to a father, I think of the daisy meadows on the way to Craggy Mountain,[3] of the birch forests of New Hampshire, of the Mississippi River at Memphis —of all of which I have been a part— and I know [51/52] there is nothing so commonplace, so dull, that is not touched with nobility and dignity. And I intend to wreak out my soul on paper and express it all. This is what my life means to me: I am at the mercy of this thing and I will do it or die. I never forget; I have never forgotten. I have tried to make myself conscious of the whole of my life since first the baby in the basket became conscious of the warm sunlight on the porch, and saw his sister go up the hill to the girl's school on the corner (the first thing I remember). Slowly out of the world of infant darkness things take shape, the big terrifying faces become familiar,—I recognize my father by his bristly moustache. Then the animal books and the Mother Goose poetry which I memorize before I can read, and recite for the benefit of admiring neighbors every night, holding my book upside down. I become conscious of Santa Claus and send scrawls up the chimney. Then St. Louis.[1] A flight of stairs at the Cincinnati rail road station which must be gone up,—the World's Fair, the Ferris Wheel, Grover at the Inside Inn, the Delmar Gardens where you let me taste beer which I spit out, a ride on a bus-automobile—over the Fair Grounds with Effie—it is raining, raining—the Cascades in the rain—a ride in the scenic railway—scared at the darkness and the hideous faces—eating a peach in the back yard (St. Louis)—I swallow a fly and am sick—and one of my brothers laughs at me. Two little boys who ride tricycles up and down the street—they dress in white and look alike—their father injured or killed in elevator accident (wasn't he) —I "commit a nuisance" on the narrow step of side yard and the policeman sees me and reports me—the smell of tea at the East India House—I'll never forget

[P. 51] [1] This refers to Tom's father, whose illness and death are recorded in *Of Time and the River.*

[P. 51] [2] The reference is to Tom's brother Ben whose death from pneumonia is recounted in *Look Homeward[,] Angel.*

[P. 51] [3] A favorite place for picnics near Asheville, N. C.

[P. 52] [1] Because of the opening of the World's Fair in St. Louis in 1904, Mrs. Wolfe took all her children there and conducted a rooming house at Fairmount and Academy Streets called The Carolina House.

[P. 53] [1] Grover, Ben's twin, came down with typhoid and died on November 16th. The events of this summer are recorded in *Look Homeward, Angel* and Grover's death is also the basis of a story, "The Lost Boy," contained in *The Hills Beyond,* published by Harper & Brothers, New York.

[**52/53**] it—Grover's[1] sickness and death —I am wakened at midnight by Mabel and she says "Grover's on the cooling board." I don't know what a cooling board is but am curious to see. I don't know what death is but have a vague, terrified sensation that something awful has happened —then she takes me in her arms and up the hall.—Disappointed at the cooling board—it's only a table— the brown mole on his neck—the trip home—visitors in the parlor with condolences—Norah Israel[2] was there—Then it gets fairly plain thereafter, and I can trace it step by step.

This is why I think I'm going to be an artist. The things that really mattered sunk in and left their mark. Sometimes only a word—sometimes a peculiar smile —sometimes death—sometimes the smell of dandelions in Spring—once Love. Most people have little more mind than brutes: they live from day to day. I will go everywhere and see everything. I will meet all the people I can. I will think all the thoughts, feel all the emotions I am able, and I will write, write, write.

I won't say whether my play was good or bad. Some people in the staid Workshop Audience were shocked, most were enthusiastic, and a great many said it was the best play written here. Good or bad, win or lose, [*The fragment ends here— Ed.*]

[2] A neighbor, and mother of one of Tom's childhood playmates.

The Story of a Novel*

THOMAS WOLFE was "visiting novelist" at the University of Colorado's Writers' Conference at Boulder from July 21 to August 9, 1935, the summer following the publication of *Of Time and the River*. While he was at Boulder, Wolfe delivered a formal lecture for which he used a greatly rewritten form of a preface he had prepared for *Of Time and the River* but was dissuaded by Maxwell Perkins from using. The lecture took one hour and forty minutes; Wolfe had difficulty during the first fifteen minutes overcoming his tendency to stammer, but after that he "did the job up pretty brown," he said. The lecture was published in three installments in the *Saturday Review of Literature* on December 14, 21, and 28, 1935, and as a small book on April 21, 1936.

An editor, who is also a good friend of mine, told me about a year ago that he was sorry he had not kept a diary about the work that both of us were doing, the whole stroke, catch, flow, stop, and ending, the ten thousand fittings, changings, triumphs, and surrenders that went into the making of a book. This editor remarked that some of it was fantastic, much incredible, all astonishing, and he was also kind enough to say that the whole experience was the most interesting he had known during the twenty-five years he had been a member of the publishing business.

I propose to tell about this experience. I cannot tell any one how to write books; I cannot attempt to give any one rules whereby he will be enabled to get his books published by publishers or his stories accepted by high-paying magazines. I am not a pro- [1/2] fessional writer; I am not even a skilled writer; I am just a writer who is on the way to learning his profession and to discovering the line, the structure, and the articulation of the language which I must discover if I do the work I want to do. It is for just this reason, because I blunder, because every en- ergy of my life and talent is still involved in this process of discovery, that I am speaking as I speak here. I am going to tell the way in which I wrote a book. It will be intensely personal. It was the most intense part of my life for several years. There is nothing very literary about it. It is a story of sweat and pain and despair and partial achievement. I don't know how to write a story yet. I don't know how to write a novel yet. But I have learned something about myself and about the work of writing, and if I can, I am going to try to tell what it is.

I don't know when it occurred to me first that I would be a writer. I suppose that like a great many other children in this [2/3] country of my generation, I may have thought that it would be a fine thing because a writer was a man like Lord Byron or Lord Tennyson or Longfellow or Percy Bysshe Shelley. A writer was a man who was far away like these people I have mentioned, and since I was myself an American and an American not of the wealthy or university-going sort of people, it seemed to me that a writer was a man from a kind of remote people that I could never approach.

I think this has happened to us all— or almost all of us here in America. We're still more perturbed by the strangeness of the writing profession than any other people I have known on the earth. It is for this reason, I think, that one finds among a great number of our people, I mean the laboring, farming sort of people from which I came, a kind of great wonder and doubt and romantic feeling about writers so that it is hard for them to understand that a writer may be one of them and not a man far away like Lord Byron or Tennyson or [3/4] Percy Bysshe Shelley. Then there is another kind of American who has come from the more educated, university-going kind of people, and these people also become fascinated with the glamor and difficulty of writing, but in a different way. They get more involved or fancy than the most involved and fancy European people of this sort. They become more "Flauberty" than Flaubert. They establish little magazines that not only split a hair with the best of them, but they split more hairs than Europeans think of splitting. The Europeans say: "Oh God, where did these people, these æsthetic Americans, ever come from?" Well, we have known it all. I think all of us who have tried to write in this country may have fallen in between these two groups of well meaning and misguided people, and if we become writers finally, it is in spite of each of them.

I don't know how I became a writer, but I think it was because of a certain force in me that had to write and that finally burst [4/5] through and found a channel. My people were of the working class of people. My father, a stonecutter, was a man with a great respect and veneration for literature. He had a tremendous memory, and he loved poetry, and the poetry that he loved best was naturally of the rhetorical kind that such a man would like. Nevertheless it was good poetry, Hamlet's Soliloquy, "Macbeth," Mark Antony's Funeral Oration, Grey's "Elegy," and all the rest of it. I heard it all as a child; I memorized and learned it all.

He sent me to college to the state university. The desire to write, which had been strong during all my days in high school, grew stronger still. I was editor of the college paper, the college magazine, etc., and in my last year or two I was a member of a course in playwriting which had just been established there. I wrote several little one-act plays, still thinking I would become a lawyer or a newspaper man, never daring to believe I could seriously become a writer. [5/6] Then I went to Harvard, wrote some more plays there, became obsessed with the idea that I had to be a playwright, left Harvard, had my plays rejected, and finally in the autumn of 1926, how, why, or in what manner I have never exactly been able to determine, but probably because the force in me that had to write at length sought out its channel, I began to write my first book in London. I was living all alone at that time. I had two rooms—a bedroom and a sitting room—in a little square in Chelsea in which all the houses had that familiar, smoked brick and cream-yellow-plaster look of London houses. They looked exactly alike.

As I say, I was living alone at that time and in a foreign country. I did not know why I was there or what the direction of my life should be, and that was the way I began to write my book. I think that is one of the hardest times a writer goes through. There is no standard, no outward judgment, by which he can measure what he has done. By day I would write for hours in big ledgers [6/7] which I had bought for the purpose; then at night I would lie in bed and fold my hands behind my head and think of what I had done that day and hear the solid, leather foot beat of the London bobby as he came by my window, and remember that I was born in North Carolina and wonder why the hell I was now in London lying in the darkened bed, and thinking about words I had that day put down on paper. I would get a great, hollow, utterly futile feeling inside me, and then I would get up and switch on the light and read the words had written that day, and then I would wonder: why am I here now? why have I come?

By day there would be the great, dull roar of London, the gold, yellow, foggy light you have there in October. The man-swarmed and old, weblike, smoky London! And I loved the place, and I loathed it and abhorred it. I knew no one there, and I had been a child in North Carolina long ago, and I was living there in two rooms in the huge octopal and illimitable web of that [7/8] overwhelming city. I did not know why I had come, why I was there.

I worked there every day with such feelings as I have described, and came back to America in the winter and worked here. I would teach all day and write all night, and finally about two and a half years after I had begun the book in London, I finished it in New York.

I should like to tell about this, too. I was very young at the time, and I had the kind of wild, exultant vigor which a man has at that period of his life. The book took hold of me and possessed me. In a way, I think it shaped itself. Like every young man, I was strongly under the influence of writers I admired. One of the chief writers at that time was Mr. James Joyce with his book *Ulysses*. The book that I was writing was much influenced, I believe, by his own book, and yet the powerful energy and fire of my own youth played over and, I think, possessed it all. Like Mr. Joyce, I wrote about things that I had known, the imme- [8/9] diate life and experience that had been familiar to me in my childhood. Unlike Mr. Joyce, I had no literary experience. I had never had anything published before. My feeling toward writers, publishers, books, that whole fabulous far-away world, was almost as romantically unreal as when I was a child. And yet my book, the characters with which I had peopled it, the color and the weather of the universe which I had created, had possessed me, and so I wrote and wrote with that bright flame with which a young man writes who never has been published, and who yet is sure all

will be good and must go well. This is a curious thing and hard to tell about, yet easy to understand in every writer's mind. I wanted fame, as every youth who ever wrote must want it, and yet fame was a shining, bright, and most uncertain thing.

The book was finished in my twenty-eighth year. I knew no publishers and no writers. A friend of mine took the huge manuscript—it was about 350,000 words [9/10] long—and sent it to a publisher whom she knew. In a few days, a week or two, I received an answer from this man saying that the book could not be published. The gist of what he said was that his house had published several books like it the year before, that all of them had failed, and that, further, the book in its present form was so amateurish, autobiographical, and unskilful that a publisher could not risk a chance on it. I was, myself, so depressed and weary by this time, the illusion of creation which had sustained me for two and a half years had so far worn off, that I believed what the man said. At that time I was a teacher in one of New York's great universities, and when the year came to a close, I went abroad. It was only after I had been abroad almost six months that news came to me from another publisher in America that he had read my manuscript and would like to talk to me about it as soon as I came home.

I came home on New Year's Day that [10/11] year. The next day I called up the publisher who had written me. He asked me if I would come to his office and talk to him. I went at once, and before I had left his office that morning, I had signed a contract and had a check for five hundred dollars in my hand.

It was the first time, so far as I can remember, that any one had concretely suggested to me that anything I had written was worth as much as fifteen cents, and I know that I left the publisher's office that day and entered into the great swarm of men and women who passed constantly along Fifth Avenue at 48th Street and presently I found myself at 110th Street, and from that day to this I have never known how I got there.

For the next six or eight months I taught at the university and worked upon the manuscript of my book with this editor. The book appeared in the month of October, 1929. The whole experience still had elements of that dream-like terror and un- [11/12] reality that writing had had for me when I had first begun it seriously and had lain in my room in London with my hands below my head and thought, why am I here? The awful, utter nakedness of print, that thing which is for all of us so namelessly akin to shame, came closer day by day. That I had wanted this exposure, I could not believe. It seemed to me that I had shamelessly exposed myself and yet that subtle drug of my desire and my creating held me with a serpent's eye, and I could do no other. I turned at last to this editor who had worked with me and found me, and I asked him if he could foretell the end and verdict of my labor. He said that he would rather tell me nothing, that he could not prophesy or know what profit I would have. He said, "All that I know is that they cannot let it go, they cannot ignore it. The book will find its way."

And that fairly describes what happened. I have read in recent months that this first book was received with what is called a [12/13] "storm of critical applause," but this really did not happen. It got some wonderful reviews in some places; it got some unfavorable reviews in others, but it unquestionably did have a good reception for a first book, and what was best of all, as time went on, it continued to make friends among people who read books. It continued to sell over a period of four or five years in the publisher's edition, and later in a cheaper edition, The Modern Library, it renewed its life and began to sell again. The upshot of it was that after the publication of this book in the autumn of 1929, I found myself with a position as a writer. And here one of the first of my great lessons as a writer began.

Up to this time I had been a young man who wanted to be a writer more than anything on earth and who had created his first book in the great blaze of illusion which a young writer must feel when he has no evidence except his hope to drive him on. Now, in a certain measure, this had changed. I had been a writer in hope and in desire [13/14] before and now I was a writer in fact. I would read about myself, for example, as one of the "younger American writers." I was a person who, some of the critics said, was to be watched. They were looking forward to my future book with interest and with a certain amount of apprehension. Here, too, my education as a writer was increasing all the time. Now, indeed, I could hear myself discussed, and somehow the fact was far more formidable than I had dreamed that it could be. It worried me, confused me, gave me a strange feeling of guilt and responsibility. I was a young American writer, and they had hopes and fears about my future, and what would I do, or would it be anything, nothing, much, or little? Would the faults which they had found in my work grow worse or would I conquer them? Was I another flash in the pan? Would I come through? What would happen to me?

I let it worry me. I would go home at night and look around my room and see that [14/15] morning's coffee cup still unwashed and books on the floor and a shirt where I had thrown it the night before and great stacks of manuscript and everything so common and familiar looking and so disorderly, and then I would think that I was now "a young American writer"; that somehow I was practising an imposture on my readers and my critics because my shirt looked the way it did and my books and my bed—not, you understand, because they were disorderly, common, familiar, but just because they looked the way they did.

But now another fact began to gnaw a way into my consciousness.

The critics had begun to ask questions about the second book, and so now I had to think about the second one as well. I had always wanted to think about the second one and the thirty-second one and the fifty-second one. I had been sure that I had a hundred books in me, that all of them would be good, that each of them would make me famous. But here again was a strange and [15/16] jolting transition from wild hope and exultant conviction; and plain, blazing fact remained. Now that I had actually written one book and *they*, the actual readers and critics who had read it, were looking for a second, I was up against it. I was not up against it the way I dreaded, I was just up against it cold and hard as one comes up against a wall. I was a writer. I had made the writer's life my life; there was no going back; I had to go on. What could I do? After the first book there had to be a second book. What was the second book to be about? Where would it come from?

This inexorable fact, although it became more and more pressing, did not bother me so much at first. Rather I was concerned with many other things that had to do with the publication of that first book, and as before, I had foreseen none of them. In the first place, I had not foreseen one fact which becomes absolutely plain after a man has written a book, but which he cannot foresee until he has written one. This fact is that [16/17] one writes a book not in order to remember it, but in order to forget it, and now this fact was evident. As soon as the book was in print, I began to forget about it, I wanted to forget about it, I didn't want people to talk to me or question me about it. I just wanted them to leave me alone and shut up about it. And yet I longed desperately for my book's success. I wanted it to have the position of proud esteem and honor in the world that I longed for it to have —I wanted, in short, to be a successful and a famous man, and I wanted to lead the same kind of obscure and private life I'd always had and not to be told about my fame and success.

From this problem, another painful and difficult situation was produced. I had written my book, more or less, directly from the experience of my own life, and, furthermore, I now think that I may have written it with a certain naked intensity of spirit which is likely to characterize the earliest work of a young writer. At any rate, I can [17/18] honestly say that I did not foresee what was to happen. I was surprised not only by the kind of response my book had with the critics and the general public, I was most of all surprised with the response it had in my native town. I had thought there might be a hundred people in that town who would read the book, but if there were a hundred outside of the negro population, the blind, and the positively illiterate who did not read it, I do not know where they are. For months the town seethed with a fury of resentment which I had not believed possible. The book was denounced from the pulpit by the ministers of the leading churches. Men collected on street corners to denounce it. For weeks the women's clubs, bridge parties, teas, receptions, book clubs, the whole complex fabric of a small town's social life was absorbed by an outraged clamor. I received anonymous letters full of vilification and abuse, one which threatened to kill me if I came back home, others which were merely obscene. One venerable [18/19] old lady, whom I had known all my life, wrote me that although she had never believed in lynch law, she would do nothing to prevent a mob from dragging my "big overgroan karkus" across the public square. She informed me further, that my mother had taken to her bed "as white as a ghost" and would "never rise from it again."

There were many other venomous attacks from my home town and for the first time I learned another lesson which every young writer has got to learn. And that lesson is the naked, blazing power of print. At that time it was for me a bewildering and almost overwhelming situation. My joy at the success my book had won was mixed with bitter chagrin at its reception in my native town. And yet I think I learned something from that experience, too. For the first time I was forced to consider squarely this problem: where does the material of an artist come from? What are the proper uses of that material, and how far must his freedom in the use of that material be controlled by [19/20] his responsibility as a member of society? This is a difficult problem, and I have by no means come to the bottom of it yet. Perhaps I never shall, but as a result of all the distress which I suffered at that time and which others may have suffered on account of me, I have done much thinking and arrived at certain conclusions.

My book was what is often referred to as an autobiographical novel. I protested against this term in a preface to the book upon the grounds that any serious work of creation is of necessity autobiographical and that few more autobiographical works than *Gulliver's Travels* have ever been written. I added that Dr. Johnson had remarked that a man might turn over half the volumes in his library to make a single book, and that in a similar way, a novelist might turn over half the characters in his native town to make a single figure for his novel. In spite of this the people in my native town were not persuaded or appeased, and the charge of autobiography was brought against me in many other places. [20/21]

As I have said, my conviction is that all serious creative work must be at bottom autobiographical, and that a man must use the material and experience of his own life if he is to create anything that has substantial value. But I also believe now that the young writer is often led through inexperience to a use of the materials of life which are, perhaps, somewhat too naked and direct for the purpose of a work of art. The thing a young writer is likely to do is to confuse the limits between actuality and reality. He tends unconsciously to describe an event in such a way because it actually happened that way, and from an artistic point of view, I can now see that this is wrong. It is not, for example, important that one remembers a beautiful woman of easy virtue as having come from the state of Kentucky in the year 1907. She could perfectly well have come from Idaho or Texas or Nova Scotia. The important thing really is only to express as well as possible the character and quality of the beautiful woman of easy virtue. But the young [21/22] writer, chained to fact and to his own inexperience, as yet unliberated by maturity, is likely to argue, "she must be described as coming from Kentucky because that is where she actually did come from."

In spite of this, it is impossible for a man who has the stuff of creation in him to make a literal transcription of his own experience. Everything in a work of art is changed and transfigured by the personality of the artist. And as far as my own first book is concerned, I can truthfully say that I do not believe that there is a single page of it that is true to fact. And from this circumstance, also, I learned another curious thing about writing. For although my book was not true to fact, it was true to the general experience of the town I came from and I hope, of course, to the general experience of all men living. The best way I can describe the situation is this: it was as if I were a sculptor who had found a certain kind of clay with which to model. Now a farmer who knew well the neighborhood [22/23] from which this clay had come might pass by and find the sculptor at his work and say to him, "I know the farm from which you got that clay." But it would be unfair of him to say, "I know the figure, too." Now I think what happened in my native town is that having seen the clay, they became immediately convinced that they recognized the figure, too, and the results of this misconception were so painful and ludicrous that the telling of it is almost past belief.

It was my experience to be assured by people from my native town not only that they remembered incidents and characters in my first book, which may have had some basis in actuality, but also that they remembered incidents which so far as I know had no historical basis whatever. For example, there was one scene in the book in which a stonecutter is represented as selling to a notorious woman of the town a statue of a marble angel which he has treasured for many years. So far as I know, there was no basis in fact for this story, and yet I was [23/24] informed by several people later that they not only remembered the incident perfectly, but had actually been witnesses to the transaction. Nor was this the end of the story. I heard that one of the newspapers sent a reporter and a photographer to the cemetery and a photograph was printed in the paper with a statement to the effect that the angel was the now famous angel which had stood upon the stonecutter's porch for so many years and had given the title to my book. The unfortunate part of this proceeding was that I had never seen or heard of this angel before, and that this angel was, in fact, erected over the grave of a well known Methodist lady who had died a few years before and that her indignant family had immediately written the paper to demand a retraction of its story, saying that their mother had been in no way connected with the infamous book or the infamous angel which had given the infamous book its name. Such, then, were some of the unforeseen difficulties with which I was con- [24/25] fronted after the publication of my first book.

Month was passing into month; I had had a success. The way was opened to me. There was only one thing for me to do and that was work, and I was spending my time consuming myself with anger, grief, and useless passion about the reception the book had had in my native town, or wasting myself again in exuberant elation because of the critics and the readers' praise, or in anguish and bitterness because of their ridicule. For the first time, I realized the nature of one of the artist's greatest conflicts, and was faced with the need of meeting it. For the first time I saw not only that the artist must live and sweat and love and suffer and enjoy as other men, but that the artist must also work as other men and that furthermore, he must work even while these common events of life are going on. It seems a simple and banal assertion, but I learned it hardly, and in one of the worst moments of my life. There is no such thing [25/26] as an artistic vacuum; there is no such thing as a time when the artist may work in a delightful atmosphere, free of agony that other men must know, or if the artist ever does find such a time, it is something not to be hoped for, something not to be sought for indefinitely.

At any rate, while my life and energy were absorbed in the emotional vortex which my first book had created, I was getting almost no work done on the second. And now I was faced with another fundamental problem which every young writer must meet squarely if he is to continue. How is a man to get his writing done? How long should he work at writing, and how often? What kind of method, if any, must he find in following his work? I suddenly found myself face to face with the grim necessity of constant, daily work. And as simple as this discovery may seem to every one, I was not prepared for it. A young writer without a public does not feel the sense of necessity, the pressure of time, as does a writer who [26/27] has been published and who must now begin to think of time schedules, publishing seasons, the completion of his next book. I realized suddenly with a sense of definite shock that I had let six months go by since the publication of my first book and that, save for a great many notes and fragments, I had done nothing. Meanwhile, the book continued to sell slowly but steadily, and in February, 1930, about five months after its publication, I found it possible to resign from the faculty of New York University and devote my full time to the preparation of a second book. That spring I was also fortunate enough to be awarded the Guggenheim Fellowship which would enable me to live and work abroad for a year. And accordingly at the beginning of May, I went abroad again.

I was in Paris for a couple of months, until the middle of July, and although I now compelled myself to work for four or five hours a day, my effort at composition [27/28] was still confused and broken, and there was nothing yet that had the structural form and unity of a book. The life of the great city fascinated me as it had always done, but also aroused all the old feelings of naked homelessness, rootlessness, and loneliness which I have always felt there. It was, and has always remained for me, at least, the most homesick city in the world; the place where I have felt mostly an alien and a stranger, and certainly for me as fascinating and seductive as the city is, it has never been a good place to work. But here I would like to say something about places to work because that is another problem which causes young writers a great deal of doubt, uncertainty, and confusion, and I think, uselessly.

I had gone through the whole experience and now I was almost done with it. I had come to Paris first six years before, a youth of twenty-four, filled with all the romantic faith and foolishness which many young men at that time felt when they saw Paris. [28/29] I had come there that first time, so I told myself, to work, and so glamorous was the magic name of Paris at that time, that I really thought one could work far better there than anywhere on earth; that it was a place where the very air was impregnated with the energies of art; where the artist was bound to find a more fortunate and happy life than he could possibly find in America. Now I had come to see that this was wrong. I had come to understand very plainly that what many of us were doing in those years when we fled from our own country and sought refuge abroad was not really looking for a place to work, but looking for a place where we could escape from work; that what we were really fleeing from in those years was not the Philistinism, the materialism, and ugliness in American life which we said we were fleeing from, but from the necessity of grap-

pling squarely with ourselves and the necessity of finding in ourselves, somehow, the stuff to live by, to get from our own lives and our own ex- [29/30] perience the substance of our art which every man who ever wrote a living thing has had to get out of himself and without which he is lost.

The place to work! Yes, the place to work *was* Paris; it *was* Spain; it *was* Italy and Capri and Majorca, but great God, it was also Keokuk, and Portland, Maine, and Denver, Colorado, and Yancey County, North Carolina, and wherever we might be, if work was there within us at the time. If this was all that I had learned from these voyages to Europe, if the price of all this wandering had been just this simple lesson, it would have been worth the price, but that was not all. I had found out during these years that the way to discover one's own country was to leave it; that the way to find America was to find it in one's heart, one's memory, and one's spirit, and in a foreign land.

I think I may say that I discovered America during these years abroad out of my very need of her. The huge gain of this [30/31] discovery seemed to come directly from my sense of loss. I had been to Europe five times now; each time I had come with delight, with maddening eagerness to return, and each time how, where, and in what way I did not know, I had felt the bitter ache of homelessness, a desperate longing for America, an overwhelming desire to return.

During that summer in Paris, I think I felt this great homesickness more than ever before, and I really believe that from this emotion, this constant and almost intolerable effort of memory and desire, the material and the structure of the books I now began to write were derived.

The quality of my memory is characterized, I believe, in a more than ordinary degree by the intensity of its sense impressions, its power to evoke and bring back the odors, sounds, colors, shapes, and feel of things with concrete vividness. Now my memory was at work night and day, in a way that I could at first neither check nor control and that swarmed unbidden in a [31/32] stream of blazing pageantry across my mind, with the million forms and substances of the life that I had left, which was my own, America. I would be sitting, for example, on the terrace of a café watching the flash and play of life before me on the Avenue de l'Opéra and suddenly I would remember the iron railing that goes along the boardwalk at Atlantic City. I could see it instantly just the way it was, the heavy iron pipe; its raw, galvanized look; the way the joints were fitted together. It was all so vivid and concrete that I could feel my hand upon it and know the exact dimensions, its size and weight and shape. And suddenly I would realize that I had never seen any railing that looked like this in Europe. And this utterly familiar, common thing would suddenly be revealed to me with all the wonder with which we discover a thing which we have seen all our life and yet have never known before. Or again, it would be a bridge, the look of an old iron bridge across an American river, the sound the train [32/33] makes as it goes across it; the spoke-and-hollow rumble of the ties below; the look of the muddy banks; the slow, thick, yellow wash of an American river; an old flat-bottomed boat half filled with water stogged in the muddy bank; or it would be, most lonely and haunting of all the sounds I know, the sound of a milk wagon as it entered an American street just at the first gray of the morning, the slow and lonely clopping of the hoof upon the street, the jink of bottles, the sudden rattle of a battered old milk can, the swift and hurried footsteps of the milkman, and again the jink of bottles, a low word spoken to his horse, and then the great, slow, clopping hoof receding into silence, and then quietness and a bird song rising in the street again. Or it would be a little wooden shed out in the country two miles from my home town where people waited for the street car, and I could see and feel again the dull and rusty color of the old green paint and see and feel all of the initials that had been carved out with [33/34] jackknives on the planks and benches within the shed, and smell the warm and sultry smell so resinous and so thrilling, so filled with a strange and nameless excitement of an unknown joy, a coming prophecy, and hear the street car as it came to a stop, the moment of brooding, drowzing silence; a hot thrum and drowsy stitch at three o'clock; the smell of grass and hot sweet clover; and then the sudden sense of absence, loneliness and departure when the street car had gone and there was nothing but the hot and drowsy stitch at three o'clock again.

Or again, it would be an American street with all its jumble of a thousand ugly architectures. It would be Montague Street or Fulton Street in Brooklyn, or Eleventh Street in New York, or other streets where I had lived; and suddenly I would see the gaunt and savage webbing of the elevated structure along Fulton Street, and how the light swarmed through in dusty, broken bars, and I could remember the old, familiar [34/35] rusty color, that incomparable rusty color that gets into so many things here in America. And this also would be like something I had seen a million times and lived with all my life.

I would sit there, looking out upon the Avenue de l'Opéra and my life would ache with the whole memory of it; the desire to see it again; somehow to find a word for it; a language that would tell its shape, its color, the way we have all known and felt and seen it. And when I understood this thing, I saw that I must find for myself the tongue to utter what I knew but could not say. And from the moment of that discovery, the line and purpose of my life was shaped. The end toward which every energy of my life and talent would be henceforth directed was in such a way as this defined. It was as if I had discovered a whole new universe of chemical elements and had begun to see certain relations between some of them but had by no means begun to organize the whole series into a harmonious and co- **[35/36]** herent union. From this time on, I think my efforts might be described as the effort to complete that organization, to discover that articulation for which I strove, to bring about that final coherent union. I know that I have failed thus far in doing so, but I believe I understand pretty thoroughly just where the nature of my failure lies, and of course my deepest and most earnest hope is that the time will come when I shall not fail.

At any rate, from this time on the general progress of the three books which I was to write in the next four and a half years could be fairly described in somewhat this way. It was a progress that began in a whirling vortex and a creative chaos and that proceeded slowly at the expense of infinite confusion, toil, and error toward clarification and the articulation of an ordered and formal structure. An extraordinary image remains to me from that year, the year I spent abroad when the material of these books first began to take on an articulate form. It seemed that I had inside me, **[36/37]** swelling and gathering all the time, a huge black cloud, and that this cloud was loaded with electricity, pregnant, crested, with a kind of hurricane violence that could not be held in check much longer; that the moment was approaching fast when it must break. Well, all I can say is that the storm did break. It broke that summer while I was in Switzerland. It came in torrents, and it is not over yet.

I cannot really say the book was written. It was something that took hold of me and possessed me, and before I was done with it—that is, before I finally emerged with the first completed part— it seemed to me that it had done for me. It was exactly as if this great black storm cloud I have spoken of had opened up and, mid flashes of lightning, was pouring from its depth a torrential and ungovernable flood. Upon that flood everything was swept and borne along as by a great river. And I was borne along with it.

There was nothing at first which could

be called a novel. I wrote about night and **[37/38]** darkness in America, and the faces of the sleepers in ten thousand little towns; and of the tides of sleep and how the rivers flowed forever in the darkness. I wrote about the hissing glut of tides upon ten thousand miles of coast; of how the moonlight blazed down on the wilderness and filled the cat's cold eye with blazing yellow. I wrote about death and sleep, and of that enfabled rock of life we call the city. I wrote about October, of great trains that thundered through the night, of ships and stations in the morning; of men in harbors and the traffic of the ships.

I spent the winter of that year in England from October until March, and here perhaps because of the homely familiarity of the English life, the sense of order and repose which such a life can give one, my work moved forward still another step from this flood tide chaos of creation. For the first time the work began to take on the lineaments of design. These lineaments were still confused and broken, sometimes utterly lost, but now I really did get the sense at last **[38/39]** that I was working on a great block of marble, shaping a figure which no one but its maker could as yet define, but which was emerging more and more into the sinewy lines of composition.

From the beginning—and this was one fact that in all my times of hopelessness returned to fortify my faith in my conviction—the idea, the central legend that I wished my book to express had not changed. And this central idea was this: the deepest search in life, it seemed to me, the thing that in one way or another was central to all living was man's search to find a father, not merely the father of his flesh, not merely the lost father of his youth, but the image of a strength and wisdom external to his need and superior to his hunger, to which the belief and power of his own life could be united.

Yet I was terribly far away from the actual accomplishment of a book—how far away I could not at that time foresee. But four more years would have to pass before the first of a series of books on which I was [39/40] now embarked would be ready for the press, and if I could have known that in those next four years there would be packed a hundred lives of birth and death, despair, defeat, and triumph and the sheer exhaustion of a brute fatigue, I do not know whether or not I could have found the power within msyelf to continue. But I was still sustained by the exuberant optimism of youth. My temperament, which is pessimistic about many things, has always been a curiously sanguine one concerning time, and although more than a year had now gone by and I had done no more than write great chants on death and sleep, prepare countless notes and trace here and there the first dim outlines of a formal pattern, I was confident that by the spring or the fall of the next year my book would somehow miraculously be ready.

So far as I can describe with any accuracy, the progress of that winter's work in England was not along the lines of planned design, but along this line that I have [40/41] mentioned—writing some of the sections which I knew would have to be in the book. Meanwhile what was really going on in my whole creative consciousness, during all this time, although I did not realize it at the moment, was this: What I was really doing, what I had been doing all the time since my discovery of my America in Paris the summer before, was to explore day by day and month by month with a fanatical intensity, the whole material domain of my resources as a man and as a writer. This exploration went on for a period which I can estimate conservatively as two years and a half. It is still going on, although not with the same all-absorbing concentration, because the work it led to, the work that after infinite waste and labor it helped me wonderfully to define, that work has reached such a state of final definition that the immediate task of finishing it is the one that now occupies the energy and interest of my life.

In a way, during that period of my life,

I think I was like the Ancient Mariner who [41/42] told the Wedding Guest that his frame was wrenched by the woeful agony which forced him to begin his tale before it left him free. In my own experience, my wedding guests were the great ledgers in which I wrote, and the tale which I told to them would have seemed, I am afraid, completely incoherent, as meaningless as Chinese characters, had any reader seen them. I could by no means hope to give a comprehensive idea of the whole extent of this labor because three years of work and perhaps a million and a half words went into these books. It included everything from gigantic and staggering lists of the towns, cities, counties, states, and countries I had been in, to minutely thorough, desperately evocative descriptions of the undercarriage, the springs, wheels, flanges, axle rods, color, weight, and quality of the day coach of an American railway train. There were lists of the rooms and houses in which I had lived or in which I had slept for at least a night, together with the most accurate and evocative descriptions of those [42/43] rooms that I could write—their size, their shape, the color and design of the wallpaper, the way a towel hung down, the way a chair creaked, a streak of water rust upon the ceiling. There were countless charts, catalogues, descriptions that I can only classify here under the general heading of Amount and Number. What were the total combined populations of all the countries in Europe and America? In how many of those countries had I had some personal and vital experience? In the course of my twenty-nine or thirty years of living, how many people had I seen? How many had I passed by on the streets? How many had I seen on trains and subways, in theatres, at baseball or football games? With how many had I actually had some vital and illuminating experience, whether of joy, pain, anger, pity, love, or simple casual companionship, however brief?

In addition, one might come upon other sections under some such cryptic heading as "Where now?" Under such a heading as this, there would be brief notations of those [43/44] thousands of things which all of us have seen for just a flash, a moment in our lives, which seem to be of no consequence whatever at the moment that we see them, and which live in our minds and hearts forever, which are somehow pregnant with all the joy and sorrow of the human destiny, and which we know, somehow, are therefore more important than many things of more apparent consequence. "Where now?" Some quiet steps that came and passed along a leafy nighttime street in summer in a little town down South long years ago; a woman's voice, her sudden burst of low and tender laughter; then the voices and the footsteps going, silence, the leafy rustle of the trees. "Where now?" Two trains that met and paused at a little station at some little town at some unknown moment upon the huge body of the continent; a girl who looked and smiled from the window of the other train; another passing in a motor car on the streets of Norfolk; the winter boarders in a little boarding house down South twenty years [44/45] ago; Miss Florrie Mangle, the trained nurse; Miss Jessie Rimmer, the cashier at Reed's drug store; Doctor Richards, the clairvoyant; the pretty girl who cracked the whip and thrust her head into the lion's mouth with Johnny J. Jones Carnival and Combined Shows.

"Where now?" It went beyond the limits of man's actual memory. It went back to the farthest adyt of his childhood before conscious memory had begun, the way he thought he must have felt the sun one day and heard Peagram's cow next door wrenching the coarse grass against the fence, or heard the street car stop upon the hill above his father's house at noon; and Earnest Peagram coming home to lunch, his hearty voice in midday greeting; and then the street car going, the sudden lonely green-gold silence of the street car's absence and an iron gate slamming, then the light of that lost day fades out. "Where now?" He can recall no more and does not know if what he has recalled is fact or fable or a fusion of the two. [45/46] Where now—in these great ledger books, month after month, I wrote such things as this, not only the concrete, material record of man's ordered memory, but all the things he scarcely dares to think he has remembered; all the flicks and darts and haunting lights that flash across the mind of man that will return unbidden at an unexpected moment: a voice once heard; a face that vanished; the way the sunlight came and went; the rustling of a leaf upon a bough; a stone, a leaf, a door.

It may be objected, it has been objected already by certain critics, that in such research as I have here attempted to describe there is a quality of intemperate excess, an almost insane hunger to devour the entire body of human experience, to attempt to include more, experience more, than the measure of one life can hold, or than the limits of a single work of art can well define. I readily admit the validity of this criticism. I think I realize as well as any one the fatal dangers that are consequent to such a raven- [46/47] ous desire, the damage it may wreak upon one's life and on one's work. But having had this thing within me, it was in no way possible for me to reason it out of me, no matter how cogently my reason worked against it. The only way I could meet it was to meet it squarely, not with reason but with life.

It was part of my life; for many years it was my life; and the only way I could get it out of me was to live it out of me. And that is what I did. I have not wholly succeeded in that purpose yet, but I have succeeded better than I at one time dared to hope. And now I really believe that so far as the artist is concerned, the unlimited extent of human experience is not so important for him as the depth and intensity with which he experiences things. I also know now that it is a great deal more important to have known one hundred living men and women in New York, to have understood their lives, to have got, somehow, at the root and source from which their natures came than to have seen or passed or talked with [47/48] 7,000,000 people upon the city streets. And what finally I should most like to say about this research which I have attempted to describe is this: That foolish and mistaken as much of it may seem, the total quality, end, and impact of that whole experience was not useless or excessive. And from my own point of view, at least, it is in its whole implication the one thing I may have to tell about my experience as a writer which may be of some concrete value to other people. I consider this experience on the whole the most valuable and practical in my whole writing life thus far. With all the waste and error and confusion it led me into, it brought me closer to a concrete definition of my resources, a true estimate of my talents at this period of my life, and, most of all, toward a rudimentary, a just-beginning, but a living apprehension of the articulation I am looking for, the language I have got to have if, as an artist, my life is to proceed and grow, than any other thing that has ever happened to me. **[48/49]**

I know the door is not yet open. I know the tongue, the speech, the language that I seek is not yet found, but I believe with all my heart that I have found the way, have made a channel, am started on my first beginning. And I believe with all my heart, also, that each man for himself and in his own way, each man who ever hopes to make a living thing out of the substances of his one life, must find that way, that language, and that door—must find it for himself as I have tried to do.

When I returned to America in the spring of 1931, although I had three or four hundred thousand words of material, I had nothing that could be published as a novel. Almost a year and a half had elapsed since the publication of my first book and already people had begun to ask that question which is so well meant, but which as year followed year was to become more intolerable to my ears than the most deliberate mockery: "Have you finished your next book **[49/50]** yet?" "When is it going to be published?"

At this time I was sure that a few months of steady work would bring the book to completion. I found a place, a little basement flat in the Assyrian quarter in South Brooklyn, and there I went about my task.

The spring passed into the summer; the summer, into autumn. I was working hard, day after day, and still nothing that had the unity and design of a single work appeared. October came and with it a second full year since the publication of my first book. And now, for the first time, I was irrevocably committed so far as the publication of my book was concerned. I began to feel the sensation of pressure, and of naked desperation, which was to become almost maddeningly intolerable in the next three years. For the first time I began to realize that my project was much larger than I thought it would be. I had still believed at the time of my return from Europe that I was writing a single book, which would be comprised within the limits of about 200,000 words. Now as scene **[50/51]** followed scene, as character after character came into being, as my understanding of my material became more comprehensive, I discovered that it would be impossible to write the book I had planned within the limits I had thought would be sufficient.

All of this time I was being baffled by a certain time element in the book, by a time relation which could not be escaped, and for which I was now desperately seeking some structural channel. There were three time elements inherent in the material. The first and most obvious was an element of actual present time, an element which carried the narrative forward, which represented characters and events as living in the present and moving forward into an immediate future. The second time element was of past time, one which represented these same characters as acting and as being acted upon by all the accumulated impact of man's experience so that each moment of their lives was conditioned not only by what they experienced in that moment, but by all that they had experi- [51/52] enced up to that moment. In addition to these two time elements, there was a third which I conceived as being time immutable, the time of rivers, mountains, oceans, and the earth; a kind of eternal and unchanging universe of time against which would be projected the transience of man's life, the bitter briefness of his day. It was the tremendous problem of these three time elements that almost defeated me and that cost me countless hours of anguish in the years that were to follow.

As I began to realize the true nature of the task I had set for myself, the image of the river began to haunt my mind. I actually felt that I had a great river thrusting for release inside of me and that I had to find a channel into which its flood-like power could pour. I knew I had to find it or I would be destroyed in the flood of my own creation, and I am sure that every artist who ever lived has had the same experience.

Meanwhile, I was being baffled by a fixed and impossible idea whose error at the time [52/53] I did not fully apprehend. I was convinced at that time that this whole gigantic plan had to be realized within the limits of a single book which would be called "The October Fair." It was not until more than a year had passed, when I realized finally that what I had to deal with was material which covered almost 150 years in history, demanded the action of more than 2000 characters, and would in its final design include almost every racial type and social class of American life, that I realized that even the pages of a book of 200,000 words were wholly inadequate for the purpose.

How did I finally arrive at this conclusion? I think it is not too much to say that I simply wrote myself into it. During all that year, I was writing furiously, feeling now the full pressure of inexorable time, the need to finish something. I wrote like mad; I finished scene after scene, chapter after chapter. The characters began to come to life, to grow and multiply until they were numbered by the hundreds, but

so huge was [53/54] the extent of my design, as I now desperately realized, that I can liken these chapters only to a row of lights which one sometimes sees at night from the windows of a speeding train, strung out across the dark and lonely countryside.

I would work furiously day after day until my creative energies were utterly exhausted, and although at the end of such a period I would have written perhaps as much as 200,000 words, enough in itself to make a very long book, I would realize with a feeling of horrible despair that what I had completed was only one small section of a single book.

During this time I reached that state of naked need and utter isolation which every artist has got to meet and conquer if he is to survive at all. Before this I had been sustained by that delightful illusion of success which we all have when we dream about the books we are going to write instead of actually doing them. Now I was face to face with it, and suddenly I realized [54/55] that I had committed my life and my integrity so irrevocably to this struggle that I must conquer now or be destroyed. I was alone with my own work, and now I knew that I had to be alone with it, that no one could help me with it now no matter how any one might wish to help. For the first time I realized another naked fact which every artist must know, and that is that in a man's work there are contained not only the seeds of life, but the seeds of death, and that that power of creation which sustains us will also destroy us like a leprosy if we let it rot stillborn in our vitals. I had to get it out of me somehow. I saw that now. And now for the first time a terrible doubt began to creep into my mind that I might not live long enough to get it out of me, that I had created a labor so large and so impossible that the energy of a dozen lifetimes would not suffice for its accomplishment.

During this time, however, I was sustained by one piece of inestimable good fortune. I had for a friend a man of immense [55/56] and patient wisdom and a gentle but unyielding fortitude. I think that if I was not destroyed at this time by the sense of hopelessness which these gigantic labors had awakened in me, it was largely because of the courage and patience of this man. I did not give in because he would not let me give in, and I think it is also true that at this particular time he had the advantage of being in the position of a skilled observer at a battle. I was myself engaged in that battle, covered by its dust and sweat and exhausted by its struggle, and I understood far less clearly than my friend the nature and the progress of the struggle in which I was engaged. At this time there was little that this man could do except observe, and in one way or another keep me at my task, and in many quiet and marvelous ways he succeeded in doing this.

I was now at the place where I must produce, and even the greatest editor can do little for a writer until he has brought from the secret darkness of his own spirit into the [56/57] common light of day the completed concrete accomplishment of his imagining. My friend, the editor, has likened his own function at this painful time to that of a man who is trying to hang on to the fin of a plunging whale, but hang on he did, and it is to his tenacity that I owe my final release.

Meanwhile, my creative power was functioning at the highest intensity it had ever known. I wrote at times without belief that I would ever finish, with nothing in me but black despair, and yet I wrote and wrote and could not give up writing. And it seemed that despair itself was the very goad that urged me on, that made me write even when I had no belief that I would ever finish. It seemed to me that my life in Brooklyn, although I had been there only two and a half years, went back through centuries of time, through ocean depths of black and bottomless experience which no ordinary scale of hours would ever measure. People have sometimes asked me what happened to my life during these years. They have asked [57/58] me

how I ever found time to know anything that was going on in the world about me when my life was so completely absorbed by this world of writing. Well, it may seem to be an extraordinary fact, but the truth is that never in my whole life have I lived so fully, have I shared so richly in the common life of man as I did during these three years when I was struggling with the giant problem of my own work.

For one thing, my whole sensory and creative equipment, my powers of feeling and reflection—even the sense of hearing, and above all, my powers of memory, had reached the greatest degree of sharpness that they had ever known. At the end of the day of savage labor, my mind was still blazing with its effort, could by no opiate of reading, poetry, music, alcohol, or any other pleasure, be put at rest. I was unable to sleep, unable to subdue the tumult of these creative energies, and as a result of this condition, for three years I prowled the streets, explored the swarming web of the million-footed city [58/59] and came to know it as I had never done before. It was a black time in the history of the nation, a black time in my own life and, I suppose, it is but natural that my own memory of it now should be a pretty grim and painful one.

Everywhere around me, during these years, I saw the evidence of an incalculable ruin and suffering. My own people, the members of my own family, had been ruined, had lost all the material wealth and accumulation of a lifetime in what was called the "depression." And that universal calamity had somehow struck the life of almost every one I knew. Moreover, in this endless quest and prowling of the night through the great web and jungle of the city, I saw, lived, felt, and experienced the full weight of that horrible human calamity.

I saw a man whose life had subsided into a mass of shapeless and filthy rags, devoured by vermin; wretches huddled together for a little warmth in freezing cold squatting in doorless closets upon the foul seat of a pub- [59/60] lic latrine within the very shadow, the cold shelter of palatial and stupendous monuments of wealth. I saw acts of sickening violence and cruelty, the menace of brute privilege, a cruel and corrupt authority trampling ruthlessly below its feet the lives of the poor, the weak, the wretched, and defenseless of the earth.

And the staggering impact of this black picture of man's inhumanity to his fellow man, the unending repercussions of these scenes of suffering, violence, oppression, hunger, cold, and filth and poverty going on unheeded in a world in which the rich were still rotten with their wealth left a scar upon my life, a conviction in my soul which I shall never lose.

And from it all, there has come as the final deposit, a burning memory, a certain evidence of the fortitude of man, his ability to suffer and somehow to survive. And it is for this reason now that I think I shall always remember this black period with a kind of joy that I could not at that time have be- [60/61] lieved possible, for it was during this time that I lived my life through to a first completion, and through the suffering and labor of my own life came to share those qualities in the lives of people all around me. And that is another thing which the making of a book has done for me. It has given my life that kind of growth which I think the fulfilment of each work does give the artist's life, and insofar as I have known these things, I think that they have added to my stature.

The early winter of 1933 arrived and with it, it seemed to me, the final doom of an abysmal failure. I still wrote and wrote, but blindly, hopelessly, like an old horse who trots around in the unending circle of a treadmill and knows no other end nor purpose for his life than this. If I slept at night, it was to sleep an unceasing nightmare of blazing visions that swept across my fevered and unresting mind. And when I woke, it was to wake exhausted, not knowing anything but work, lashing myself on into a hopeless [61/62] labor, and so furiously at it through the day; and then night again, a frenzied prowling of a thousand streets, and so to bed and sleepless sleep again, the nightmare pageantry to which my consciousness lay chained a spectator.

There was a kind of dream which I can only summarize as dreams of Guilt and Time. Chameleon-like in all their damnable and unending fecundities, they restored to me the whole huge world that I had known, the billion faces and the million tongues, and they restored it to me with the malevolent triumph of a passive and unwanted ease. My daily conflict with Amount and Number, the huge accumulations of my years of struggle with the forms of life, my brutal and unending efforts to record upon my memory each brick and paving stone of every street that I had ever walked upon, each face of every thronging crowd in every city, every country with which my spirit had contested its savage and uneven struggle for supremacy [62/63]—they all returned now— each stone, each street, each town, each country—yes, even every book in the library whose loaded shelves I had tried vainly to devour at college—they returned upon the wings of these mighty, sad, and somehow quietly demented dreams—I saw and heard and knew them all at once, was instantly without pain or anguish, with the calm consciousness of God, master of the whole universe of life against whose elements I had contended vainly for all-knowledge for so many years. And the fruit of that enormous triumph, the calm and instant passivity of that inhuman and demented immortality, was somehow sadder and more bitter than the most galling bitterness of defeat in my contention with the multitudes of life had ever been.

For above that universe of dreams there shone forever a tranquil, muted, and unchanging light of time. And through the traffic of those thronging crowds—whose faces, whose whole united and divided life was now [63/64] instantly and without an effort of the will, my *own*—there rose forever the sad unceasing murmurs of the body of this life, the vast recessive fadings of the shadow of man's death that breathes forever with its dirge-like sigh around the huge shores of the world.

And *beyond, beyond*—forever *above, around, behind* the vast and tranquil consciousness of my spirit that now held the earth and all her elements in the huge clasp of its effortless subjection—there dwelt forever the fatal knowledge of my own inexpiable *guilt*.

I did not know what I had done—I only knew that I had ruinously forgotten time, and by so doing had betrayed my brother men. I had been long from home—why, how, or in what way, I could not know—but drugged there in the drowsy fumes of some green country of the witches' magic, with something in me dark and full of grief I could not quite remember. And suddenly I was home again—walking alone beneath that light of tranquil, quiet, and unchanging [**64/65**] brown, walking the roads, the hill-slopes, and the streets of my familiar country—sometimes the *exact* and *actual* lineaments of home, my childhood, and my native town, so that not only all that I had known and remembered—each familiar street and face and house and every cobblestone upon the pavement—but countless things I never knew that I had seen, or had forgotten that I ever knew—a rusty hinge upon the cellar door, the way a stair creaked, or an old cracked blister of brown paint upon the woodwork by the grate, an oak tree trunk upon the hill all hollowed out upon one side by a knotted hole, the glazed pattern of the glass in the front door, the brass handle of a street-car brake-control, quite rubbed to silver on one side by the hard grip of the motorman, and covered by a cloth tobacco sack—such things as these, together with a million others, returned now to torment my sleep.

And even more than these, more, more familiar even than these scenes of memory and inheritance, were those landscapes that some- [**65/66**] how had been *derived* from them—the streets, the towns, the houses and the faces that I saw and imagined not the way they *were*, but the way

they *should* be in the unfathomed, strange, and unsuspected logics of man's brain and heart—and that were, on this account, more real than real-ness, and more true than home.

I had been long from home—I had grown old in some evil and enchanted place, I had allowed my life to waste and rot in the slothful and degrading surfeits of Circean time. And now my life was lost —my work undone—I had betrayed my home, my friends, my people in the duties of some solemn and inviolable trust—and suddenly I was home again, and *silence* was my answer!

They did not look at me with looks of bitterness and hate, they did not lash me with the fierce opprobrium of scorn, or curse me with the menaces of vengeance and reprisal—oh, if they had, what balm of anguish and of judgment even curses would have had!—but instead their look was silence, and [**66/67**] their tongue was mute. And again, again, I walked the streets of that familiar town, and after years of absence saw again the features of familiar faces, and heard familiar words, the sounds of well-known voices once again, and with a still and deep amazement saw the shift and interplay of action, the common familiarity of day, the traffic of the streets, and saw that it was all as it had always been, I had forgotten nothing —until I passed them, and death fell.

I walked among them, and their movements ceased, I walked among them, and their tongues were still, I walked among them and they neither moved nor spoke until I passed, and if they looked at me, their eyes were blank with silence and no memory; there was no reproach, no grief, and no contempt, there was no bitterness and scorn—if I had died, there should at least have been the ghost of memory, but it was as if I never had been born. And so I passed them by, and everywhere I trod was death, and when I had gone by, behind me I could hear their [**67/68**] voices start again; the clamours of the street, and all the traffic of bright day awoke—but only after I had passed them by!

And so the whole town flowed around me, was behind me, and at once, without a bridge or instant of transition, I was walking on a barren road, across the huge sweep of a treeless waste and barren vacancy and that tranquil, sad and fatal light shone on me from the horror of a planetary vacancy, the lidless and remorseless eye of an unperturbed sky that ate into my naked spirit constantly the acid of unuttered shame.

Another and more pertinent variety of these dreams of Guilt and Time would take this form: It seemed to me that I had gone abroad, was living there, and yet was conscious that I was still employed as an instructor at the university. Remote from all the violence and turmoil of America, the harsh impact of its daily life, remote too from the rasping jargon of the university, its corridors packed with swarthy faces, loud with strident tongues, away from all the jar [68/69] and rush and hurly-burly of its fevered life, its unwholesome tensions and its straining nerves, I lived my life in foreign luxuries of green and gold. I dreamed my life away in ancient Gothic towns, or in the pleasant romance of a château country, my spirit slid from land to land, from one enchantment to another, my life was passing by in spells of drowsy magic—and yet I was forever haunted by a consciousness of Time and Guilt, the obscure gnawing of forsaken trust. And suddenly I would seem to wake into a full and frenzied consciousness: I had been gone from home a year —my classes at the university had been waiting on me—and instantly I was there again, rushing through those swarming corridors, hurrying frantically from one classroom to another, trying desperately to find the classes I had so forgotten. There was a grotesque and horrible quality of humor in these dreams, which unfortunately I could not appreciate: I was somehow convinced my forlorn classes had been seeking for me for a year, I saw them [69/70] searching through the mazes of the corridors, prowling among the swarming myriads of their 30,000 fellow students,

sitting in patient dejection at the hours appointed for our meetings in classrooms where their absent teacher never entered. And finally—and most horrible of all— I saw the mounting pile of unmarked student themes—those accursed themes that grew in number week by week—that piled up in mountainous and hopeless accumulations—whose white backs were hideously innocent of the scrawled comment with which I had once—tormented by twin agonies of boredom and conscience— covered every scrap of their surface. And now it was too late! Even a month, two weeks, a week—some miracle of time and frenzied labor—might have served somehow to retrieve myself—but now it was the last day of the term, the last class ended, the last irrevocable moment of salvation had gone by. I found myself suddenly standing there in the offices of the English faculty, struck dumb with horror, confronted by the [70/71] great white mountain of those unmarked themes. I turned, a ring of silent forms encircled me, not staring, not harsh with scorn or anger, and not thrusting close, but just looking at me with the still surveyal of their condemnation. My little Jews stood first, their dark eyes fixed on me with a dejected but unwavering reproach, and behind them stood the jury of my peers, the outer circle of instructors.

They were all there—students, instructors, friends, enemies, and the huge damnation of that pile of unmarked themes —there was no word spoken, nothing but their quiet look of inflexible and unpardoning accusal.

This dream returned to torture sleep a hundred times: Each time I would awake from it in a cold sweat of anguish and of horror, and so strong was the impression of the dream, so real and terrible the spell of its conviction, that sometimes I would wake out of this dream and lie for minutes in cold terror while my mind fought with the phantoms of my sleep to argue me back into reality. [71/72]

Nor were these dreams of Guilt and Time the only ones: my mind and memory in sleep blazed with a fiery river of unending images: the whole vast reservoirs of memory were exhumed and poured into the torrents of this fiery flood, a million things, once seen and long forgotten, were restored and blazed across my vision in this stream of light—and a million million things unseen, the faces, cities, streets, and landscapes yet unseen and long imagined—the unknown faces yet more real than these that I had known, the unheard voices more familiar than the voices I had heard forever, the unseen patterns, masses, shapes and landscapes in their essence far more real than any actual or substantial fact that I had ever known —all streamed across my fevered and unresting mind the flood of their unending pageantry—and suddenly I knew that it would never end.

For sleep was dead forever, the merciful, dark and sweet oblivions of childhood sleep. [**72/73**] The worm had entered at my heart, the worm lay coiled and feeding at my brain, my spirit, and my memory— I knew that finally I had been caught in my own fire, consumed by my own hungers, impaled on the hook of that furious and insatiate desire that had absorbed my life for years. I knew, in short, that one bright cell in the brain or heart or memory would now blaze on forever—by night, by day, through every waking, sleeping moment of my life, the worm would feed and the light be lit,—that no anodyne of food or drink, or friendship, travel, sport or women could ever quench it, and that nevermore until death put its total and conclusive darkness on my life, could I escape.

I knew at last I had become a writer: I knew at last what happens to a man who makes the writer's life his own.

Such was the state my life had come to in the early winter of 1933, and even at that moment, although I could not see it, the end of my huge labor was in sight. In the mid- [**73/74**] dle of December of that year the editor, of whom I have spoken, and who, during all this tormented period, had kept a quiet watch upon me, called me to his home and calmly informed me that my book was finished. I could only look at him with stunned surprise, and finally I only could tell him out of the depth of my own hopelessness, that he was mistaken, that the book was not finished, that it could never be completed, that I could write no more. He answered with the same quiet finality that the book was finished whether I knew it or not, and then he told me to go to my room and spend the next week in collecting in its proper order the manuscript which had accumulated during the last two years.

I followed his instructions, still without hope and without belief. I worked for six days sitting in the middle of the floor surrounded by mountainous stacks of typed manuscript on every side. At the end of a week I had the first part of it together, and just two days before Christmas, 1933, I [**74/75**] delivered to him the manuscript of "The October Fair," and a few days later, the manuscript of "The Hills Beyond Pentland." The manuscript of "The Fair" was, at that time, something over 1,000,000 words in length. He had seen most of it in its dismembered fragments during the three preceding years, but now, for the first time, he was seeing it in its sequential order, and once again his intuition was right; he had told me the truth when he said that I had finished the book.

It was not finished in any way that was publishable or readable. It was really not a book so much as it was the skeleton of a book, but for the first time in four years the skeleton was all there. An enormous labor of revision, weaving together, shaping, and, above all, cutting remained, but I had the book now so that nothing, not even the despair of my own spirit, could take it from me. He told me so, and suddenly I saw that he was right.

I was like a man who is drowning and who [**75/76**] suddenly, at the last gasp of his dying effort, feels earth beneath his feet again. My spirit was borne upward by the greatest triumph it had ever known, and although my mind was tired, my body exhausted, from that moment on I felt equal to anything on earth.

It was evident that many problems were before us, but now we had the thing, and we welcomed the labor before us with happy confidence. In the first place there was the problem of the book's gigantic length. Even in this skeletonized form the manuscript of "The October Fair" was about twelve times the length of the average novel or twice the length of *War and Peace*. It was manifest, therefore, that it would not only be utterly impossible to publish such a manuscript in a single volume, but that even if it were published in several volumes, the tremendous length of such a manuscript would practically annihilate its chances of ever finding a public which would read it.

This problem now faced us, and the editor grappled with it immediately. As his exam- [76/77] ination of the manuscript of "The October Fair" proceeded, he found that the book did describe two complete and separate cycles. The first of these was a movement which described the period of wandering and hunger in a man's youth. The second cycle described the period of greater certitude, and was dominated by the unity of a single passion. It was obvious, therefore, that what we had in the two cyclic movements of this book was really the material of two completely different chronicles, and although the second of the two was by far the more finished, the first cycle, of course, was the one which logically we ought to complete and publish first, and we decided on this course.

We took the first part first. I immediately prepared a minutely thorough synopsis which described not only the course of the book from first to last, but which also included an analysis of those chapters which had been completed in their entirety, of those which were completed only in part, [77/78] and of those which had not been written at all, and with this synopsis before us, we set to work immediately to prepare the book for press. This

work occupied me throughout the whole of the year 1934. The book was completed at the beginning of 1935, and was published in March of that year under the title of *Of Time and the River*.

In the first place, the manuscript, even in its unfinished form, called for the most radical cutting, and because of the way in which the book had been written, as well as the fatigue which I now felt, I was not well prepared to do by myself the task that lay ahead of us.

Cutting had always been the most difficult and distasteful part of writing to me; my tendency had always been to write rather than to cut. Moreover, whatever critical faculty I may have had concerning my own work had been seriously impaired, for the time being at least, by the frenzied labor of the past four years. When a man's work has poured from him for almost five years like [78/79] burning lava from a volcano; when all of it, however superfluous, has been given fire and passion by the white heat of his own creative energy, it is very difficult suddenly to become coldly surgical, ruthlessly detached.

To give a few concrete illustrations of the difficulties that now confronted us: The opening section of the book describes the journey of a train across the State of Virginia at night. Its function in the book is simply to introduce some of the chief characters, to indicate a central situation, to give something of the background from which the book proceeds, and perhaps through the movement of the train across the stillness of the earth to establish a certain beat, evoke a certain emotion which is inherent to the nature of the book. Such a section, therefore, undoubtedly serves an important function, but in proportion to the whole purport of the book, its function is a secondary one and must be related to the whole book in a proportionate way.

Now in the original version, the manu- [79/80] script which described the journey of the train across Virginia at night was considerably longer than the average novel. What was needed was just an introductory chapter or two, and what I had written was over 100,000 words in length, and this same difficulty, this lack of proportion, was also evident in other parts of the manuscript.

What I had written about the great train was really good. But what I had to face, the very bitter lesson that every one who wants to write has got to learn, was that a thing may in itself be the finest piece of writing one has ever done, and yet have absolutely no place in the manuscript one hopes to publish. This is a hard thing, but it must be faced, and so we faced it.

My spirit quivered at the bloody execution. My soul recoiled before the carnage of so many lovely things cut out upon which my heart was set. But it had to be done, and we did it.

The first chapter in the original manuscript, a chapter which the editor, himself, [80/81] admitted was as good a single piece of writing as I had ever done, was relentlessly kicked out, and the reason it was kicked out was that it was really not a true beginning for the book but merely something which led up to the true beginning; therefore it had to go. And so it went all up and down the line. Chapters 50,000 words long were reduced to ten or fifteen thousand words, and having faced this inevitable necessity, I finally acquired a kind of ruthlessness of my own, and once or twice, myself, did more cutting than my editor was willing to allow.

Another fault that has always troubled me in writing is that I have often attempted to reproduce in its entirety the full flood and fabric of a scene in life itself. Thus, in another section of the book, four people were represented as talking to each other for four hours without a break or intermission. All were good talkers; often all talked, or tried to talk, at the same time. The talk was wonderful and living talk because I knew the life and character and the vocabu- [81/82] lary of all these people from its living source, and I had forgotten nothing. Yet all the time, all that was actually happening in this scene was that a young woman had got out of her husband's motor car and gone into her mother's house and kept calling to the impatient man outside every time he honked his horn, "All right, all right. I'll be with you in five minutes." These five minutes really lengthened into four hours, while the unfortunate man outside honked upon his horn, and while the two women and two young men of the same family inside carried on a torrential discourse and discussed exhaustively the lives and histories of almost everyone in town, their memories of the past, adventures of the present, and speculations of the future. I put it all down in the original manuscript just as I had seen and known and lived it a thousand times, and even if I do say so myself, the nature of the talk, the living vitality and character of the language, the utter naturalness, the floodtide river of it all was wonderful, but I had [82/83] made four people talk 80,000 words—200 printed pages of close type in a minor scene of an enormous book, and of course, good as it was, it was all wrong and had to go.

Such, then, were some of our major difficulties with the manuscript we had in hand, and although since its publication there have been many declarations to the effect that the book would have benefited by a much more radical cutting, the cutting we did do was much more drastic than I had dreamed was possible.

Meanwhile I was proceeding at full speed with the work of completing my design, finishing the unfinished parts and filling in the transition links which were essential.

This in itself was an enormous job and kept me writing all day long as hard as I could go for a full year. Here again the nature of my chief fault was manifest. I wrote too much again. I not only wrote what was essential, but time and time again my enthusiasm for a good scene, one of those en- [83/84] chanting vistas which can open up so magically to a man in the full flow of his creation, would overpower me, and I would write thousands of words upon a scene which contributed nothing of vital importance to a book whose greatest need already was ruthless condensation.

During the course of this year, I must have written well over a half million words of additional manuscript, of which, of course, only a small part was finally used.

The nature of my method, the desire fully to explore my material, had led me into another error. The whole effect of those five years of incessant writing had been to make me feel not only that everything had to be used, but that everything had to be told, that nothing could be implied. Therefore, at the end, there were at least a dozen additional chapters which I felt had to be completed to give the book its final value. A thousand times I debated this question desperately with my editor. I told him that these chapters had to go in simply because I felt the [84/85] book would not be complete without them, and with every argument he had, he tried to show me that I was wrong. I see now that on the whole he was right about it, but at the time I was so inextricably involved in my work, that I did not have the detachment necessary for a true appraisal.

The end came suddenly—the end of those five years of torment and incessant productivity. In October I took a trip to Chicago, a two weeks' vacation, my first in over a year. When I returned I found that my editor had quietly and decisively sent the manuscript to the press, the printers were already at work on it, the proof was beginning to come in. I had not foreseen it; I was desperate, bewildered. "You can't do it," I told him, "the book is not yet finished. I must have six months more on it."

To this he answered that the book was not only finished, but that if I took six months more on it, I would then demand another six months and six months more beyond that, and that I might very well become so ob- [85/86] sessed with this one work that I would never get it published. He went on to say, and I think with complete justice, that such a course was wrong for me. I was not, he said, a Flaubert kind of writer. I was not a perfectionist. I had twenty, thirty, almost any number of books in me, and the important thing was to get them produced and not to spend the rest of my life in perfecting one book. He agreed that with six months' additional work upon the book, I might achieve a certain finish and completeness, but he did not think that the benefit would be nearly as great as I thought it would be, and his own deep conviction was that the book should be published at once without further delay, that I should get it out of me, forget about it, turn my life to the final completion of the work which was already prepared and ready, waiting for me. He told me, furthermore, exactly what the nature of the criticism would be, the criticism of its length, its adjectives, its overabundance, but he told me not to despair. [86/87]

He told me finally that I would go on and do better work, that I would learn to work without so much confusion, waste, and useless torment, that my future books would more and more achieve the unity, sureness, and finality that every artist wants his work to have, but that I had to learn in the way I had learned, groping, struggling, finding my own way for myself, that this was the only way to learn.

In January, 1935, I finished the last of my revisions on the proof; the first printed copies came from the press in February. The book was released for final publication early in March. I was not here when it came out. I had taken a ship for Europe the week before, and as the ship got farther and farther from the American shores, my spirits sank lower and lower, reaching, I think, the lowest state of hopeless depression they had ever known. This, I believe, was largely a physical reaction, the inevitable effect of relaxation upon a human organism which had for five years been strained to its utmost [87/88] limit. My life seemed to me to be like a great spring which had been taut for years and which was now slowly uncoiling from its tension. I had the most extraordinary sense of desolation I had ever known when I thought about my book. I had never realized until now how close I had been to it, how much a part of me it had become, and now that it had been taken away from me, my life felt utterly futile, hollow as a shell. And now that the book was gone, now that there was nothing more that I could do about it, I felt the most abysmal sensation of failure. I have always been somewhat afraid of print, although print is a thing I have tried so hard to achieve. Yet it is literally true that with everything I have ever written, I have felt when the hour of naked print drew nigh a kind of desperation and have even entreated my publisher not only to defer the publication of my book until another season, but have asked the editors of magazines to put off the publication of a story for another month or two until I had a [88/89] chance to work on it some more, do something to it, I was not always sure what.

Now I had an overwhelming sense of shame greater than any I had felt before. I felt as if I had ruinously exposed myself as a pitiable fool who had no talent and who once and for all had completely vindicated the prophecies of the critics who had felt the first book was just a flash in the pan. It was in this frame of mind that I arrived in Paris on March 8, the day the book was to be published in America. I had come away to forget about it, and yet I thought about it all the time. I walked the streets from dawn to dark, from night to morning, at least a dozen times in two short weeks I heard the celebration of mass at Sacré Cœur, and then would walk the streets again and come back to my hotel at ten o'clock and lie upon the bed, and still I could not sleep.

After several days of this, I steeled myself to go to the office of the travel agency where a message might be waiting for me. I found a cablegram there. It was from my [89/90] publisher, and it said simply: "Magnificent reviews somewhat critical in ways expected, full of greatest praise." I read it the first time with a feeling of almost intolerable joy but as I continued to read and reread it, the old dark doubt began to creep across my mind and by the time night had come I was convinced that this wonderful cable was just a sentence of doom, and that my editor, out of the infinite compassion of his spirit, had taken this means of breaking the news to me that my book was a colossal failure.

Three days passed in which I prowled the streets of Paris like a maddened animal, and of those three days I could later remember almost nothing. At the end of that time I sent a frenzied cablegram to that editor in which I told him I could stand anything better than this state of damnable uncertainty and pleaded with him to give me the blunt truth no matter how bitter it might be. His answer to this cable was such that I could no longer doubt him or the reception which the book had had at home. [90/91]

This completes, as far as I can remember it, the story of the making of a book and what happened to its maker. I know it is too long a story; I know, also, that it must seem to be a story filled with the record of a man's blunders and ludicrous mistakes, but simply because it is that kind of story, I hope that it may have some value. It is a story of the artist as a man and as a worker. It is a story of the artist as a man who is derived out of the common family of earth and who knows all the anguish, error, and frustration that any man alive can know.

The life of the artist at any epoch of man's history has not been an easy one. And here in America, it has often seemed to me, it may well be the hardest life that man has ever known. I am not speaking of some frustration in our native life, some barrenness of spirit, some arid Philistinism which contends against the artist's life and which prevents his growth. I do not speak of these things because I do not put the same belief in them that I once did. I am speaking as I [91/92] have tried to speak from first to last in the concrete terms of the artist's actual experience, of the nature of the physical task before him. It seems to me that the task is one whose physical proportions are vaster and more difficult here than in any other nation on the earth. It is not merely that in the cultures of Europe and of the Orient the American artist can find no antecedent scheme, no structural plan, no body of tradition that can give his own work the validity and truth that it must have. It is not merely that he must make somehow a new tradition for himself, derived from his own life and from the enormous space and energy of American life, the structure of his own design; it is not merely that he is confronted by these problems; it is even more than this, that the labor of a complete and whole articulation, the discovery of an entire universe and of a complete language, is the task that lies before him.

Such is the nature of the struggle to which henceforth our lives must be devoted. Out [**92/93**] of the billion forms of America, out of the savage violence and the dense complexity of all its swarming life; from the unique and single substance of this land and life of ours, must we draw the power and energy of our own life, the articulation of our speech, the substance of our art.

For here it seems to me in hard and honest ways like these we may find the tongue, the language, and the conscience that as men and artists we have got to have. Here, too, perhaps, must we who have no more than what we have, who know no more than what we know, who are no more than what we are, find our America. Here, at this present hour and moment of my life, I seek for mine.

No Door: A Story of Time and the Wanderer*

THOMAS WOLFE in 1933 completed a short novel which was based, he said, on his "own life for the last ten or fifteen years," and submitted it to *Scribner's Magazine*. One portion, entitled *No Door* was published in the July, 1933, issue; and another, entitled "The House of the Far and the Lost," in the August, 1934, issue. Wolfe wanted to publish *No Door* as a small book and Scribner's agreed at first and then decided against such publication. Portions of *No Door* were used in fragmented form in *Of Time and the River, From Death to Morning,* and *You Can't Go Home Again.* The complete work was published as a unit for the first time in *The Short Novels of Thomas Wolfe* in 1961. The passages reprinted here are from the second section, "October: 1923," dealing with the return of the protagonist to his home in the hills of Old Catawba (North Carolina) after the death of his father. In a modified form they appear in *Of Time and the River* (New York: Charles Scribner's Sons, 1935), pp. 327-328, 329-332, 333-334.

. . . .

October had come again, and that year it was sharp and soon: frost was early, burning the thick green on the mountain sides to massed brilliant hues of blazing colors, painting the air with sharpness, sorrow, and delight. Sometimes, and often, there was warmth by day, an ancient drowsy light, a golden **[46/47]** warmth and pollenated [*sic*] haze in afternoon, but over all the earth there was the premonitory breath of frost, an exultancy for all the men who were returning, a haunting sorrow for the buried men, and for all those who were gone and would not come again.

My father was dead, and now it seemed to me that I had never found him. He was dead, and yet I sought him everywhere, and could not believe that he was dead, and was sure that I would find him. It was October and that year, after years of ab-

sence and of wandering, I had come home again.

I could not think that he had died, but I had come home in October, and all the life that I had known there was strange and sorrowful as dreams. And yet I saw it all in shapes of deathless brightness—the town, the streets, the magic hills, and the plain prognathous faces of the people I had known as if I had revisited the shores of this great earth with a heart of fire, a cry of pain and ecstasy, a memory of intolerable longing and regret for all that glorious and exultant life which I must visit now forever as a fleshless ghost, never to touch, to hold, to have its palpable warmth and substance for my own again. I had come home again, and yet I could not believe that he was dead, and I thought I heard his great voice ringing in the street again, and that I would see him striding toward me across the Square with his gaunt earth-devouring stride, or find him waiting every time I turned the corner,

*Thomas Wolfe, "No Door," *Scribner's Magazine*, XCIV (July 1933) 7-12, 46-56. Copyright 1933 Charles Scribner's Sons; renewal copyright © 1961. Reprinted in part in *Of Time and the River*, pp. 327-334, by Thomas Wolfe and in its entirety in *The Short Novels of Thomas Wolfe*, edited by C. Hugh Holman (New York: Charles Scribner's Sons, 1961) pp. 157-231. Used by permission of the publisher.

or lunging toward the house bearing the tremendous provender of his food and meat, bringing to us all the deathless security of his strength and power and passion, bringing to us all again the roaring message of his fires that shook the firefull chimney throat with their terrific blast, giving to us all again the exultant knowledge that the good days, the magic days, the golden weather of our lives would come again, and that this dream-like and phantasmal world in which I found myself would waken instantly, as it had once, to all the palpable warmth and glory of the earth, if only my father would come back to make it live, to give us life, again.

Therefore, I could not think that he was dead. And at night, in my mother's house, I would lie in my bed in the dark, hearing the wind that rattled dry leaves along the empty pavement, hearing far-off across the wind, the barking of a dog, feeling dark time, strange time, dark secret time, as it flowed on around me, remembering my life, this house, and all the million strange and secret visages of time, dark time, thinking, feeling, thinking:

"October has come again, has come again. . . . I have come home again, and found my father dead . . . and that was time . . . time . . . time. . . . Where shall I go now? What shall I do? For October has come again, but there has gone some richness from the life we knew, and we are lost." [*Ellipses in Wolfe's text*].

Storm shook the house at night—the old house, my mother's house—where I had seen my brother die. The old doors swung and creaked in darkness, darkness pressed against the house, the darkness filled us, filled the house at night, it moved about us soft and secret, palpable, filled with a thousand secret presences of sorrowful time and memory, moving about me as I lay below my brother's room in darkness, while storm shook the house and something creaked and rattled in the wind's strong blast.

. . . .

And I would lie there thinking:

. . . .

"Now October has come again which in our land is different from October in the other lands. The ripe, the golden month has come again, and in Virginia the chinkapins are falling. Frost sharps the middle music of the seasons, and all things living on the earth turn home again. The country is so big you cannot say the country has the same October. In Maine, the frost comes sharp and quick as driven nails, just for a week or so the woods, all of the bright and bitter leaves, flare up: the maples turn a blazing bitter red, and other leaves turn yellow like a living light, falling about you as you walk the woods, falling about you like small pieces of the sun, so that you cannot say where sunlight shakes and flutters on the ground, and where the leaves.

"Meanwhile the Palisades are melting in massed molten colors, the season swings along the nation, and a little later in the South dense woodings on the hill begin to glow and soften, and when they smell the burning woodsmoke in Ohio children say: 'I'll bet that there's a forest fire in Michigan.' And the mountaineer goes hunting down in North Carolina, he stays out late with mournful flop-eared hounds, a rind of moon comes up across the [**47/48**] rude lift of the hills: what do his friends say to him when he stays out late? Full of hoarse innocence and laughter, they will say: 'Mister, yore ole woman's goin' to whup ye if ye don't go home.' "

Oh, return, return!

"October is the richest of the seasons: the fields are cut, the granaries are full, the bins are loaded to the brim with fatness, and from the cider-press the rich brown oozings of the York Imperials run. The bee bores to the belly of the yellowed grape, the fly gets old and fat and blue, he buzzes loud, crawls slow, creeps heavily to death on sill and ceiling, the sun goes down in blood and pollen across the bronzed and mown fields of old October.

"The corn is shocked: it sticks out in hard yellow rows upon dried ears, fit now for great red barns in Pennsylvania, and the big stained teeth of crunching horses. The indolent hoofs kick swiftly at the boards, the barn is sweet with hay and leather, wood and apples. This, and the clean dry crunching of the teeth, is all: the sweat, the labor, and the plow are over. The late pears mellow on a sunny shelf; smoked hams hang to the warped barn rafters; the pantry shelves are loaded with three hundred jars of fruit. Meanwhile the leaves are turning, turning up in Maine, the chestnut burrs plop thickly to the earth in gusts of wind, and in Virginia the chinkapins are falling.

"There is a smell of burning in small towns in afternoon, and men with buckles on their arms are raking leaves in yards as boys come by with straps slung back across their shoulders. The oak leaves, big and brown, are bedded deep in yard and gutter: they make deep wadings to the knee for children in the streets. The fire will snap and crackle like a whip, sharp acrid smoke will sting the eyes, in mown fields the little vipers of the flame eat past the black coarse edges of burnt stubble like a line of locusts. Fire drives a thorn of memory in the heart.

"The bladed grass, a forest of small spears of ice, is thawed by noon: summer is over but the sun is warm again, and there are days throughout the land of gold and russet. But summer is dead and gone, the earth is waiting, suspense and ecstasy are gnawing at the hearts of men, the brooding prescience of frost is there. The sun flames red and bloody as it sets, there are old red glintings on the battered pails, the great barn gets the ancient light as the boy slops homeward with warm foaming milk. Great shadows lengthen in the fields, the old red light dies swiftly, and the sunset barking of the hounds is faint and far and full of frost: there are shrewd whistles to the dogs of frost and silence—this is all. Wind scuffs and rattles at the old brown eaves, and through the night the great oak leaves keep falling.

"Trains cross the continent in a swirl of dust and thunder, the leaves fly down the tracks behind them: the great trains cleave through gulch and gulley, they rumble with spoked thunder of the bridges over the powerful brown wash of mighty rivers, they toil through hills, they skirt the rough brown stubble of shorn fields, they whip past empty stations in the little towns and their great stride pounds its even pulse across America. Field and hill and lift and gulch and hollow, mountain and plain and river, a wilderness with fallen trees across it, a thicket of bedded brown and twisted undergrowth, a plain, a desert, and a plantation, a mighty landscape with no fenced niceness, an immensity of fold and convolution that can never be remembered, that can never be forgotten, that has never been described—weary with harvest, potent with every fruit and ore, the immeasurable richness embrowned with autumn, rank, crude, unharnessed, careless of scars or beauty, everlasting and magnificent, a cry, a space, an ecstasy!—American earth in old October.

"And the great winds howl and swoop across the land: they make a distant roaring in great trees, and boys in bed will stir in ecstasy, thinking of demons and vast swoopings through the earth. All through the night there is the clean, the bitter rain of acorns, and the chestnut burrs are plopping to the ground.

"And often in the night there is only the living silence, the distant frosty barking of a dog, the small clumsy stir and feathery stumble of the chickens on limed roosts, and the moon, the low and heavy moon of autumn, now barred behind the leafless poles of pines, now at the pinewood's brooding edge and summit, now falling with ghost's dawn of milky light upon rimed clods of fields and on the frosty scurf on pumpkins, now whiter, smaller, brighter, hanging against the church spire's slope, hanging the same way in a million streets, steeping all the earth in frost and silence.

"Then a chime of frost-cold bells may peal out on the brooding air, and people lying in their beds will listen. They will not speak or stir, silence will gnaw the darkness like a rat, but they will whisper in their hearts:

" 'Summer has come and gone, has come and gone. And now—?' But they will say no more, they will have no more to say: they will wait listening, silent and brooding as the frost, to time, strange ticking time, dark time that haunts us with the briefness of our days. They will think of men long dead, of men now buried in the earth, of frost and silence long ago, of a forgotten face and moment of lost time, and they will think of things they have no words to utter.

"And in the night, in the dark, in the living sleeping silence of the towns, the million streets, they will hear the thunder of the fast express, the whistles of great ships upon the river.

"What will they say then? What will they say?"

Only the darkness moved about me as I lay there thinking; feeling in the darkness: a door creaked softly in the house. **[48/49]**

.   .   .   .

"Come to us, father, in the watches of the night, come to us as you always came, bringing to us the invincible sustenance of your strength, the limitless treasure of your bounty, the tremendous structure of your life that will shape all lost and broken things on earth again into a golden pattern of exultancy and joy. Come to us, father, while the winds howl in the darkness, for October has come again bringing with it huge prophecies of death and life and the great cargo of the men who will return. For we are ruined, lost, and broken if you do not come, and our lives, like rotten chips, are whirled about us onward in the darkness to the sea."

So, thinking, feeling, speaking, I lay there in my mother's house, but there was nothing in the house but silence and the moving darkness: storm shook the house and huge winds rushed upon us, and I knew then that my father would not come again, and that all the life that I had known was now lost and broken as a dream.

Suddenly I knew that every man who ever lived has looked, is looking, for his father, and that even when his father dies, his son will still search furiously the streets of life to find him, and that he never loses hope but always feels that some day he will see his father's face again. I had come home again in October and there were no doors, there were no doors for me to enter and I knew now that I could never make this life my own again. Yet, in all the huge unrest that was goading me to flight I had no place or door or dwelling-place on earth to go, and yet must make for myself a life different from the one my father made for me or die myself.

Storm shook the house at night and there was something calling in the wind. It spoke to me and filled my heart with the exultant prophecies of flight, darkness, and discovery, saying with a demon's whisper of unbodied joy:

"Away! Away! Away! There are new lands, morning, and a shining city! Child, child, go find the earth again!"

.   .   .   .

The Wolfe at the Door*

CLIFTON FADIMAN (1940-   ), American literary critic, essayist, and radio and television performer, has been a devoted and outspoken surveyor of the literary scene for more than three decades. His parody of Thomas Wolfe's writing is based upon a portion of the Bascom Pentland sequence in *Of Time and the River* (New York: Charles Scribner's Sons, 1935), pp. 175-194. An earlier version of the Bascom Pentland material appeared in the short novel *A Portrait of Bascom Hawke*, in *Scribner's Magazine*, April, 1932, and is reprinted in *The Short Novels of Thomas Wolfe* (New York: Charles Scribner's Sons, 1961), pp. 4-71.

There they were, two dark wandering atoms.

Uncle Habbakuk, one of the legendary, far-wandering Gants, and full of their dark, illimitable madness, was of but average stature, being only eight or nine feet high. He lifted his fork from one of his characteristic disgusting, unsavory, and nauseating messes. It consisted of old iron filings, chopped twine, oats, and clippings *hachis* from the *Times* classified ads section. With his hard, bony fore-finger he prodded Aunt Liz. Ceaselessly he prodded her, hungrily, savagely. But she gave no sign. She was lost (Oh lost! lost! who shall point out the path?) in a dream of time.

"Phuh! Phuh!" howled Uncle Habbakuk, the goat-cry welling up like a madness out of the vine of his throat. "Phuh! Phuh! Ow—ooh! *Beep!*"

Uncle Habbakuk, with demonic, fore-fingered energy, continued to lift up his idiotic, wordless and exultant howl. It was monstrous, yet somehow lovely, not to say fated, this gaunt confrontation of these two lonely atoms. . . . How strange and full of mystery life is! One passes another in the street, or a face flashes past as the great huge train-projectiles of Amer-ica hurtle by, in all their thrill and men-ace, over the old brown earth, and the soul fills with sadness and irrecoverable memories. Why is this? Is it because we are the sons of [455/456] our fathers and the nieces and nephews of our aunts and uncles?

Who will answer our questions, satisfy our furious impatience, allay our elemen-tal desires, soothe our tormented unrest, and check our heavy baggage? Who?

"*Beep!*" barked Uncle Habbakuk in his coruscating and indefinite way. "What is man that thou—*whah!*—art mindful of him?"

"Whoo-oop," chirped and sniggled Aunt Liz. Sly and enigmatic, she picked up a morsel of bread and hurled it savagely upon the table, with a gesture old as time itself, and secret with the secretiveness of a thousand secretive, lovely and mysteri-ous women, all secret. Then she relapsed into her dream of time. She was entranced in one of her brooding and incalculable states— (O the States, O Alabama, Ari-zona, Arkansas, and California; O Colo-rado, Connecticut, Delaware, and Florida; O Georgia, Idaho, Illinois, and Indiana; O Iowa, Kansas, Kentucky, and Louisiana;

* Clifton Fadiman, "The Wolfe at the Door," *Party of One: The Selected Writings of Clifton Fadiman* (New York: The World Publishing Company, 1955), pp. 455-460. Reprinted with the permission of the World Publishing Company.

O Maine, Maryland, Massachusetts, and Michigan; O Minnesota, Mississippi, Missouri, and Montana; O Nebraska, Nevada, New Hampshire, and New Jersey; O New Mexico, New York, North Carolina, and North Dakota; O Ohio, Oklahoma, Oregon, and Pennsylvania; O Rhode Island, South Carolina, South Dakota, and Tennessee; O Texas, Utah, Vermont, and Virginia; O Washington, West Virginia, Wisconsin, and Wyoming; and O! O! the District of Columbia!)

At this very moment, so pregnant and prescient with the huge warp of fate and chance, the dark, terrific weaving of the threads of time and destiny, there was heard one of the loveliest and most haunting of all sounds, to echo in the ears of Americans forever, surging in the adyts of their [456/457] souls and drumming in the conduits of their blood. The doorbell tinkled.

"A moment's—*beep!*—peace for all of us before we die," snarled, bellowed, and croaked gaunt Uncle Habbakuk, prodding himself violently in the midriff with his hard bony fore-finger. "Give the goat-cry!"

"Phuh-phuh! Ow-ooh! *Beep!*" came the goat-cry from without, and Aunt Liz opened the door. It was he, the youth, of the tribe of the Gants, eleven feet, eight inches high, with slabsided cheeks, high, white, integrated forehead, long, savage, naked-looking ears, thirty-two teeth, and that strange, familiar, native, alien expression common to all the Gants, wandering forever and the earth again. It was the youth, but no less was it Jason and Faustus and Antaeus and Kronos and Telemachus and Synopsis and all those shining young heroes who have hungered amid the *Gewirr* of life and sought their fathers in the congeries of the compacted habitations of man, hot for the alexin of our cure and amorous of the unknown river and a thousand furious streets.

With a loose and powerful gesture Uncle Habbakuk, in frenzied despair, luminous hope, and frantic entreaty, welcomed the youth, snuffling.

"Where have you *been*, youth? Have you touched, tasted, heard, *and seen* everything? Have you *smelt everything?* Have you come from out the *wilderness,* the buried past, the lost *America?* Are you bringing up Father out of the *River?* Have you done any delicate *diving* for the *Greeks?* Have you embraced *life* and *devoured* it? Tell me! Open the adyts of your soul. Beep."

"Beep," chirped the youth somberly. "I have been making mad journeys, peril-fraught and passion-laden, on the Hud- [457/458] son River Day Line, watching my lost, million-visaged brothers and sisters. I have been lying in my upper berth above good-looking women in the lower berth on a thousand train-wanderings. They were all of them tall and sensual-looking Jewesses, proud, potent, amber, dark, and enigmatic. I always felt they would not rebuff me if I spoke to them, but yet I did not speak. Later on, however, I wondered about their lives. Yet I have been with a thousand women, their amber thighs spread amorously in bright golden hay.

"Pent in my dark soul I have sought in many countries my heart's hope and my father's land, the lost but unforgotten half of my own soul. In the fierce, splendid, strange and secret North have I sought; and, on the other hand, in the secret, strange, splendid and fierce South. In the fatal web of the City strangely and bitterly have I savored the strange and bitter miracle of life and wondered darkly at the dark wonder of man's destiny. Amid this phantasmagoric chaos, in a thousand little sleeping towns built across the land (O my America! O my!) I have pursued my soul's desire, looking for a stone, a leaf, a door we never found, feeling my Faustian life intolerably in my entrails. I have quivered a thousand times in sensual terror and ecstatic joy as the 5:07 pulled in. I have felt a wild and mournful sorrow at the thought, the wonderful thought, that everything I have seen and known (and have I not known and seen all that is to be seen and known upon this dark, brooding continent?) has come out of my own life, is indeed I, or me, the youth eternal, many-visaged and many-volumed.

"Whatever it may be, I have sought it through my kaleidoscopic days and velvet-and-duvetyn-breasted nights, and in my dark, illimitable madness, in my insatiate and huge [458/459] unrest, in my appalling and obscene fancies, in my haunting and lonely memories (for we are all lonely) , in my grotesque, abominable and frenzied prodigalities, I have always cried aloud—"

"Whoo-oops," gargled, snorted, and snuffled Aunt Liz from out her dream of time.

"What is it that we know so well and cannot speak?" continued the youth, striding a thousand strides across a hundred floors. "What is it that we speak so well and cannot know? Why this ceaseless pullulation stirring in my branching veins, not to be stilled even by the white small bite and tigerish clasp of secret women, of whom I have had one thousand in round figures? Whence the savagery, the hunger and the fear? I have sought the answer in four hundred and twelve libraries, including the Mercantile, the 42nd Street Public, the Muhlenberg Branch, and the Brooklyn—ah, Brooklyn, vast, mysterious, and never-to-be-forgotten Brooklyn and its congeries of swarming, unfathomable life, O Brooklyn! I have read in ten years at least twenty thousand books, devouring them twelve hours a day, no holidays, four hundred pages to a book, or in other words,—and I am furiously fond of other words—I have read thirty-three pages a minute, or a page every two seconds. Yet during this very same period I managed with ease to prowl ten thousand wintry, barren, and accursed streets, to lie with one thousand women, and take any number of train-trips. (Oh! the dark earth stroking forever past the huge projectile!) This is it to be a Gant! Questing my destiny lying ever before me, I have been life's beauty-drunken lover, and kept women and notebooks in a hundred cities, yet have I never found the door or turned the knob or slipped the bolt or torn off the leaf or [459/460] crossed the road or climbed the fence. I have seen fury riding in the mountains, but who will show me the door?"

"Phuh! Phuh!" howled Uncle Habbakuk from out his illimitable loneliness; and "Whoo-oop!" came from Aunt Liz, lost in her dream of time. Both lost, all lost, lost forever, forever lost.

PART TWO

WOLFE'S WRITING METHODS

Thomas Wolfe*

MAXWELL E. PERKINS (1884-1947) was in the editorial department of Charles Scribner's Sons from 1910 until his death. He accepted *Look Home-ward, Angel* for publication and worked with Wolfe in organizing *Of Time and the River.* The essay from which selections are reprinted here was pre-pared by Perkins just before his death and was first published in the *Harvard Library Bulletin* in the Autumn, 1947, issue.

. . . .

The first time I heard of Thomas Wolfe I had a sense of foreboding. I who love the man say this. Every good thing that comes is accompanied by trouble. It was in 1928 when Madeleine Boyd, a literary agent, came in. She talked of several man-uscripts which did not much interest me, but frequently interrupted herself to tell of a wonderful novel about an American boy. I several times said to her, 'Why don't you bring it in here, Madeleine?' and she seemed to evade the question. But finally she said, 'I will bring it, if you promise to read every word of it.' I did promise, but she told me other things that made me realize that Wolfe was a tur-bulent spirit, and that we were in for turbulence. When the manuscript came, I was fascinated by the first scene where Eugene's father, Oliver W. Gant [*sic*], with his brother, two little boys, stood by a roadside in Pennsylvania and saw a divi-sion of Lee's Army on the march to Gettysburg.

But then there came some ninety-odd pages about Oliver Gant's life in New-port News, and Baltimore, and elsewhere. All this was what Wolfe had heard, and had no actual association with which to reconcile it, and it was inferior to the first episode, and in fact to all the rest of the book. I was turned off to other work and

gave the manuscript to Wallace Meyer, thinking, 'Here is another promising novel that probably will come to nothing.' Then Meyer showed me that wonderful night scene in the cafe where Ben was with the Doctors, and Horse Hines, the undertaker, came in. I dropped everything and began to read again, and all of us were reading the book simultaneously, you might say, including John Hall Wheelock, and there never was the slightest disagreement among us as to its importance. [**270/271**]

After some correspondence between me and Wolfe, and between him and Made-leine Boyd, from which we learned how at the October Fair in Germany he had been almost beaten to death—when I real-ized again that we had a Moby Dick to deal with—Wolfe arrived in New York and stood in the doorway of my boxstall of an office leaning against the door jamb. When I looked up and saw his wild hair and bright countenance—although he was so altogether different physically—I thought of Shelley. *He* was fair, but his hair was wild, and his face was bright and his head disproportionately small.

We then began to work upon the book and the first thing we did, to give it unity was to cut out that wonderful scene i began with and the ninety-odd pages tha followed, because it seemed to me, and he agreed, that the whole tale should be un

*Maxwell E. Perkins, from "Thomas Wolfe," *Harvard Library Bulletin*, I (Autumn, 1947), 269-277. Reprinte by permission of the President and Fellows of Harvard College.

folded through the memories and senses of the boy, Eugene, who was born in Asheville. We both thought that the story was compassed by that child's realization; that it was life and the world as he came to realize them. When he had tried to go back into the life of his father before he arrived in Asheville, without the inherent memory of events, the reality and the poignance were diminished—but for years it was on my conscience that I had persuaded Tom to cut out that first scene of the two little boys on the roadside with Gettysburg impending.

And then what happened? In *Of Time and the River* he brought the scene back to greater effect when old Gant was dying on the gallery of the hospital in Baltimore and in memory recalled his olden days. After that occurred I felt much less anxiety in suggesting cuts: I began then to realize that nothing Wolfe wrote was ever lost, that omissions from one book were restored in a later one. An extreme example of this is the fact that the whole second half of *The Web and the Rock* was originally intended to be the concluding episode in *Of Time and the River.* But most, and perhaps almost all, of those early incidents of Gant's life were worked into *The Web and the Rock* and *You Can't Go Home Again.*

I had realized, for Tom had prefaced his manuscript with a statement to that effect, that *Look Homeward, Angel* was autobiographical, but I had come to think of it as being so in the sense that *David Copperfield* is, or *War and Peace,* or *Pendennis.* But when we were working together, I suddenly saw that it was often almost literally autobiographical—that these people in it were his people. I am sure my face took on a [271/272] look of alarm, and Tom saw it and he said, 'But Mr. Perkins, you don't understand. I think these people are *great* people and that they should be told about.' He was right. He had written a great book, and it had to be taken substantially as it was. And in truth, the extent of cutting in that book has

somehow come to be greatly exaggerated. Really, it was more a matter of reorganization. For instance, Tom had that wonderful episode when Gant came back from his far-wandering and rode in early morning on the trolley car through the town and heard about who had died and who had been born and saw all the scenes that were so familiar to Tom or Eugene, as the old trolley rumbled along. This was immediately followed by an episode of a similar kind where Eugene, with his friends, walked home from school through the town of Asheville. That was presented in a Joycean way, but it was the same sort of thing—some one going through the town and through his perceptions revealing it to the reader. By putting these episodes next to each other the effect of each was diminished, and I think we gave both much greater value by separating them. We did a great deal of detailed cutting, but it was such things as that I speak of that constituted perhaps the greater part of the work.

Of Time and the River was a much greater struggle for Tom. Eventually, I think it was on Thanksgiving Day 1933, he brought me in desperation about two feet of typescript. The first scene in this was the platform of the railroad station in Asheville when Eugene was about to set out for Harvard, and his family had come to see him off. It must have run to about 30,000 words and I cut it to perhaps 10,000 and showed it to Tom. He approved it. When you are waiting for a train to come in, there is suspense. Something is going to happen. You must, it seemed to me, maintain that sense of suspense and you can't to the extent of 30,000 words. There never was any cutting that Tom did not agree to. He knew that cutting was necessary. His whole impulse was to utter what he felt and he had no time to revise and compress.

So then we began a year of nights of work, including Sundays, and every cut, and change, and interpolation, was argued about and about. The principle that I was working on was that this book, too, got its unity and its form through the senses of Eugene, and I remember how, if I had had my way, we should, by sticking to that principle, have lost one of the most wonderful episodes Wolfe ever wrote—the death of Gant. [**272/273**] One night we agreed that certain transitions should be written in, but instead of doing them Wolfe brought on the next night some five thousand words about Eugene's sister in Asheville when her father was ill, and a doctor there and a nurse. I said, 'Tom, this is all outside the story, and you know it. Eugene was not there, he was in Cambridge; all of this was outside his perception and knowledge at the time.' Tom agreed with me, but the next night, he brought me another five thousand words

or so which got up into the death of Gant. And then I realized I was wrong, even if right in theory. What he was doing was too good to let any rule of form impede him.

It is said that Tolstoy never willingly parted with the manuscript of *War and Peace*. One could imagine him working on it all through his life. Certainly Thomas Wolfe never willingly parted from the proofs of *Of Time and the River*. He sat brooding over them for weeks in the Scribner library and not reading. John Wheelock read them and we sent them to the printer and told Tom it had been done. I could believe that otherwise he might have clung to them to the end.

.   .   .   .

A Note on Thomas Wolfe*

EDWARD C. ASWELL (1900-1958) was a member of the editorial department of Harper and Brothers, from 1935 to 1947, and vice-president of McGraw-Hill, from 1947 until his death. Aswell became Wolfe's editor when the novelist moved from Scribner's to Harper's, and it was he who assembled the materials left by Wolfe upon his death into *The Web and the Rock, You Can't Go Home Again,* and *The Hills Beyond.* Upon Perkins' death in 1947, Aswell became administrator of the Wolfe literary estate. In "A Note on Thomas Wolfe," which was appended to *The Hills Beyond,* Aswell explained his procedures in editing Wolfe's manuscript remains.

. . . .

Illuminating as is *The Story of a Novel,* much still remains to be said about Thomas Wolfe's unusual techniques. No one, I think, ever went about the job of writing as he did. His strengths and his weak- **[351/352]** nesses, his brilliant achievements in probing to the roots of human character and in evoking the sights, sounds, smells, and very feel of his America, as well as his constant preoccupation with the elusive mysteries of communication and of form—all were implicit in his methods. He often said that he never learned anything except by experience, by trial and error, by finding out for himself. This was true. He had to do everything the hard way. And it was as true of his writing habits as of anything else. He had read many books and articles in which other writers told how they did it—and he found no help in them for himself. . . . In the end he always came back to that. So he borrowed nothing from others. First and last, his methods were his very own. He invented them—because he had to.

. . . .

Till the day he died he was always as honest in speaking of his un- **[352/353]** certainties and self-doubts as he was in affirming what he knew. So it happened that I, his last editor, became the most convenient receptacle during the final year of his life for his long and earnest confidences about the work he had done and was doing, and how he was doing it. Throughout that year I probably saw him more frequently than anyone, and what I have to say here is based in large measure upon the things he told me. Beyond that it became my duty after his death to edit his unpublished manuscript, which, when stacked in one pile, stood breast high from the floor. The better part of three years went into studying and editing it. This was a rare experience, which shed a great deal of new light on Thomas Wolfe's methods. So, although I cannot speak with first-hand knowledge of how he wrote his first three creative books, I think I have a fairly clear idea of how he wrote his last three. . . . **[353/354]**

. . . .

. . . Of course there is nothing mysterious about the ends which his writing was meant to serve. The motives which drove him to write, and which lent such singular integrity to everything he wrote, can

*Edward C. Aswell, from "A Note on Thomas Wolfe," *The Hills Beyond* by Thomas Wolfe (New York: Harper and Brothers, 1941), pp. 349-386. Copyright 1941 by Maxwell Perkins as Executor. Reprinted by permission of Harper and Brothers.

be read clearly enough in his books. But his techniques are more obscure, and often cannot be derived from the evidence that is visible in his printed pages. His methods were certainly unusual, if not unique in literature. Very few [354/355] people know anything about them. Perhaps that is one reason why there are so many misconceptions about Thomas Wolfe.

For example, some of his readers seem to think that when Tom was in the throes of composition, all he had to do was to open the sluice gates and the words tumbled forth in an irresistible torrent like the surge of pent-up waters suddenly released. True, he wrote like one possessed. His first drafts were always done in longhand with a pencil, and when he had a secretary, as he did throughout his last year, one of her chores was to keep a dozen pencils sharpened and ready for his need. With amazing speed he would fill innumerable sheets of paper with his vigorous scrawl, and toss them aside to fall on the floor for his secretary to pick up, put in order, and transcribe. He never hesitated for a word: the words came too fast for him, and in his effort to keep up with them he would often form only the first letter and the last with a wriggle between, so that only the initiated could decode his sentences.

But the analogy by which this process has been compared to the opening of sluice gates becomes very misleading if left without qualification. To understand what was happening with Tom when he was writing, one needs to remember all the years through which his experience and observation had slowly accumulated. One also needs to be reminded of his acute self-tortures of thought and feeling about everything he had experienced and observed. He could not put anything that had happened to him out of his consciousness until he had rehearsed it in memory a thousand times, going back over it again and again in every detail until he had got at the core of it and had extracted the last shred of meaning out of it on every level. One needs to be told,

too, of his ingenious experiments with different ways of saying what he wanted to say, sometimes only worked out in his head, sometimes roughly sketched on paper. All of this preceded the moment of spate-writing and made it possible.

Beyond this, one needs to know—and the fact may come as a surprise—that Tom had become a tireless reviser and rewriter. Whether this was true of him in his younger days I cannot say, but it was certainly true of him later. Much as he had told me and shown me of what he had been doing in those last years, I was not quite prepared to dis- [355/356] cover, when I came to deal with the whole manuscript, how vitally essential rewriting had become to his whole method. Far more often than not I found that there would be at least two different versions of the same episode, and sometimes there were as many as four or five versions. There would be a first draft hastily sketched out, then later drafts that filled in the details, and it was fascinating to see how the thing had changed and grown under his hand. When he was dissatisfied with a scene or character he would not, as a rule, simply revise his draft and get it recopied: he would put it aside and rewrite it some different way from start to finish. He would pace the floor over it, and he might dictate the revision straight to the typewriter—then his secretary would have an exhausting day trying to keep up. In editing the manuscript it was very puzzling to come upon these variant versions because they were not marked (the pages were frequently out of order and were not even numbered), and only a careful comparison of the internal evidence could determine which was the last draft and the most complete realization of his intentions. . . . [356/365]

. . . .

It is strange but true that not one of his creative books was written as the volume it ultimately turned out to be. *Look Homeward, Angel* came closest to it. Tom said that that book "almost wrote itself," by which he meant that its line of movement was clear to him from the start, and that he wrote it fairly easily, without even being aware of many of the problems that were to arise to plague him in the preparation of the later books. Even so, however, Maxwell E. Perkins of Scribner's, Tom's first editor, tells me that a large section at the beginning of the manuscript of *Look Homeward, Angel* was cut out, since it covered at length the early life of old Gant, and lacked the feeling of instant warmth and reality which came into Tom's writing as soon as the story moved on to Eugene and his immediate family background. The later books did not "write themselves" in any sense of the word, and were not planned as individual books. *The Story of a Novel* confirms this fact about *Of Time and the River,* and the same thing holds for the posthumous books. Tom always spoke of the whole mass of manuscript from which those later volumes were taken simply as "the book." He did not know whether in the end it would make one book or a dozen, and he didn't much care. That seemed to him the publisher's problem, and he was right about it. What went into each volume was largely a matter of convenience and practicability.

This may seem to contradict what I have said about form in Wolfe's writing, but there is no real contradiction. For, although Tom did not plan the various parts of his story as the published books which we know, he did plan the parts in themselves, and planned each part in relation to all the other parts. What is more, he planned the whole from first to last, and the whole was complete within him before he ever began to write. Not that he could at that time have given anyone an exact blueprint of the books that were to come. His knowledge was more fundamental than that, much more central to his purpose. He knew what kind of books he was going to write, he knew what they [365/366] were to be about, and he knew precisely what effect he wanted them to have on his readers. . . . [366/372]

. . . .

Since he had the whole conception of his work clear in his mind, he did not have to follow his nose in order to find out where he was going. In the main his chronology was fixed by the order of his experience, so he knew where the parts joined and did not have to write chapters six and seven before he could tackle eight and nine. This left him free to write each day whatever scene he most felt like writing that day. Yesterday he might have been working on something out of the Brooklyn period of his life, but if in the night his mind happened to go back thirty years to some remembered episode of his childhood, he would get up today to work on that, and the Brooklyn material would be laid aside until he felt like returning to it. In this way he might cover within a month various unrelated events and characters widely scattered throughout the time cycle of his story. In this way, too, while writing the individual parts he was also working on the whole thing all the time.

When one entered the front room of his three-room suite at the Chelsea the first thing that met the eye was the incongruous sight of two huge wooden packing cases which always stood in the middle of the floor. These were his bank, his repository for manuscript. When he finished writing anything and had got it typed out, he would salt it away in these boxes. Everything he had was in them, the sketch he had done yesterday together with all the unpublished material that dated back through the years to the very beginning—crisp white sheets fresh [372/373] from the typewriter mixed in with old manuscript yellowed with the deposits of time and torn and dog-eared by much handling. It looked like a grab-bag, hopeless to disentangle, but he knew what was there and could quickly lay his hands on anything he wanted.

From time to time he would stop his writing for several days and go through the packing cases, taking out certain portions of manuscript and putting them together. If some fragment written six years before belonged with something he had just recently done he would weave them into a single piece, rewriting them when necessary. Then they were salted away again to await the day when they would again be dug out and fitted into still larger continuities. The process was, I imagine, something like that by which mosaics are constructed: first each individual bead or jewel was fashioned; then, when there were enough of them to work with, they were sorted out and put together to form a part of the pattern for which they had been designed.

. . . .

Thomas Wolfe's Characters: Portraits from Life*

FLOYD C. WATKINS (1920-   ) is professor of English at Emory University. He is an editor of the anthology *The Literature of the South* and co-author, with John B. Cullen, of *Old Times in the Faulkner Country.* His *Thomas Wolfe's Characters* was the result of extensive research in Asheville, North Carolina, into the actual persons and events portrayed in *Look Homeward, Angel* and others of Wolfe's works.

Identification of names is certainly not definition of the creative powers of a writer, but in the works of Wolfe such delving turns up facts with several significances. His artful naming of his characters was one of the traits that led to such a furious reception of *Look Homeward, Angel,* and his method of changing names is an indication of the amount of autobiography in his work.

Many places are given names entirely different in sound from the real names but very similar in meaning, and the comparisons are interesting etymologically. Raleigh, North Carolina, for example, retains the name of an Elizabethan courtier and becomes *Sydney,* just as Old Fort, a town near Asheville, is in Wolfe's works *Old Stockade.* Chapel Hill is *Pulpit Hill,* and Spruce Street, the address of Mrs. Wolfe's boardinghouse, the Old Kentucky Home, becomes *Spring Street,* the address of Eliza Gant's *Dixieland.* Government Street Wolfe calls *Federal Street. Altamont,* the name for Asheville, connotes altitude and mountains, but appropriate as the name is, it is imaginary only as a name for Asheville, because there is a small town called Altamont in western North Carolina.

The nationality of names and of the characters in the novels is in almost every instance unchanged: Jeannerett becomes *Jannadeau;* Sternberg, *Greenberg;* Guischard, *Deshaye;* Finkelstein, *Stein;* Lipinski, *Rosalsky.*

Because of their vast estates and mansion near Asheville, the Vanderbilts have played significant roles in the life of the town and in Wolfe's novels. When he wrote about them, he associated the name of their sire, old "Commodore" Vanderbilt, the railroad baron, with that of another robber baron of the post-Civil War period, Jay Gould. Vanderbilt thus became *Goulderbilt.* [7/8]

The connotation of grain as well as the *t-o-n* is preserved in the change from Wheaton to *Barton.* When Clara Paul became *Laura James,* as Mrs. Wolfe notes in *The Marble Man's Wife,* a similar ending for the first name was retained, and the last name was changed to that of a different disciple of Christ.

In many names one syllable is changed while another remains the same: Woodfin Street, where Wolfe was born, becomes *Woodson Street* in the novels. Biltmore, the Vanderbilt estate, is called *Biltburn;* Redwood, *Redmond;* Brigman, *Tugman.* The *Tarkington* family in *Look Homeward, Angel* were really Perkinsons; Israel became, obviously and logically, *Isaacs.* The fictitious *Montgomery Avenue* is in reality Asheville's Montford Avenue.

Only the initials are changed in many

* Floyd C. Watkins, from *Thomas Wolfe's Characters: Portraits from Life* (Norman: University of Oklahoma Press, 1957), pp. 7-11. Used by permission of the University of Oklahoma Press.

names: Bus Woody is changed to *Gus Moody;* Patton Avenue, to *Hatton Avenue;* Jarrett, to *Garrett.* Wolfe enjoyed playing with names in changing Reuben Rawls to *Ralph Rolls,* in reversing Charles French Toms to get *Tom French.*

Sometimes only one name is changed while the other, although it may be extremely unusual, is retained. Changes of this sort are numerous: Pearl Shope to *Pearl Hines;* Charlie Mascari to *Pete Mascari;* Cassius or "Cash" Gudger to *Saul Gudger;* Rufus Woodcock to *Gilbert Woodcock;* Charles L. Sluder to *Fagg Sluder;* Julius Martin to *Julius Arthur;* James Barnard to *Dick Barnard;* Louis Graves to *George Graves;* Daniel Hodges to *Malcolm Hodges.*

The saloonkeeper O'Donnel, Wolfe calls *Tim O'Donnel,* but later in the same book he is given a different last name, *Tim O'Doyle.* Another such inconsistency is the spelling of the name of the groceryman as *Bradley* and *Bradly.* Jeweller Arthur M. Field is once called *Shields* and again *Arthur N. Wright.* [8/9]

Why Wolfe throughout his fiction used names so near to the real ones is a speculation that Asheville has often considered. That he was aware of how he followed life and how he changed it seems to be proved by his usual care in giving entirely fictitious names to those involved in great scandals. His methods of naming characters perhaps helped him avoid the extra labor of keeping hundreds of strange names straight in his head. Perhaps, on the other hand, he wished his home-town friends to know the sources of his art. Did he realize how the use of a real name or one similar to it would increase the pleasure—or the anger? His consistency indicates that surely he must have enjoyed skirting the abyss and making fiction as close to life as possible.

Even the tourist casually driving through Asheville for the first time is able to identify some of the people and places of the novels. Old residents are still able to point out a remarkable number of things that Wolfe wrote about. Careful examina-

tion of old city directories, newspapers, telephone books—reinforced by conversations with local citizens and the identifications given in articles and stories—results in nearly complete equation of fiction and fact.

There are many more than 300 characters and places mentioned by name or described in *Look Homeward, Angel,* and probably there is not an entirely fictitious person, place, or incident in the whole novel. I have been able to identify with some accuracy about 250 places and people; and in almost every instance where the problem is difficult, there is evidence that Wolfe had in mind a real character or a place. Those migrant boarders and tourists who came to the Old Kentucky Home, rocked on the porch for a spell, and then moved on are seldom identifiable. Wolfe remembered them, but the townspeople do [9/10] not; and the minor exploits of boarders rarely are recorded by the papers. The Negroes also have been forgotten. Wolfe recalled the sordid and strange details of their segregated lives, but their names in most instances are now lost. Fiction is here probably based on fact that cannot be proved. Some of Eugene's friends at the University of North Carolina have been hard to equate with those of Wolfe, but here again the research is difficult and the practice well established. On the other hand, when the character is of a type that is well known in a small town, there is hardly ever any difficulty.

When identification cannot be established for a family, a check in the city directories still reveals that Wolfe almost invariably used surnames that were prevalent in contemporary Asheville, and usually the social, economic, and racial status is unchanged in the fiction. Although there is no Tom Flack in the directories, for example, there are several Negroes with that family name.

The methods the townspeople use to identify the characters of the novels are critical comments on Wolfe's mode of creation. The temptation of the researcher is to think that everyone in Asheville was an abnormality and a strange caricature of mankind. But people, events, and places are now seen out of focus, with the books serving as a device that works all the wonders of a combination prism-camera-telescope-microscope. Wolfe remembered well, but frequently his memory adhered to the physical abnormality, the occupation, the odd personal habit, the peculiar mannerism, or the whispered story. "Wolfe makes his characters stand out—even those who have minor roles," wrote a local journalist in the *Asheville Citizen*. "He has a knack of selecting those peculiarities in characteristics which are easily forgotten by others, but which tend to bring out cer- [10/11] tain vital phases of the real person."[7] One of his uncles, for example, commented that he did not realize how often he pared his nails until his nephew described it so frequently in his book. Clarence Sumner, still a reporter for the *Citizen* and once a classmate of Wolfe at the University of North Carolina, states that "Wolfe never fictionalized except to combine, emotionalize, caricature." Thus, he created his characters, exploiting all the eccentricities of his family and of those others whom he knew well, using other townspeople for background and unimportant roles. The good-humored, deformed, and somewhat idiotic Willie Goff, the seller of pencils, is a good example. In fiction his name, personality, and deformities are described as truthfully by Wolfe as they are by the *Citizen's* reporter in a reminiscent article on local characters.[8]

[7] *Asheville Citizen*, March 23, 1932.
[8] Thomas Wolfe, *Look Homeward, Angel* (New York, Charles Scribner's Sons, 1929), 342; *Asheville Citizen*, August 22, 1948.

PART THREE

REVIEWS OF *LOOK HOMEWARD, ANGEL*

C'est Maître François*

BASIL DAVENPORT (1905-   ) is a member of the editorial board of the Book-of-the-Month Club. He has edited the *Portable Roman Reader* and a number of other anthologies, and has written a study of the science-fiction novel. This review of *Look Homeward, Angel* is reasonably typical of the combination of enthusiasm and qualification that marked the initial reception of the book.

If it were customary to head reviews with a motto, like a chapter of Walter Scott, a review of "Look Homeward, Angel" might well take a phrase from Mr. Arthur Machen's "The Secret Glory": *"C'est Maître François! Maître François en très mauvais humeur peut-être, mais Maître François tout de même!"* The analogy must not be pushed too far; there are of course many important differences, notably a violent emotional intensity in Mr. Wolfe that is entirely lacking in Rabelais, but they have the same fundamental and most unusual quality, a robust sensitiveness. Extraordinary keenness of perception usually makes a character like Roderick Usher or Des Esseintes, or, in real life, Proust, one who is forced to shut himself away from bright lights, loud sounds, and strong feelings, and occupies himself with infinitely cautious and delicate experiments upon himself. But Mr. Wolfe, like Rabelais, though plainly odors and colors and all stimuli affect him more intensely than most people, is happily able to devour sensations with an enormous vigor; his perceptions have a rare combination of fineness and largeness.

In manner, Mr. Wolfe is most akin to James Joyce, somewhere between the ascetic beauty of the "Portrait of the Artist as a Young Man" and the unpruned fecundity of "Ulysses"; but he resembles many other people by turns. His hero, Eugene Gant, amuses himself by registering at country hotels as John Milton or William Blake, or by asking for a cup of cold water and blessing the giver in his Father's name; so Mr. Wolfe amuses himself by writing here in the manner of one author and there of another. He will suddenly fall into a dada fantasia, such as often appears in *transition*, as

> A woman sobbed and collapsed in a faint. She was immediately carried out by two Boy Scouts . . . who administered first aid to her in the rest-room, one of them hastily kindling a crackling fire of pine boughs by striking two flints together, while the other made a tourniquet, and tied several knots in his handkerchief,—

and so on, and half a dozen pages later he will enumerate, in the painfully unimaginative manner of "An American Tragedy," the real holdings of Mrs. Gant:

"There were, besides, three good building-lots on Merrion Avenue valued at $2,000 apiece, or at $5,500 for all three; the house on Woodson Street valued at $5,000" and so on for a page and a half. That is, it seems to be the great gift of Mr. Wolfe that everything is interesting, valuable, and significant to him. It must be confessed that he has just missed the greatest of gifts, that of being able to convey his interest to the ordinary reader.

Upon what was his vitality nourished? Rabelais fed on all the fulness of the

*Basil Davenport, "C'est Maître François," Saturday Review of Literature, VI (December 21, 1929), 584. Used by permission of the Saturday Review of Literature.

French Renaissance, a dawn in which it was bliss to be alive; what would he have been like if he had been a poor boy in a small southern town, with a drunken father, a shrewish mother, and a family of quarrelling brothers and sisters? Mr. Wolfe's answer seems to be that, in his childhood at least, he would have done unexpectedly well. Eugene, in pitifully cramped surroundings, somehow has a greater fulness of life than most boys have. From his father, especially, he draws some sense of Dionysian madness, of Falstaffian greatness. The teaching he has is very bad, but he gets somewhere, from it or from himself, a real feeling for Latin and Greek. His first money is earned on a paper route that takes him through the Negro quarter, his first knowledge of women comes from a Negress who is in arrears to his company, yet he is never without a sense of the wonder and pain of desire and hunger. Years ago Mr. Tarkington said: "There's just as many kinds of people in Kokomo as there is in Pekin," but he carried little conviction, for his melodrama was too obviously arranged. It is Mr. Wolfe's contribution that he has drawn an unsparing picture of character and emotion. For those who can see it, there is everywhere a wealth of vitality that is almost enough.

But it is the little less, after all, and his town grows more insufficient as Eugene grows older. There is one chapter, in manner probably inspired by "The Waste Land," describing an afternoon in the square, with a running comment of quotations.

"Give me a dope, too."
"I don't want anything," said Pudge Carr. Such drinks as made them nobly wild, not mad . . .
Mrs. Thelma Jarvis, the milliner, drew, in one swizzling guzzle, the last beaded chain of linked sweetness long drawn out from the bottom of her glass. Drink to me only with thine eyes. . . . She writhed carefully among the crowded tables, with a low rich murmur of contrition. Her voice was ever soft, gentle, and low—an excellent thing in a woman. The high light chatter of the tables dropped as she went by. For God's sake, hold your tongue and let me love!

It is good enough, the town and the soda-water, but it should be so much better! A great company of poets are called on to set the beauties of the world against their pitiful analogues in Altamont. Mr. Wolfe's criticism of the narrowness of his hero's surroundings is the more bitter because he has done it such abundant justice.

The bitterness grows when Eugene goes to the state university. Here Eugene, developing rapidly, becomes more difficult to understand, more difficult perhaps for his author to picture. It is often observable in books that begin with the birth of a boy that they grow confused as he approaches the age of the author. Here too the goat-foot that always belongs to the followers of Joyce is shown. Eugene becomes morbidly conscious of his physique, and yet unnaturally neglectful of it. He does not have his teeth filled or his hair cut; he does not bathe. He is naturally not popular, and he resents his want of popularity, in a way that is not far short of megalomania; he revolts against American sanitation and cleanliness, declaring that health is for fools, and great men have always shown signs in their lined faces of the disease of genius. Now this is hardly comprehensible, and hence hardly credible, even when the first two thirds of the book has given one the will to be as sympathetic as possible. There are possible reasons for Eugene's cult of dirt, ranging from a subconscious fear of impotence and a confused desire to be like the Horatian he-goat, *elentis mariti* (there is something like that in Mr. D. H. Lawrence), to a rankling sense of social inferiority, perverted by a fierce pride into a resolve to emulate the Fraternity Row aristocracy in nothing, not even in cleanliness (there is something like that in Mr. Wilbur Daniel Steele's "Meat"), through a dozen others. But Eugene here is not clear, as if Mr. Wolfe did not understand him, or understood him too well to think him worth explaining.

In the end Eugene is left wondering, with the same sense of the loneliness and greatness of the soul that informs the book from the beginning. "Look Homeward, Angel" though it has the faults of luxuriousness, has the great virtue that it always has the vision of something half-comprehensible behind the humdrum life, and that in the reading it carries conviction with it. [584]

Episcop

The Loneliness at the Core*

C. HUGH HOLMAN (1914-   ) is Kenan Professor of English and chairman of the Department of English at the University of North Carolina. He has edited *The Short Novels of Thomas Wolfe*. This essay-review was a portion of the "Re-Assessment: 1955" series, which made new critical appraisals of older works, in *The New Republic*.

Thomas Wolfe's *Look Homeward, Angel* fell on critically evil days, and they have taken their toll of its reputation, if not of its steadily increasing number of readers. It was published the month of the 1929 stock market crash, lived the first decade of its existence in the sociological and Marxist-minded thirties, and presented to politically sensitive critics a hero of whom its author approvingly wrote: ". . . he did not care under what form of government he lived—Republican, Democrat, Tory, Socialist, or Bolshevist. . . . He did not want to reform the world, or to make it a better place to live in." That hero, Eugene Gant, was hardly in tune with the intellectual temper of his times.

It is a frankly autobiographical book, "a story of the buried life," written by a man who, by his own confession, "failed to finish a single book of . . . [Henry] James." Yet its whole existence has been during a time when the technical and formal considerations of Henry James have triumphantly established themselves as the proper criteria for fiction. For a book largely devoid of the traditional fictional or dramatic structure, almost naïvely innocent of "crucial plot," and seemingly dedicated to the lyrical expression of emotion not very tranquilly recollected, the age of Jamesian criticism has proved patronizingly hostile.

As Herbert Muller, by no means an unfriendly critic of Wolfe, has said:

> His limitations may be exposed most clearly on his own ground, by setting his novels beside such other autobiographical novels as *Sons and Lovers, Of Human Bondage, The Portrait of the Artist as a Young Man* and *Remembrance of Things Past*. In these the hero is a creation, not a *nom de plume*, and his life a work of art, not a flood of memories. In this company Wolfe appears a very artless young man.

In such a context of critical opinion it has required effort to maintain a serious attitude toward Wolfe and his first book, *Look Homeward, Angel,* which is almost universally acknowledged to be his best novel—effort that few serious critics have made.

I believe that my experience is fairly typical. I belong to the generation that read *Look Homeward, Angel* when it was new and they were very young. It wove for me an evocative spell as complete as any book ever has. It seemed to me that this was not a book; it was life and life as I knew it. I brought to it, a very young book, the naïve and uncritical response of the very young. Such an attitude did not survive, and in a very few years I became aware of the irresponsibility, the rhetorical excess, and the formless confusion of the book.

* C. Hugh Holman, from "The Loneliness at the Core," *The New Republic*, CXXXIII (October 10, 1955), 16-17. Used by permission of *The New Republic*.

To go back to *Look Homeward, Angel* in 1955 and seriously to read it has been an experience in some ways as startling as the initial reading was, and it has made me aware that it is a different book from what I had thought and a much better one.

The standard view of *Look Homeward, Angel* has assumed one of three attitudes: that literal autobiography very thinly disguised constitutes the important portion of the book; that what form it has was given it by the editor Maxwell Perkins rather than its author; and that the book is most interesting in terms of Wolfe's acknowledged and pervasive debt to James Joyce.

The first attitude has resulted in a mass of biographical data, but, as Louis D. Rubin has recently pointed out, the value of the book must ultimately be determined in terms of its quality as *novel* rather than its accuracy as personal history. The second attitude reached the epitome of critical severity with Bernard DeVoto's "Genius is not Enough," and Wolfe is today generally credited with the major, if not the sole part in determining the form of his first two books.

The debt to Joyce, although everywhere obvious, seems to me almost nowhere truly significant. The least admirable portions of *Look Homeward, Angel* are those very portions where the ghost of *Ulysses* hovers visibly on the sidelines—portions such as the well-known record of the schoolboys' trip home from school, with its ironic pattern of mixed quotations so reminiscent of Joyce.

I think the first thing that strikes the mature reader who goes back to *Look Homeward, Angel* is the realization that it is a book enriched by a wealth of humor and saved from mawkishness by a pervasive comic spirit. This quality of the book is usually lost on its young readers, because the young very seldom see much amusing in themselves. Yet everywhere in this book one is aware that it is a very young book, not because its attitudes are themselves very young, but because it is

a record of the inner and outer life of a very young boy.

The author looks back at youth with longing and love, but also with a steady but tolerant amusement. This is nowhere more apparent than in the hyperbolically presented day-dreams of "Bruce-Eugene" and in the very youthful posturing of the college student so earnestly set upon dramatizing himself. The humor is itself sometimes very poor and very seldom of the highest order. It is satire directed with crude bluntness; it is hyperbole lacking in finesse; it is *reductio ad absurdum* without philosophical seriousness. Wolfe is not a great comic writer, but his comic sense gives distance and depth to his picture of his youthful self.

For all its rhetorical exclamation about emotion, *Look Homeward, Angel* is a book firmly fixed in a sharply realized and realistically presented social environment. The book comes to us almost entirely through Eugene Gant's perceptions, but what he perceives is very often Altamont and Pulpit Hill (Asheville and Chapel Hill, N. C.) and he perceives them with a wealth of accurate detail. At this stage of his career, Thomas Wolfe had few serious pronouncements to make about man as a social animal (in his later career he was to attempt to make many), but he had a realist's view of his world.

It is a view colored, too, by a broadly [16/17] Agrarian attitude, however much he was contemptuous of the Agrarians as a group. His picture of Altamont is a picture of a place mad with money and size, of a people submerging everything of value in valueless wealth. This view, the sword on which Eliza Gant is first hoist and then eviscerated, extends from the family to the life of the town and finally to the imagery of the whole book. As an example (and it is but one of hundreds), when he hears his idol-brother Ben talking sententious businessman nonsense, "Eugene writhed to hear this fierce condor prattle this stale hash of the canny millionaires, like any obedient parrot in a teller's cage."

Further, we perceive as a rediscovery that beneath the extravagant rhetoric, the badly and baldly rhythmic passages—the ones that eager young men reprint as bad free verse—there is a truly lyric quality in Wolfe's writing. With an abnormally keen memory for sensory perceptions, what Wolfe called his "more than ordinary . . . power to evoke and bring back the odors, sounds, colors, shapes, and feel of things with concrete vividness," he is able to bring to bear vicariously on our five senses the precise content of a given scene and to make it poignantly and palpably real.

And here he works, not as a rhetorician asking us to imagine an emotion, but as an imagist rubbing "the thing" against our exposed nerve ends and thereby calling forth the feeling. It is, perhaps, in this ability to use authentically "the thing" to evoke emotion that the finest aspect of Wolfe's very uneven talent appears.

A new look at *Look Homeward, Angel* shows us that it is a book, not only of Eugene's "buried life," but one about tragic loneliness. Few lonelier pictures exist than the ones here that show the insularity within which Eliza and W. O.

Gant live. This W. O. Gant, a rich and hungry man in spirit, who was never called by his wife Eliza anything except "Mr. Gant," strove by rhetoric, invective, alcohol, and lust to make somehow an impress on the unresponsive world around him. He is the ultimate tragic center of a book which deals with spiritual isolation almost everywhere.

Certainly the book lacks formal novelistic structure. If its core, as I believe, is W. O. Gant, then it contains a wealth of unresolved irrelevancy. If its central pattern is somehow linked up with brother Ben, as Wolfe seems to feel that it is, then we must regretfully assert that Brother Ben is a failure, the only really dead person in a book noteworthy for the vitality of its characters.

. . . .

Unless we demand that all novels be neat and concise, *Look Homeward, Angel* has much to offer us still: a clear, detailed picture of a town; two extravagantly drawn but very living people, Eliza and W. O. Gant; a comic sense that lends aesthetic distance; a poignantly lyrical expression of the physical world of youth; and a picture of the individual's incommunicable loneliness.

re-read
whole

Thomas Wolfe and the Kicking Season*

PAMELA HANSFORD JOHNSON (1912-   ), a British novelist, is the wife of Sir Charles P. Snow, himself a novelist of distinction. She has been an interested reader of Wolfe's work for a number of years. In this essay-review she examines his current reputation in England on the occasion of the publication of a new edition of Look Homeward, Angel and a selection of his letters.

To nearly every successful and serious writer, either during his lifetime or within a short period after it, there comes the Kicking Season. This is not arranged or concerted by villains in committee; it just happens because something is abroad in the air, a sense that it is high time somebody got his come-uppance, was "reappraised," or simply, in his own best interests, given a temporary check. I remember it happening to Hemingway when *Across the River and Into the Trees* came out. I detected a faint whiff of it—very faint— over Mr. Eliot's last play. The higher they rise. . . . Yes, one day it will even be the turn of Scott Fitzgerald. Even of Mr. E. M. Forster. At the moment, it is the turn of poor Tom Wolfe.

"This man is not a novelist," wrote Mr. Cyril Connolly, on September 14th last, when a new edition of *Look Homeward, Angel* and Wolfe's *Selected Letters* were issued together,† "he is an obsessional neurotic with a gift for words who could write only about himself and who cannot create other people. He is the Benjamin Robert Haydon of American literature." The late Edwin Muir headed his article, "The Pretender," and wrote, "His novels have become almost unreadable," quoting, to prove it, a good deal of Wolfe's old nonsense and little of his excellence. In the whole of *Look Homeward, Angel* he

found only one convincing character, "Elizabeth Gant." It is odd to see her as Elizabeth. She was Eliza to us.

By "us," I mean a group of young men and girls at the beginning of the 'thirties, either just within or just out of their teens, reared in a London suburb, good grammar school products, liking to roll back the carpet in the evenings and dance, and to flow through successive crazes for successive writers. What writers? Well, there was a long run on Dostoievsky; on O'Flaherty; a short but (for me) painful one on Nietzsche; and then, one day, *Look Homeward, Angel* burst upon us like the radiance from a lighthouse newly erected upon some very sticky rocks. We ate, drank, and dreamed it. We weren't fools. We had some taste, we knew that some of it was guff. . . .

But that book spoke for us: spoke, not in spite of its sprawlings, its bawlings, its youthful yellings and howlings about the family, the silver cord, the "incommunicable prison of this earth," love itself, but because of those things. We were not articulate ourselves, though we had much we wanted to say. Wolfe had far too much to say, but he said it with our voices.

In the *Manchester Guardian* of October

† *Look Homeward, Angel.* By Thomas Wolfe. Heinemann. 21s. *Selected Letters of Thomas Wolfe*, edited, with an Introduction by Elizabeth Nowell. Heinemann, 25s

* Pamela Hansford Johnson, from "Thomas Wolfe and the Kicking Season," *Encounter* (England), XII (April, 1959), 77-80. Reprinted with the permission of Lady Snow and *Encounter*.

3rd last, Mrs. Doris Lessing, that soberly diagnostic critic, wrote with her usual sense, her usual lack of flummery, that Wolfe was a myth-maker: "He did not write *about* adolescence: to read him is to re-experience adolescence. . . . I have yet to meet a person born into any kind of Establishment who understood Wolfe, I have yet to meet a provincial who has cracked open a big city who does not acknowledge that Wolfe expressed his own struggle for escape into larger experience."

And there you have it, pat: "the *whole* thing," as Starwick would have said.

For it is no good denying one's enthusiasms, once they have been excited. There must have been something to back them, in proportion to their violence. These boys and girls I have spoken of didn't even mind the rhetoric—"O lost, and by the wind grieved, ghost, come back again . . ."—and it was encouraging to me to find a positive response to this threnody by an otherwise stern young man in *Granta,* at the end of last year. So he should respond, unless he were dead already. We did. We couldn't help it.

The Times Literary Supplement, in an excellent middle article, paid Wolfe the tribute of taking him seriously, and praising where praise was due. This mentioned his "gift of mimicry" [77/78] (first-class, by the way), and his masterly ability to transfer the flavour of a person to the printed page. The writer also, and this was salutary, reminded us of Faulkner's almost wildly generous praise of Wolfe. He "put Wolfe first" among his contemporaries: "We all fail, but Wolfe made the best failure because he tried hardest to say the most." Mr. Faulkner is not an ass. He would not have been so carried away by a writer who was an ass—utterly.

What Wolfe had, however, was the splendid capacity to lend dignity and marmoreal stature to the fact of being young. Aldous Huxley succeeded by flattering the youth of his day. The young people who loved him were not (they knew) as clever as he; but he held out the hope that if they used their brains hard enough they might one day hope to respond to him on more or less equal terms. He did not speak as one of them: but he never talked down. Wolfe spoke from among them: he was a great, bossy, tormented voice in their crowd. He spoke for them: they cried Hooray. Out of their dumb, secreted music he made a big noisy song.

If the word "artist" has any meaning at all, of course Wolfe was one. He did not know how to order the whole of his vast material, but he did know how to turn a death in the family, a humiliation in love, into art. I cannot conceive how anyone can read of the death of Ben Gant, the episodes with Abe Jones at N.Y.U., the [78/79] nightmare quartet in Paris, Eugene, Eleanor, Ann, and Starwick, the first excitement of prowling the book-stacks at Harvard, without accepting the fact. I wrote in my own book: "There are three deaths in literature comparable for power and pity and horror with the death of Ben: the death of Oliver Gant, in *Of Time and the River,* of the father in Roger Martin du Gard's *Les Thibault,* and of the grandmother in *A la Recherche du Temps Perdu.* The nervous strain of it, the appalling grief, and above all the pervasive *bad temper* are suggested with an extraordinary nakedness and force."

I don't feel like going back on that. The scene is wonderful because it is autobiography, because it is personally felt: but art has arranged it. After all, the majority of mankind manage to feel. Only a small number can convey their emotions to others.

The trouble with Wolfe now is that he runs counter to anything we have learned recently to respect. He is pre-eminently Bad Form—or would be if he had a form. He is politically reprehensible—or would be if he had any coherent politics. He throws up bizarre additional difficulties by his hidden ambivalence. . . .

I am inclined to think that, so far as he

is concerned, this is *merely* a Kicking Season, and not a definite reappraisal. What we shall have to do, eventually, is to sort Wolfe down. We must sort him down in our own minds while we read him, even as we sort Balzac down, accepting the work as a whole (because both the good and the bad make up the whole of any writer), while keeping our own reservations. Wolfe came nearer than any other writer to producing the "Great American Novel" in its mythopoeic sense. His is a young book risen out of a young culture; it attempts too much, just as he, poor devil, attempted too much when he tried to read all at once all the books ever written. But William Faulkner must still have the last word on him. What he said may have been the overspill of an enormous impulse of generosity: yet he meant it at the time, as we who were young when the 'thirties began meant our enthusiasm at the time. And such praise, such grateful affection, doesn't spring out of nothing. Wolfe, at times, writes like Hell or James Joyce. At others, he writes like a great novelist. How many writers can do as much?

. . . .

PART FOUR

WOLFE'S STYLE

The Style*

PAMELA HANSFORD JOHNSON in 1947 published the first British book-length critique of Thomas Wolfe, under the title *Thomas Wolfe: A Critical Study,* a book which appeared in America the following year under the title *Hungry Gulliver.* For biographical data see "Thomas Wolfe and the Kicking Season" (p. 60).

. . . .
We read Wolfe primarily for his rhetorical poetry, which he delivers from his great height with the authority of a prophet who has seen the clouds open to reveal a calligraphy of fire upon the white spaces of the air.

To him all things are marvellous. He never learned [20/21] the sophistication that brings fear of an audience. He never doubted his own vision, never paused to think, "Yes, this all seems very marvellous to me, but these older and wiser persons sitting around—are they likely to smile at me because the things that fill me with wonder are things at which they wondered only in their youth, and have now set aside with all the other commonplace marvels of human experience?" . . . [21/22]

. . . .
Wolfe's feeling for the colour, the music and the shape of words is extraordinary; there is no American writer to whom language in itself means so much. He couples for onomatopoeic effect words not strictly onomatopoeic in themselves, but having that significance for him. For example, "the glut and hiss of tides." "Hiss" is an onomatopoeic word, "glut" is not; but "glut," for Wolfe, had the slap and suck of a heavy driving wave, and is here a word of sound. And again—"the million sucks and scoops and hollows of the shore." All these three nouns Wolfe has *heard.* What he sees is not the static image of sands scooped out by the sea, but the sea itself actually in the process of sculpting them. By infusing the idea of sound into these visual words, he has telescoped the process of days and years into an action that we can watch in moments. His prose reduces to our immediate comprehension not only the spaces of the world, but also its eternal evolution. [22/23]

. . . .
Wolfe prefaces each one of his novels with a prose poem, and poetry is mingled as inextricably with the body of his work as it is with the narrative of the Old Testament. The style of it derives, indeed, from the poetic books of the Bible and is influenced also, so far as rhythm and sonority are concerned, by Whitman. In its very distinctiveness, in the grandiose flow, the rhetoric, the choice of the harsh, the round and glowing word, the startling image, it is fair game for the parodist and the imitator; but the force that is in it, a force freed by Wolfe's intense desire to achieve on paper the highest possible expression of the grandeur he saw upon earth, is inimitable, and beyond mockery.

Could I make tongue say more than tongue could utter! Could I make brain grasp more than brain could think! Could I weave into immortal denseness some small brede of words, pluck out of sunken depths the roots of living,

* Pamela Hansford Johnson, from "The Style" (Chapter 2), *Hungry Gulliver: An English Critical Appraisal of Thomas Wolfe* (New York: Charles Scribner's Sons, 1948), pp. 20-39. Used by permission of Charles Scribner's Sons, Lady Snow, and Curtis Brown Ltd.

some hundred thousand magic words that were as great as all my hunger, and hurl the sum of all my living out upon three hundred pages![1]

The words strike response from the heart as the sun strikes arrows of bronze from the shield. In their [23/24] clangour, their gasping weight of effort, they force the imagination to the realisation of Wolfe's whole being and desire as narrowly, as nearly, as the battering ram breaches the walls that will not quite yield. It is the effort of Hotspur, whom the lines remember:

> By heaven, methinks it were an easy leap
> To pluck bright honour from the pale-faced
> moon;
> Or dive into the bottom of the deep
> Where fathom-line could never touch the
> ground,
> And pluck up drowned honour by the locks.

Wolfe's words: pluck, sunken, depths, roots, hurl. Hotspur's: leap, pluck, dive, deep, drowned, locks. All these words imply descent into the mind to bring up the drowned Idea.

Wolfe writes vast cumbrous passages of monumental beauty, prose poems as wild, as disturbing as anything in America's literature. When he speaks of Loss—"O lost and by the wind grieved, ghost come back again!"[2]—he speaks not merely of his own loss, but of some lost secret for which the millions of America are forever in milling search. . . . "Of wandering for ever and the earth again . . . of seedtime, bloom, and the mellow-dropping harvest. And of the big flowers, the rich flowers, the strange, unknown flowers. . . . Who owns the earth? Did we want the earth that we should wander on it? Did we need the earth that we were never still upon it?" [3] [24/25]

Strangest and most evocative poem of all is this prophecy, which occurs in the final paragraph of the final book, concluding the "Letter to Foxhall Edwards":

Something has spoken to me in the night, burning the tapers of the waning year; some-

thing has spoken in the night, and told me I shall die. I know not where. Saying:

"To lose the earth you know, for greater knowing: to lose the life you have, for greater life; to leave the friends you love, for greater loving; to find a land more kind than home, more large than earth—

"Whereon the pillars of this earth are founded, towards which the conscience of the world is tending—a wind is rising, and the rivers flow."[4]

This is instantly moving because of its "supernatural" quality. Whatever it was that inspired the statement, it has upon it the command and hush of prophecy. Yet it is not a statement that flowed straight from the mind to the paper; it is most exquisitely and curiously formed. It is interesting to notice the dominant shapes that appear in Wolfe's image. First there are the converging rivers and then, rising above them, the uprights: the tapers of the year, the pillars of the earth. In a shadowy fashion, these shapes give to this passage the visual quality so pronounced in the whole of Wolfe's work. [25/26]

The passage opens with an announcement, twice repeated, of the revelation of the author's imminent death. This is followed by a poem, beautiful and formal in design (three pentameters, one hexameter, three pentameters) which expresses the idea of joy and fulfilment beyond death. The words used are very simple, in Wolfe's New Testament and not Old Testament mood: "earth," "land," "life," "friends," "home," "pillars," "conscience," "rivers." The poem summarizes the desire from which his life's work springs: the desire for homecoming; and is one of the most

[1 *The Web and the Rock* (Harper & Brothers, 1939), p. vi.]
[2 *Look Homeward, Angel* (Charles Scribner's Sons, 1929), p. 2, *et passim.*]
[3 *Of Time and the River* (Charles Scribner's Sons, 1935), p. 2.]
[4 It should be noted that this passage was actually written in reference to Nazi Germany and not to his own death, as Lady Snow here assumes. It first appeared in the short novel, "I Have a Thing to Tell You," in *The New Republic*, March 10, 17, 24, 1937. This selection is from Thomas Wolfe, *You Can't Go Home Again* (New York: Harper and Brothers, 1940), p. 743. See also *The Short Novels of Thomas Wolfe*, ed. C. Hugh Holman (New York, 1961), pp. 235-278; particularly the headnote, pp. 235-236, and the conclusion, p. 278.]

flawless conclusions to any novel in the English language.

Wolfe's poetry derives from Whitman, the unexpected image, the positive statement, the towering authority; but is fundamentally divorced from the philosophy.

I believe a leaf of grass is no less than the
  journey work of the stars,
And the pismire is equally perfect, and a grain of
  sand, and the egg of the wren,
And the tree-toad is a chef-d'oeuvre for the
  highest,
And the running blackberry would adorn the
  parlours of heaven,
And the narrowest hinge in my hand puts to
  scorn all machinery,
And the cow crunching with depressed head sur-
  passes any statue, [26/27]
And a mouse is miracle enough to stagger sextillions of infidels.[5]

The images of the adorning blackberry, the hinge of the hand, the sextillions of infidels, would have been possible to Wolfe, and so would the pairing and contrasting of the nature-words and man-words:

| tree-toad | blackberry | hand | cow |
| chef d'oeuvre | parlours | machinery | statue |

but the thoroughgoing Brahma philosophy would not. Wolfe did not believe that in himself he was all things; he believed that he himself as a man, was higher than all things. . . . [27/28]

. . . .

With the dialogue of a physical passion Wolfe is ever uneasy, and he takes refuge in a kind of voluptuous rowdyism.

The dialogue of ordinary human intercourse, however, he achieves with the ease that arises from an ear perfectly attuned to the shorthand of daily speech, the serviceable omission, the preservation of breath by the labour-saving glance or shrug.

His mother and his sister Helen are seeing the young Eugene off on the train that will take him to the University. Eliza, sad, nagging, an inveterate hinter, is talking to her soured daughter, who is dully and childlessly married, bitter, illumined only by her own coarse, warm, desperate humour. They have been speaking of some friend who bore her baby at the age [28/29] of forty-four. Helen says, with her air of "rough banter" and a look full of sadness, that in this case there may yet be a chance for her.

"Chance!" the mother cried strongly, with a little scornful pucker of the lips—"why, of course there is! If I was your age again I'd have a dozen—and never think a thing of it." For a moment she was silent, pursing her reflective lips. Suddenly a faint sly smile began to flicker at the edges of her lips, and turning to the boy, she addressed him with an air of sly and bantering mystery:
"Now, boy," she said—"there's lots of things that you don't know . . . you always thought you were the last—the youngest—didn't you?"
"Well, wasn't I?" he said.
"H'm" she said with a little scornful smile and an air of great mystery—"There's lots that I could tell you—"
"Oh, my God!" he groaned, turning towards his sister with an imploring face. "More mysteries! . . . The next thing I'll find that there were five sets of triplets after I was born—Well, come on, Mama," he cried impatiently. "Don't hint around all day about it . . . What's the secret now—how many were there?"
"H'm!" she said with a little bantering, scornful, and significant smile.
"O Lord!" he groaned again—"Did she ever tell you what it was?" Again he turned imploringly to his sister.
She snickered hoarsely, a strange high-husky [29/30] and derisive falsetto laugh, at the same time prodding him stiffly in the ribs with her big fingers.
"Hi, hi, hi, hi, hi," she laughed. "More spooky business, hey? You don't know the half of it. She'll be telling you next you were only the fourteenth."
"H'm!" the old woman said, with a little scornful smile of her pursed lips. "Now I could tell him more than that! The fourteenth! Pshaw!" she said contemptuously—"I could tell him—"
"O God!" he groaned miserably. "I knew it! . . . I don't want to hear it."
"K, k, k, k, k," the younger woman sniggered derisively, prodding him in the ribs again.[6]

This is all perfectly realistic, accurately heard and recorded.

[5 Walt Whitman, *Song of Myself*, lines 663-669.]
[6 Thomas Wolfe, *Of Time and the River* (Charles Scribner's Sons, 1935), pp. 6-7.]

The sister's interjections—"hi, hi, hi," "k, k, k, k," have more derisive an effect than any which could be made by words, by comment, or by the routine laughter-symbols. The stammer of Eugene's brother Luke is reproduced with the same economy, the same sparing of the eye that might be troubled by too many small dashes on the printed page.

It may be noted, from this passage, how Wolfe employed the repetition of certain words to force a mood into the reader's mind. "Banter" is used three times; "sly," twice; "scornful," three times; "imploring," twice; "groaned," three times. It is a curious and deliberate trick of emphasis, extraordinarily effective and sometimes cinematic. The attention is concentrated [30/31] upon Eliza's face as if it were shown in close-up. Her lips "pucker," are "reflective," a "faint, sly smile" flickers at their edges, they are scornfully "pursed." The repetition of the word "lips" four times in the passage quoted does not seem redundant, but instead gives the effect of an intense visual clarity. . . . [31/33]

. . . .

. . . Indeed, Wolfe's dialogue and narrative *is* unemphatic and straightforward save when there is some special effect to be made: and the passages of poetry are thereby thrown into a stronger relief. Yet they are never separated from the main body of the story, but grow as naturally out of it as shoots from the trunk of a tree, firmly rooted, and of a kind with it. . . . [33/34]

. . . .

. . . The poetic passages are obviously the result of great concentration, but narrative and dialogue sweep along in a torrent, and there are slacknesses to be found in them. Wolfe is a stylist where Dreiser is not; but, like Dreiser, he does not consider himself bound by the orthodoxies of English composition. Conjunctions and prepositions fall as they will; the author is striving for the maximum force of expression, and not the maximum of elegance.

They got out of the car. Joel took his valise, and like a person walking in a dream, he followed him across the porch, into a large and dimly lit entrance-hall. Joel put his valise down in the hall, and turning, whispered . . . [7]

This passage, with its repetitions and ambiguities, shows Wolfe's casual routine fashion of crossing the space between one important incident and another. It is preceded by a long complex sentence of great visual beauty:

It was a dream-house, a house such as one sees only in a dream—the moonlight slept upon its soar- [34/35] ing wings, its white purity, and gave the whole enormous structure an aerial delicacy, a fragile loveliness like some enchanted structure that one sees in dreams . . . [8]

—and is followed by the description of Eugene's entry into the Pierce mansion:

He nodded, unable to speak, and in silence followed his guide down the hall and through the house. Joel opened a door: the blazing moonlight fell upon the vast, swarded lawn and sleeping woods of that magic domain known as Far Field Farm. And that haunting and unearthly radiance fell as well upon the white wings of that magic house and on a group of its fortunate inhabitants who were sitting on the terrace.
The two young men went out: forms rose to greet them. [9]

The connecting link between these two passages is so perfunctory as to cause a momentary break in mood, and there are flaws of a similar kind throughout Wolfe's entire work. [35/39]

. . . .

To Wolfe, richness is all. He loads every rift with ore until, at times, the whole work comes dangerously near to cracking under the strain. Life is to him so lavish of wealth that he is forever straining to repay the debt with the currency of language. A greater "taste," as we accept this proud and finical word, would have saved him from the cannibalistic love-scenes

[7 *Ibid.*, p. 515.]
[8 *Ibid.*]
[9 *Ibid.*]

with Esther, the abusive apostrophising of Ann, the bellows, the howls, the fist-clenchings, the bursts of rolling and windy verbosity; but had he possessed it, he would have been infinitely less the man and less the genius. He had sufficient confidence not to care for the scribbled stricture in the margin, the pencilled underlining and exclamation mark, the little smiling deprecation, the quibble of the critic European and Fancy; his very faultiness is a part of his power, and this he realised, and of this made a matter for pride. It is significant that he was really angry with the reviewer who wrote of his "barbaric yawp."

The trouble with much of our own writing today is not any lack of "taste"; it is rather an inhibiting excess of it.

Thomas Wolfe: Of Time and Neurosis*

W. M. FROHOCK (1908-   ) is professor and chairman of the Department of Romance Languages and Literatures at Harvard University. For many years he has studied the contemporary French and American novel critically. This essay is from a collection of his critical estimates of the major twentieth-century American novelists. It originally appeared in the *Southwest Review* in 1948.

. . . .
The rhetoric is essential. One reads much more about Wolfe's breadth of vocabulary and his obviously sensuous pleasure in words, and of what someone has called his multitudinous garrulity, than about the way he used his gift. He has the distinction of being the one writer of his generation who truly dared pull out all the stops. Dos Passos cannot compete with him in this respect, because Dos Passos' method of seeing and recording impressions calls for finding the perfectly right word, and the perfectly right word is obscured if associated with a half-dozen approximately right words; and besides, the completely successful word for Dos Passos needs the least possible rhetorical support: where each word stands completely for an impression the only real linkage needed is that of consciousness, proximity [61/62] to the word which denotes the preceding impression in the series. Hemingway cannot compete because his instinctive emotional key, subdued and uneloquent, will not permit, and because his favorite characters are frequently talkative but rarely eloquent people.

Wolfe and his characters, on the other hand, have the native eloquence of an old-time political orator. He needs every resource of rhetorical structure to support the great weight of his enormous enumerations, which are as heavy as Dreiser's. It is extraordinary how often the rhetoric of his own sentences is identical with the drunken rhetoric which he puts in the sonorous mouth of the old man Gant, the great difference of course being that Gant has the rhetorical structure he needs, but not the words to go with it; whereas Wolfe has the words.

The hands had given to the interminable protraction of his living death a kind of concrete horror that it otherwise would not have had. For as his powerful gaunt figure waned and wasted under the ravages of the cancer that was consuming him until he had become only the enfeebled shadow of his former self, his gaunt hands, on which there was so little which death could consume, lost none of their former rock-like heaviness, strength and shapely power. Thus, even when the giant figure of the man had become nothing but a spectral remnant of itself, sunk in a sorrow of time, awaiting death, those great, still-living hands of power and strength hung incredibly, horribly, from that spectral form of death to which they were attached.

The words are here. And so also are most of the faults against which the manuals of English continually warn: prolixity, punning, cliché, repetitiousness and the rest. What saves it? It seems to me that in passages like this Wolfe skates

* W. M. Frohock, from "Thomas Wolfe: Of Time and Neurosis" (Chapter 3), *The Novel of Violence in America 1900-1950* (Dallas: Southern Methodist University Press, 1950), pp. 47-66. Reprinted by permission of Southern Methodist University Press.

determinedly around the edges of the hackneyed, rescuing himself each time through the presence of the particular word which redeems the rest and keeps the phrase from being irremediable cliché: in the first sentence "interminable protraction" saves the hackneyed "living death"; in the [**62/63**] second, the appearance of the verb "waned"—entirely unexpected and acquiring from its context a meaning it never quite had before—stands in relation to the other verb, "wasted," as "enfeebled" stands to the rest of what would otherwise be the deadly cliché, "shadow of his former self." Such rhetorical repetitions as "spectral remnant," which picks up the earlier "shadow," and "spectral forms" which in turns picks up "spectral remnant," are the sources of a freshness which is all the more perceptible because on analysis we are convinced that it comes from reviving what, except in the hands of Thomas Wolfe, would be entirely beyond hope of resuscitation.

All of this is related to Wolfe's habit of taking up some of the most familiar lines of the literary heritage and making them new and strange by the changing of a word or so: "It was unbelievable that an old cancer-riddled spectre of a man should have so much blood in him." I can remember offhand three separate places where he plays variations on the old man with so much blood in him. Despite our awareness that Wolfe abuses this device—as for that matter he abuses, sooner or later, most other rhetorical devices—its value to him is palpable. The essence of this we find in Shakespeare himself, in such lines as

> . . . the feet
> That fourteen hundred years ago were nailed
> For our advantage to the bitter cross

wherein a word like "bitter," common as dirt itself, of its own strength lifts an ordinary prose discourse into poetry. Wolfe's gift is of the same kind. The result is the sort of boldness which allows him to get away with the obvious—note the repeated

pun on Gant's name in the passage above, and the association of "rock-like heaviness" with the hands of a man who has always been a stonecutter. This is the [**63/64**] kind of eloquence that Wolfe brings to the themes of time and of death, time's child.

It is impossible to read Wolfe and like him without becoming something of an anthologist. And since each reader of Wolfe has his own favorite selections, I am offering here at least one example of his poetry of time:

> . . . it is not the slow, the punctual sanded drip of the unnumbered days that we remember best, the ash of time; nor is it the huge monotone of the lost years, the unswerving schedules of the lost life and the well-known faces, that we remember best . . .

This is the poetry of a theme on which John Dos Passos, with a poet's discipline turned to his special uses, was writing the prose.

There is no point in denying that often Wolfe let go to print much that should never have gone. Those of us who like him believe that there was a god in him, but a very unruly god who gave him no peace and at times went away without warning, as people sometimes go away and leave a radio with the switch turned on playing in an empty tenement. He was an enthusiast who had, as old Gant had, "a tragic consciousness of time," and of death. Like the people in *Look Homeward, Angel* he was a fanatic, and time and death were his obsessions. Consequently, in those moments when the god is absent he sounds like a hysterical woman who insists on feeling unloved, while life slips away without anything really stable appearing amid the flow of existence—a hysterical woman whose life is a great conspiracy to frustrate her.

Much that he wrote proves that the critics who were hell-bent to show what really needed no demonstration, i.e., that he did not know how to compose, were right, and is evidence of the compulsive frenzy in which he wrote. It was often more important to him to finish saying some- [64/65] thing and get on to saying something else, than to take care for the nicety of the saying.) Edward Aswell has done his best to dispel the legend that Wolfe never rewrote, and other critics who have examined Wolfe's style closely have found a change appearing in the later work; but there remains abundant proof he did not rewrite enough. Words obsess him, and rhetoric sweeps him away. Such things as Francis Starwick's having a "rather womanish" voice almost *ad infinitum,* the appearance of words like "octopal" in and out of acceptable context on so many occasions, the inability to stop ringing the changes on lines like the one about the old man with all the blood in him, the multiple repetitions of such an intuition as that Uncle Bascom's head is like Emerson's—and so on indefinitely— simply mar his work. They also testify to the great truth of Wolfe's own remark that at times when he wrote it felt as if a great black cloud had discharged itself inside him. Wolfe knew his weakness; he was haunted by the example of Flaubert, and grateful to Maxwell Perkins for assuring him that it was not necessary to be "the Flaubert kind of writer." He finally changed from Scribner to Harper in order to prove to his detractors that he, and not Maxwell Perkins, was the one who put the books together. Our criticism of him will become more cogent as we give over arguing about this incontrovertible weakness and go on to define, as precisely as we can, Wolfe's great strength.

A long time ago the French philosopher Diderot, busy with a discussion on insti-

tutions among the savages of the South Seas, paused a moment to remark how contrary to common sense it seems, in a world where time is always at work and change is the rule, to base marriage on the assumption that love is eternal. Years later his countryman, Musset, picked up the theme in a famous poem, *Le Souvenir,* in [65/66] which he added a new ingredient: how sad and how poignant that the eternity of the love we swear is, of necessity, an illusion. The difference between the two points of view is probably the essential difference between the eighteenth century and the nineteenth; Diderot's reflection was prompted merely by the fact that he was having a certain amount of trouble with his wife—a situation which he managed somehow to take pretty much in stride—whereas Musset, frustrated in his various attempts to realize a completely satisfactory love, generalizes his predicament into an essential aspect of man's fate. This mood is Wolfe's, leaving out love or substituting for it the whole complex of man's emotions. It puts him in the tradition of Proust . . . and of Dos Passos, a very central and important tradition since it reflects in literature the great discovery of the relativity of all things which is our inheritance from the nineteenth century. But the tradition itself does not need to be eternal, and the feeling we have that after Proust and Dos Passos and Wolfe there was left, *circa* 1930, very little to be said about it, is probably the best indication we have that by that date the nineteenth century was over.

The World of Fiction*

BERNARD DEVOTO (1897-1955), American historian, novelist, critic, and essayist, was an authority on Mark Twain. Among his many volumes the best known were *Across the Wide Missouri*, which won the Pulitzer Prize for History, and *Mark Twain's America*. He edited the *Saturday Review of Literature* in 1936, 1937, and 1938. *The World of Fiction*, from which this selection is taken, is a study of the devices of fiction in relation to the psychological relationship of the reader to the work.

In the later novels of Sherwood Anderson a characteristic kind of passage becomes increasingly common. I refer not to the communal disrobing scenes so fully criticized in Mr. Hemingway's *Torrents of Spring* but to the Whitmanesque soliloquies on birth, blood fellowship, the soul's groping for brotherhood, the pain of the mind's failure to heed its own deepest promptings, the solitude in which human life is imprisoned—on a large number of vague but passionately developed themes. Most readers find them not only unintelligible but actively and offensively dull. They have troubled a number of critics, who have devised various systems of analysis to rationalize them, but their real insufficiency is immediately revealed when they are examined technically. Such passages are anomalies. They are rich with emotion, in fact they consist of nothing but emotion, and as such they are material out of which fiction is made. But fiction has not been made of them. The emotion as it appears is [**260/261**] not the emotion of the characters but that of the author himself. It is relevant only to him, not to the people he is writing about nor the relationships in which they are placed. Fiction comes to a dead stop and Anderson feels passionately and with great eloquence before our eyes.

Thomas Wolfe's *Of Time and the River* has frequently been compared to *Moby-Dick*. A truer comparison would mention Melville's *Pierre,* which is similarly sown with long passages of unshaped emotion. At that period Melville frequently could not complete the process of creative transformation and was content to substitute rhetoric for fiction, which is what Wolfe did at his worst.

But this was the reason why these things could never be forgotten—because we are so lost, so naked, and so lonely in America. Immense and cruel skies bend over us, and all of us are driven on forever and we have no home. Therefore, it is not the slow, the punctual sanded drip of the unnumbered days that we remember best, the ash of time; nor is it the huge monotone of the lost years, the unswerving schedules of the lost life and well-known faces, that we remember best. It is a face seen once and lost forever in a crowd, an eye that looked, a face that smiled and vanished on a passing train, it is a prescience of snow upon a certain night, the laughter of a woman in a summer street long years ago, it is the memory of a single moon seen at the pine's dark edge in old October—and all of our lives is written in the twisting of a leaf upon a bough, a door that opened, and a stone.

For America has a thousand lights and weathers and we walk the streets, we walk the streets forever, we walk the streets of life alone.

It is the place of the howling winds, the hurrying of [**261/262**] *the leaves in old October, the hard clean falling to the earth of acorns.*

* Bernard DeVoto, from *The World of Fiction* (Boston: Houghton Mifflin Company, 1950), pp. 260-264. Reprinted by permission of and arrangement with Houghton Mifflin Company, the authorized publishers.

The place of the storm-tossed moaning of the wintry mountainside, where the young men cry out in their throats and feel the savage vigor, the rude strong energies; the place also where the trains cross rivers.

This sort of thing recurs periodically in the novel. For instance:

And finally, in that dark jungle of the night, through all the visions, memories, and enchanted weavings of the timeless and eternal spell of time, the moment of forever—there are two horsemen, riding, riding, riding in the night.

Who are they? Oh, we know them with our life and they will ride across the land, the moon-haunted passage of our lives forever. Their names are Death and Pity, and we know their face: our brother and our father ride ever beside us in the dream-enchanted spell and vista of the night; the hooves level time beside the rhythms of the train.

Horsed on the black and moon-maned steeds of fury, cloaked in the dark of night, the spell of time, dream-pale, eternal, they are rushing on across the haunted land, the moon-enchanted wilderness, and their hooves make level thunder with the train.[1] [262/263]

In such passages the affairs of the Gant family have evaporated and Wolfe in his own person is pulsating with superhuman —or supersyntactical—ecstasy and pain. What is wrong with them and the many similar ones is not their intensity—intensity is always welcome in a novel—but the fact that they are in Wolfe's own person. That his novel deals with the imaginary Gant family is something of a legal fiction, but the reader requires the pretense to be maintained. Once he picks up the novel he is concerned solely with the Gant family; he is not indifferent but actively hostile to Wolfe's feelings, however they might move him if they were in a non-fictional context.

It is sometimes said in praise of such passages—which are a mildew on much fiction, though not often fiction which is taken so seriously as Anderson's and Wolfe's—that they are poetic. But fiction is fiction and poetry is poetry, and each is most itself in its methods. When the methods are blended you get something different from both and much less important than either. Both call on the same

psychic resources, but fiction has to use the substance in its own way and shape it to its own purposes or the result will be disaster. Emotion in the raw can be an attribute only of the characters whose lives are engaged with one another inside the illusion. When it remains an attribute of the author it has not yet become fiction.

A passage of description that is intended to give the scene reality, a passage of analysis that is intended to interpret the behavior of characters, or a passage of exposition that is intended to give significance to the action, is fiction clumsily written. Nevertheless it is written in terms of the novel; its meaning, however imperfectly conveyed, is a meaning of [263/264] the novel, not of something outside it. But passages of emotion which have not been transformed, whose reference and relevance are not of the characters but of the novelist, are only a stage on the way to fiction, a stage that is still short of it. The same objection may be made to them as to the clumsily handled passages: they halt the movement of fiction as effectively as if pages from the telephone book had been inserted in a death scene and they destroy the illusion by bringing the novelist out of the wings. But the objection to the clumsily handled passages is to the handling only, the material in itself is acceptable. You have seen the novelist manipulating the strings and that is deplorable, but at least the puppets were giving the show. Whereas when the novelist is heaving with emotion of his own,

[1] Quite apart from the point my text discusses, I cannot forbear remarking that this is fearfully bad writing. That the first of the passages I quote has been reprinted in various anthologies supposed to exemplify the best writing of our time, and that it is referred to seriously and even analyzed for beauty and subtlety of style in critical treatments of Wolfe only make the standards of American criticism seem more amazing. I have remarked that many critics of fiction work under the handicap of not being able to think of novels from within, but surely the first obligation of a critic is to understand what prose is. The prose of these passages is inept, crude, trite, sprawling. It is as sophomoric as the emotions it more or less eructates; in [262/263] fact, only a sophomore singularly gifted with vagueness could write so badly. Just why should we waste time on a critic's imperatives about the social and esthetic obligations of fiction when he admires such stuff as this? [263].

when he is walking the streets forever in the hurrying leaves of old October or is horsed on the moon-maned steeds of fury in the dream-pale spell of time, he has become the show and there are no longer any puppets.

Technical analysis therefore is meaningless. All one can say is that the novelist has mistaken his medium or fallen short of it. He is writing something that resembles Old Testament rhapsody but differs from it in not having the living core. He most certainly is not writing fiction. Perhaps his material might eventually prove to have the highest usefulness for fiction, but before it can become fiction it must be submitted to processes that have been discussed in the first half of this book. It must stay longer in the tanning bath or the rising pan, it must be leavened—or whatever metaphor will suggest that a transformation must occur before it can acquire form. The essential thing has not yet been done to it.

Rhetoric In Southern Writing: Wolfe*

FLOYD C. WATKINS. For biographical data see *Thomas Wolfe's Characters* (p. 49). This essay was one of the papers read in a symposium on the problem of rhetoric in Southern writing, at the Third Conference on Problems in the Study of Southern Literature, held at the meeting of the Modern Language Association in Madison, Wisconsin, September 10, 1957, under the chairmanship of C. Hugh Holman. Other speakers were Robert D. Jacobs, on Poe, and William Van O'Connor, on Faulkner.

The claims that Thomas Wolfe was an expatriate Southerner who fouled his own nest are matched by claims that he befouled his own books with "turbulent and undisciplined rhetoric"—and no ten-minute paper can even clarify the issues between the attackers and the defenders of his style. Some judge him the greatest writer of modern times, some the worst, and some both the best and the worst. Faulkner, Wolfe's fellow Southern rhetorician, has "rated Wolfe first" although he was, says Faulkner, "willing to throw away style." Robert Penn Warren finds the rhetoric "astonishingly loose," "sometimes grand, . . . more often tedious and tinged with hysteria." Edwin Berry Burgum maintains that in "the periodic sentences and the consolation of abstract statement . . . indubitably Wolfe becomes one of the great stylists in the English language." If the critics disagree, the Wolfe cultists are certain that his style is one of his great accomplishments. Indeed, his poetic rhetoric has attracted the large audience to which many modern poets claim they cannot appeal.

The varying judgments by different critics, the frequent changes in the attitude of the reader toward Wolfe, and the tendency to like a passage from Wolfe at one time and to dislike it at another—all these are understandable if we view him as a poet—particularly a primitive or natural poet. Perhaps the most basic characteristic of Wolfe's prose is that it reveals a love for primitivistic sound and phrase. As a college student he once recited for days a single line from one **[79/80]** of the penny dreadfuls of his time: "The arm was hairy, hairy beyond all description." Much of his writing reveals an attraction to the mere words and rhythms of a sentence not entirely unlike the appeal to the primitive in Vachel Lindsay's "The Congo." His elaborate repetitions and pointing words and phrases are occasionally as inept as the dull reiterations of a freshman theme, often as primitive as the incremental repetition of a folk ballad, and sometimes as infinitely various as the work of a careful poet.

The long description of Altamont waking at dawn in *Look Homeward, Angel* contains an example of how Wolfe repeated phrases and figures and achieved an unusual effect by varying the combinations of colors and images. "Spring," he wrote, "lay strewn lightly like a fragrant gauzy scarf upon the earth; the night was a cool bowl of lilac darkness, filled with fresh orchard scents." In the following twelve pages he repeats in many combinations such terms as *lilac darkness, pearl*

* Floyd C. Watkins, "Rhetoric in Southern Writing: Wolfe," *Georgia Review*, XII (Spring, 1958), 79-82. Reprinted by permission of the *Georgia Review*.

light, nacreous dawn, and *blue-pearl* until the repetitions lead gradually to the full light of day, which appears suddenly in the new term *virginal sunlight*. Without such extended development, some of the descriptive passages would seem overwritten, but the activities of the waking citizens as well as the repetitions prepare for a rhapsody like the following: "Nacreous pearl light swam faintly about the hem of the lilac darkness; the edges of light and darkness were stitched upon the hills. Morning moved like a pearl-gray tide across the fields and up the hillflanks, flowing rapidly down into the soluble dark." This is one of the best examples of Wolfe's characteristic rhetorical patterning of phrases throughout a unified passage. Similarly, in the description of the death of Ben Gant, the images of the "bright and stricken thing," the cock, and the leaves are repeated with great power and accumulating effect.

Look Homeward, Angel is Wolfe's most subtle novel in imagery. He describes wonder as "the union of the ordinary and the miraculous," and in many instances he succeeds in blending the two poetically and almost metaphysically in the poetic sense. Destiny, he says for example in the first paragraph, leads "into the hills that shut in Altamont over the proud coral cry of the cock, and the soft stone smile of an angel. . . ." *Coral cry* metaphysically yokes heterogeneous elements by violence together; it may involve a description of the color of the cock, or the description of the sound as a color, or the description of the color of the dawn. And "the soft stone smile of the angel" merges **[80/81]** paradoxical terms. Oxymorons and conceits of this kind are almost omnipresent in the first novel but rather infrequent in the later works.

Wolfe's turbulent emotions and extravagant figures of speech often counterbalance his successes. That cow in *Look Homeward, Angel* which is "singing in her strong deep voice her Sunday exuberance" is an unhappy example of Wolfe's own occasional bovine mooings; and she even suggests the ineptness of the squeal and the goat-cry in the love story in *The Web and the Rock* or of characters "holding [their] . . . entrails thoughtfully in [their] . . . hands" in *Of Time and the River*. The most overdone passages in *Look Homeward, Angel* at times make the hero more ridiculous than adolescent. If the description of Eugene's paper route is on the whole a masterful accomplishment, the hero is excessively afflicted with emotions while carrying the papers: "he burst into maniacal laughter. He leaped high into the air with a scream of insane exultancy, burred in his throat idiot-animal squeals, and shot his papers terrifically into the flimsy boarding of the shacks."

What most of us too often fail to see, however, is Wolfe's frequent comic intent in his rhetorical passages. Often he succeeds in making his adult readers nostalgically long for childhood, and he amuses them in the same passages by creating comic melodrama about childhood, using deliberately high-flown rhetoric. When young Eugene Gant visualizes himself as the Dixie Ghost in a motion picture, Wolfe is not only portraying a child's imagination but also sympathetically laughing at the child and the movie. When the Ghost "found himself face to face with the little dancing girl," there was as much comedy as childhood romance: "Two smoking globes of brine welled from the pellucid depths of her pure eyes and fell with a hot splash on his bronzed hand." Later, the Ghost "pondered on love's mystery. Pure but passionate. Appearances against her, 'tis true: The foul breath of slander. She worked in a bawdy-house but her heart was clean. Outside of that, what can one say against her?"

If Wolfe depicts W. O. Gant as a tragic hero of almost gigantic proportions in some scenes, he also frequently uses rhetoric to make him a boisterous clown. When, for example, ladies compliment him because he votes for prohibition, Wolfe describes him mock-heroically: "With far-seeing statesmanship he looked westward toward Pisgah." And then W. O launches into a political oration extolling his own virtues and damning the evil whisky he loves. But this pose is shaken [81/82] by his cronies' crudeness, expressed in a style characteristic of the writings of the Old Southwest humorists: "Go on, W. O., but for God's sake, don't belch!" And Tim O'Doyle, the bartender, adds a tall tale in the homely speech of Southern folk: "I've seen him start for the door and step through the windey. When we see him coming we hire two extra bottle openers. He used to give the barman a bonus to get up early."

Look Homeward, Angel exhibits the major tendencies in Wolfe's rhetoric. It is his best book, because his rhetorical flourishes are most happily employed to describe the emotions and the imagination of a sensitive child or youth. In the next two books, the rhetoric frequently becomes bombastic descriptions of adolescent emotions of an older if not more mature hero. *You Can't Go Home Again* marks in many respects a new stage. The rhetoric appears in panoramic descriptions of the landscape of America and in passages where a lyrical style is appropriate.

The decline evident in *Of Time and the River* and *The Web and the Rock* is significantly offset by Wolfe's increasing use of his Southern origins and of Southern speech and oratory. "The Web of Earth" is one of his best works because Wolfe presents so ably the mountaineer rhetoric of Eliza Gant in what might be called a stream of conversation. Uncle John's account of the battle of Chickamauga in *The Hills Beyond* is one of the most effective representations of mountaineer speech in American literature. And the political oratory and backwoods humor of Zachariah Joyner in *The Hills Beyond* are other examples of Wolfe's growing consciousness of his Southern heritage, including Southern rhetoric.

Wolfe must be viewed as a Southern rhetorician. He was a poet in his love of sound and his use of sensuous imagery. At his worst, he is "full of sound and fury, signifying nothing"; at his best, as one of his characters says of W. O. Gant, he could "tie a knot in the tail of the English language."

The Privileged Moment: A Study in the Rhetoric of Thomas Wolfe*

MAURICE NATANSON (1924-   ) is professor of philosophy at the University of North Carolina. He is the author of *A Critique of Jean-Paul Sartre's Ontology* and *The Social Dynamics of George H. Mead*. In this article he brings certain aspects of a "phenomenology of language" to bear upon Wolfe's rhetoric.

Every language is the whole of a world, a space in which our souls live and move. Each word breathes the air of the whole. Each is open toward an unbounded horizon. A language is not an aggregate of words and rules. It is a potential world, an infinity of past and future worlds, merely a frame within which we speak and can create our world, actualizing ourselves and our language.

—*Kurt Riezler*

I

The rhetoric of Thomas Wolfe is part of his legend.[1] Building a fury of signs, he elevated words and sounds to an intensity which is qualitatively their own and unique to his style; protean and boundless, he urged language into a wildness and power that signalized his transcendent view of the world as a labyrinth of the lonely and the alone. Wolfe's style, then, is as striking as his great figure must have been; there is no critic of his work who has failed to remark its reach and also its problematics.[2] But as with so many other features of the Wolfe legend, there has been more mention of his rhetoric than there has been serious analysis of it.[3] Somehow it has been taken for granted for the very reason of its immediacy. That much has been lost in this way I hope to show; but the present essay cannot claim to be a study of Wolfe's style or an anatomy of his

language. Rather, I am here concerned with his rhetoric as a single, though crucial, facet of a phenomenology of language, a facet which will, however, lead to nuclear issues in rhetorical theory.

Although it is not within the scope of this essay to consider the problems of a phenomenology of language or the more general philosophical issues involved in clarifying the relationship of language to reality, I do wish to indicate the immediate sense in which I am using the term "rhetoric" in the present discussion. Negatively stated, I am not interested here in

[1] See Herbert J. Muller, *Thomas Wolfe* (Norfolk, Connecticut, 1947), Chapter 1.
[2] For a sympathetic treatment of Wolfe's style, see Pamela Hansford Johnson, *Thomas Wolfe: A Critical Study* (London and Toronto, 1947), pp. 17-33; the case against Wolfe is presented by Alfred Kazin, *On Native Grounds* (New York, 1942), Chapter 15. Kazin writes (p. 480): "Wolfe was the Tarzan of rhetoric, the noble lover, the antagonist of cities, the spear of fate, the Wolfe whose rhetoric, swollen with archaisms out of the English classics, can be as painful to read as a child's scrawlings. His rhetoric, pilfered recklessly from the Jacobeans and Sir Thomas Browne, James Joyce and Swinburne, Gilbert Murray and the worst traditions of Southern oratory, was a gluttonous English instructor's accumulation. He became enraptured with the altitudinous, ceremonial prose of the seventeenth century, with the vague splendors of a dozen assorted romanticisms, and united them at the pitch of his father's mountain oratory."
[3] There is no title on Wolfe's rhetoric contained in the bibliography of the secondary literature which appears in Thomas Clark Pollock and Oscar Cargill, *Thomas Wolfe at Washington Square* (New York, 1954), nor is there any article specifically concerned with Wolfe's style included in *The Enigma of Thomas Wolfe*, ed. Richard Walser (Cambridge, Mass., 1953).

* Maurice Natanson, "The Privileged Moment: A Study in the Rhetoric of Thomas Wolfe," *Quarterly Journal of Speech*, XLIII (April, 1957), 143-150. Reprinted with the permission of the *Quarterly Journal of Speech*.

anything that can be called traditional rhetoric, i.e., the history of rhetoric in Greek and Roman thought, nor am I concerned with recent discus- [143/144] sions of the status of theory of rhetoric.[4] Furthermore, I am not talking about anything which has been discussed under the rubric of rhetorical criticism or poetic. Although the style of my problem may be closest to the spirit of the "New Rhetoric," I have developed my ideas from distinctively philosophical considerations and from a particular philosophical tradition that are not proper parts of the "New Rhetoric." Positively stated, I have used "rhetoric" as an inroad to the philosophical problem of how language both fixes and realizes the complex "moments" of meaning which announce reality. Rhetoric here is developed, however, within and through the context of Wolfe's writings rather than in philosophical terms. I have started with the naive sense of rhetoric which has been used to characterize a distinctive aspect of Wolfe's style, but my point is that this sense of rhetoric as high-flown, charged, and rhapsodic usage is a clue to a profound dimension of language which has been obscured or ignored—the power of language to epiphanize transcendent meanings through its own instrumentality. The rationale of such a concept of rhetoric, the analysis of its structure, is the task of a phenomenology of language which would account for and describe the logical genesis and foundation of meaning in subjectivity. The philosophical achievement of Edmund Husserl has given us the groundwork for such an investigation. Alfred Schutz' "Symbol, Reality, and Society"[5] is a decisive contribution to recent discussion of these problems. But such phenomenological investigations of language and reality are beyond the limits of my remarks on Wolfe. Here I wish to restrict the problem to exactly what I have attempted: interpreting the rhetoric of Thomas Wolfe as the articulation of reality through privileged moments.

Our first problem is one of definition. Traditionally, by the rhetoric of Thomas Wolfe has been meant his charged language, those extensive passages throughout his works which are stylistically reminiscent of Whitman and Melville and which bear the fiery and solemn cadences of the Old Testament.[6]

Who has seen fury riding in the mountains? [Wolfe writes]. Who has known fury striding in the storm? Who has been mad with fury in his youth, given no rest or peace or certitude by fury, driven on across the earth by fury, until the great vine of the heart was broke, the sinews wrenched, the little tenement of bone, marrow, brain, and feeling in which great fury raged, was twisted, wrung, worn out, and exhausted by the fury which it could not lose or put away? Who has known fury, how it came?[7]

Such passages appear in at least two ways in the novels: they are interspersed, usually following scenes or vignettes, and serve as a kind of chorus for the works; also they are binding and bridging structures which function as motifs at the beginning of each novel, as connective tissue between sections, and as poetic finales.

As a chorus, Wolfe's chanting voice takes up again and again the central themes of his work: the self in its solitude and lostness in reality, the self in [144/145] the image of Telemachus, the self's rootedness in earth, history, and the prime memories of family and home, and, finally, the voyage of the self in search of itself through the mysteries of time and the haunting domain of death. Suffusing these passages is a sense of root loss, an *a priori* of something sought for and somewhere missed, as though what structures human experience into the relatedness of men

[4] E.g.: My article, "The Limits of Rhetoric," *QJS*, XLI (April 1955), is completely unrelated to the present essay, apart from the identity of philosophical standpoint underlying both papers.
[5] In *Symbols and Society: Fourteenth Symposium of the Conference on Science, Philosophy and Religion*, ed. Lyman Bryson, Louis Finkelstein, Hudson Hoagland, R. M. Maciver (New York, 1955).
[6] Two collections of rhetorical-poetic passages from the writings of Wolfe have appeared: John Hall Wheelock, *The Face of a Nation* (New York, 1939) and John S. Barnes, *A Stone, A Leaf, A Door* (New York, 1945).
[7] *Of Time and the River* (New York, 1944), pp. 27-28.

were itself flawed—not failure here but the impossibility of fulfillment:

Which of us has known his brother? Which of us has looked into his father's heart? Which of us has not remained forever prison-pent? Which of us is not forever a stranger and alone?[8]

As binding and bridging forces, such expressive passages are distillations of things done, places seen, persons encountered, and experiences suffered and reveled in. The connections are both immediate and indirect: they lead from one set of affairs to another in the novelist's story and they also thrust back and forth in the substance of events. Throughout *Of Time and the River*, for example, the image and theme of death is taken up in manifold ways—the deaths of the hero's father and brother are the points of central reference —and returned to through the instrument of rhetorical passages. Immediately after a comic interlude in the novel, Wolfe turns to the theme of his brother's death and resurrects his image:

And then he would hear again the voice of his dead brother, and remember with a sense of black horror, dream-like disbelief, that Ben was dead, and yet could not believe that Ben had ever died, or that he had had a brother, lost a friend. Ben would come back to him in these moments with a blazing and intolerable reality, until he heard his quiet living voice again, saw his fierce scowling eyes of bitter gray, his scornful, proud and lively face, and always when Ben came back to him it was like this: he saw his brother in a simple image, in some brief forgotten moment of the past, remembered him by a word, a gesture, a forgotten act: and certainly all that could ever be known of Ben's life was collected in that blazing image of lost time and the forgotten moment. And suddenly he would be there in a strange land, staring upward from his bed in darkness, hearing his brother's voice again, and living in the far and bitter miracle of time.[9]

After this section devoted to Ben, there is an immediate return to the earlier scene. This kind of placement can only be understood as connective ordering which illuminates the themes of a novel by rhetorical emphasis. The connection is direct to the

extent that it instantly binds together parts of a single sequence; it is indirect, however, in its very persuasion, for it calls the reader back to fragmented moments of the theme's expression at the same time that it promises a re-sounding and rearticulation in pages to come.

But defining rhetoric in this context as charged language, dominated by poetic image, and having the several stylistic functions just discussed, is far from arriving at an acceptable analysis of the problem. It is my thesis that there is much more involved in the rhetoric of Thomas Wolfe; that we must go beyond the characters of rich, compressed, and pulsating language to the interior and essential meaning born and expressed by the order of prose-poetry commonly associated with Wolfe. I wish to suggest that that meaning lies in a certain attitude toward language itself, a certain appraisal of the limits of language, and a certain refusal to accept those limits—at least not without raging. To put the entire matter in a different way: Wolfe's rhetoric involves a conception of language, its inherent powers and possibilities, and, I would add, its relation-[145/146] ship to the reality it describes and engages, and to its votaries, like Wolfe, whom it demonizes.

II

For many and divergent reasons, ours may be called the century of language: whether we consider the contributions of philosophers, psychologists, or novelists, the central impression that a new "key" (to use Susanne Langer's term) has been struck in the whole range of knowledge and art is unavoidable and undeniable. In philosophy the work of such variant thinkers as Peirce, Husserl, Cassirer, Heidegger, and Wittgenstein has created a rich literature concerned with the problems of symbol, concept, and form; in psychology

[8] *Look Homeward, Angel* (New York, 1929), motif, facing p. 3.
[9] *Of Time and the River*, pp. 200-201.

(broadly taken) the work of Freud, George H. Mead, the Gestalt school, and Kurt Goldstein has opened up a new terrain of relevances for language in its relationship to mind and action; and in literature, the revolutionary contributions of Proust and Joyce have liberated and made explicit a generative force in art.[10] Even if we restrict ourselves to literary influences, the impact of the century's discovery on the consciousness of Wolfe was enormous. Joyce's influence on Wolfe may serve as an approach to the problem of rhetoric.[11]

Only obliquely in *Ulysses* and *A Portrait of the Artist as a Young Man,* but explicitly in *Stephen Hero,* Joyce formulates his theory of *epiphany.*

By an epiphany he meant a sudden spiritual manifestation, whether in the vulgarity of speech or of gesture or in a memorable phrase of the mind itself. He believed that it was for the man of letters to record these epiphanies with extreme care, seeing that they themselves are the most delicate and evanescent of moments.[12]

An epiphany is a momentous and instantaneous manifestation of reality; it is a sudden breaking into experience with arterial force, revealing "that which is" with utter truth and candor. The greatness of an artist may be measured by the epiphanies he gives us, those revelations that turn on vast lights in our consciousness, which in searching out their hidden objects, their shadowed forms, search out in us the gift of understanding. Joyce presents his theory in quasi-satiric scholastic terms:

First we recognize that the object is *one* integral thing, then we recognize that it is an organized composite structure, a *thing* in fact: finally, when the relation of the parts is exquisite, when the parts are adjusted to the special point, we recognize that it is *that* thing which it is. Its soul, its whatness, leaps to us from the vestment of its appearance. The soul of the commonest object, the structure of which is so adjusted, seems to us radiant. The object achieves its epiphany.[13]

An epiphany may be generated out of compounded objects and experiences, however, and the moment of insight and expression goes beyond the Thomistic trinity of "wholeness, harmony, and radiance" which Joyce discusses.[14] An epiphany in the compounded sense, [146/147] generalized into the total world of experience, is the discovery of a thematic meaning which has been lost in its "sedimentations" (to borrow a term from the language of phenomenology), which has encysted in its complexity within experience, but below the threshold of explicit awareness. It is this distillation of meanings which is tapped by creative genius and brought to expression in epiphany. And, I would suggest, it is precisely the stylistic methodology of Joyce that recommends itself to Wolfe, for he too is haunted by epiphanies potential to creation, awaiting the season of their unfolding.

If the epiphanies of Joyce are revelations of Man, they are for Wolfe outpourings of the person, the self alone; yet the starting point, stylistically, is historical for both. Just as *Ulysses* is the exploration of consciousness through the single day of Leopold Bloom, a moment in time, so, it may be remarked, the novels of Wolfe begin with a dating of the action or a state-

---

[10] T. S. Eliot writes of *Ulysses:* "I hold this book to be the most important expression which the present age has found; it is a book to which we are all indebted, and from which none of us can escape." ("Ulysses, Order, and Myth," in *James Joyce: Two Decades of Criticism,* ed. Seon Givens [New York, 1948], p. 198.)

[11] See Thomas Wolfe, *The Story of a Novel* in *The Portable Thomas Wolfe,* ed. Maxwell Geismar (New York, 1946), p. 566 and also cf. Nathan L. Rothman, "Thomas Wolfe and James Joyce: A Study in Literary Influence," in *The Enigma of Thomas Wolfe.*

[12] James Joyce, *Stephen Hero* (A Part of the First Draft of A Portrait of the Artist as a Young Man), ed. Theodore Spencer (New York, 1944), p. 211; see Spencer's Introduction, *Ibid.,* pp. 16-17 and cf. Irene Hendry, "Joyce's Epiphanies," in *James Joyce: Two Decades of Criticism* and Harry Levin, *James Joyce: A Critical Introduction* (Norfolk, Connecticut, 1941), pp. 28-31 and *passim.*

[13] *Stephen Hero,* p. 213.

[14] *Ibid.,* pp. 212-213 and *A Portrait of the Artist as a Young Man* in *The Portable James Joyce,* ed. Harry Levin (New York, 1947), p. 478 ff.

ment of the historicity of the theme.[15] The beginning of *Look Homeward, Angel* is the clearest announcement of Wolfe's intentions: the prologue of the first chapter presents a colon to which the totality of the rest of the novel is a restricted, implicit remainder:

Each of us [Wolfe writes] is all the sums he has not counted: subtract us into nakedness and night again, and you shall see begin in Crete four thousand years ago the love that ended yesterday in Texas.
The seed of our destruction will blossom in the desert, the alexin of our cure grows by a mountain rock, and our lives are haunted by a Georgia slattern, because a London cutpurse went unhung. Each moment is the fruit of forty thousand years. The minute-winning days, like flies, buzz home to death, and every moment is a window on all time.
This is a moment:[16]

Each person, each event, each history of affairs is a compressed cipher for which Wolfe's art is hermeneutic. The world of each man is a microcosm in which is pressured the totality of all that ever was, implied in an almost Hegelian trail of connections that return the moment to Time, the event to Process, the individual to the Absolute. Wolfe's world is a world of moments, highly structured and individuated, yet caught up in the themes of a mutual destiny, a single attraction that gives them valence and defines their signification.

The placement of meaning and insight in the moment is inescapable to any reader of the novels: the stranger seen in the street, on the train, from afar, glimpsed for that instant of recognition and then forever vanished back into the web of anonymity, the face at the window, the brief look of the bank teller, the sight of the salesman, the suddenly-caught movement of the laborer, the craftsman, the stitch of the tailor, the trucker shifting heavy gears, the frosty face of the trainsman signalling in an early hour of winter, the soft cry of a child—all these are familiar moments in the pages of the novels, and Wolfe is unimaginable without them. But these moments are usually described

as "far and lost," as instantly gone, as "forever lost." They are instantaneous irruptions in consciousness which fill the hero with sadness and longing and despair and wonder; they are always sudden, always intense, and always remembered. It is in these moments that Wolfe's epiphanies manifest themselves.

But it is necessary to examine these [147/148] moments most rigorously if we are to go beyond the simple marking of them: what content do they inform us of, what indeed do they epiphanize? In answer to this question one commentator has suggested that the passion of the moment is in its givenness and that the meaning of the moment invariably escapes both novelist and reader.

Everything for Wolfe is in the moment [writes John Peale Bishop], he can so try to impress us with the immensity of the moment that it will take on some sort of transcendental meaning. But what that meaning is, escapes him, as it does us. And once it has passed from his mind, he can do nothing but recall another moment, which as it descends into his memory seems always about to deliver itself, by a miracle, of some tremendous import.[17]

But Bishop views these moments in an almost moral context: they represent efforts on the part of the novelist to embrace his characters and their truth as well; and since Wolfe, according to this critic, was ultimately incapable of love, those moments fail to achieve resolution: they are mounting crescendos in a symphony that moves, quickens, and elevates without ever coming to climax.

The most striking passages in Wolfe's novels [Bishop says] always represent these moments of comprehension. For a moment, but a moment only, there is a sudden release of compassion, when some aspect of suffering and bewildered humanity is seized, when the other's emotion is

[15] The opening sentences of *Of Time and the River* and *You Can't Go Home Again* date the action of the novel in terms of the hero; the opening sentence of *The Web and the Rock* and the third paragraph of the opening page of *Look Homeward, Angel* date the action in terms of the hero's ancestors.
[16] *Look Homeward, Angel*, p. 3.
[17] John Peale Bishop, "The Sorrows of Thomas Wolfe," *Kenyon Review*, I (1939), 10-11.

in a timeless completion known. Then the moment passes, and compassion fails.[18]

But I think Wolfe's moments may be viewed apart from Bishop's moral framework, that they do reveal an interior signification, and that though they lapse in the temporal movement of the novel, they remain constant in the articulation of Wolfe's vision. It is as instrumentalities of rhetoric that their import may be grasped and their positive quality seized.

III

Someone has remarked that all Wolfe's novels are about a novelist writing a novel. Whatever truth there may be in this, in addition to surface observation, it may tend to obscure a deeper truth about Wolfe's work: that much of it is self-critical in the sense of being metalinguistic. There are sections of the novels, in addition to *The Story of a Novel,* which are directly concerned with the problems of language and language users, though those sections often take the form of meditations on language and art rather than academic or philosophical critiques. In an epiphanous moment Wolfe presents the bond and power that bind the writer to his art:

At that instant he saw, in one blaze of light, an image of unutterable conviction, the reason why the artist works and lives and has his being—the reward he seeks—the only reward he really cares about, without which there is nothing. It is to snare the spirits of mankind in nets of magic, to make his life prevail through his creation, to wreak the vision of his life, the rude and painful substance of his own experience, into the congruence of blazing and enchanted images that are themselves the core of life, the essential pattern whence all other things proceed, the kernel of eternity.[19]

The epiphany Wolfe gives us is the revelation of language itself: the artist in words is more than storyteller or technician; he is in possession of the quintessence of existence if only it can be tamed into expression, worked into "the congruence of blaz-

ing and enchanted images." Language, for Wolfe, is both battering ram and castle, it is weapon and wound, for the moment's meaning is that language *is* reality, bound to it in the way of its being and in the form of its substance. Wolfe's quest for linguistic dominion is the effort to wrench from language its capacity to penetrate reality, to gain an in- [148/149] road into being, to achieve the miracle of epiphany in which language reveals itself as reality and reality reveals itself through image, form, and the magical terms of language. "Could I," Wolfe cries, "weave into immortal denseness some small brede of words, pluck out of sunken depths the roots of living, some hundred thousand magic words that were as great as all my hunger, and hurl the sum of all my living out upon three hundred pages!"[20] And this cry, itself a moment, is the confession that language is superior to any of its concretizations, that it remains, like earth and the seasons, a quest for the wanderer and a home for the lost.

The moment, then, is revealed in language because its very character is constituted of language: the image of the real *is* the real or as much of it as man can grasp, and language draws us into the vortex of full expression. The points in language when such perfection of meaning and image, of word and reality, is achieved are epiphanies; they are, we may say, *privileged moments* of consciousness. And now the full relationship of rhetoric and language may be seen, for rhetoric, as we choose to interpret it in our present framework, is the complete expression which embodies an epiphany, and makes of it a privileged moment. It is not a question of poetic expression or high-flown language; rather it is the victory of language over its object when form fixes content with purity and high purpose. The fixation intended here is the expression of consciousness divorcing from its interest, momentarily, the irrelevancies which

18 *Ibid.,* pp. 14-15.
19 *Of Time and the River,* p. 550.
20 *The Web and the Rock* (New York, 1937), motif on page preceding p. 3.

bind us to the meanings sedimented in reality. In this sense, rhetoric liberates consciousness from a burden of connections and opens it up and out into a world of unlimited truth. It re-teaches us how to *see* what is given us in experience; by its very power and elevation it draws us up to face what hitherto in seeing we have always ignored: rhetoric gives to the privileged moment a privileged status. Though his essay is concerned with different problems from those we have been dealing with here, a passage from Camus' *The Myth of Sisyphus* gives a penetrating statement of what we may call the rhetoric of privilege:

Thinking is learning all over again how to see, directing one's consciousness, making of every image a privileged place. . . . From the evening breeze to this hand on my shoulder, everything has its truth. Consciousness illuminates it by paying attention to it. Consciousness does not form the object of its understanding, it merely focuses, it is the act of attention, and, to borrow a Bergsonian image, it resembles the projector that suddenly focuses on an image. The difference is that there is no scenario, but a successive and incoherent illustration. In that magic lantern all the pictures are privileged. Consciousness suspends in experience the objects of its attention. Through its miracle it isolates them.[21]

Consciousness attains to the privileged moment through its capacity to fix it in symbols, to announce its coherence through the coherence of language itself. In this sense, rhetoric as "fixative" is a special moment, a privileged moment, in linguistic expression, and in the purest

form it can attain, it transcends itself into poetry.

If we have presented rhetoric in a rather unusual light, it is no less the case that we have turned to perhaps curious features of language and consciousness itself. The world examined in these terms is hardly the world as it **[149/150]** is ordinarily regarded. Our excuse, if one is necessary, is that the world as it truly presents itself to human experience is elusive and that the privilege of epiphany commends itself in making substantive to consciousness what otherwise remains tormentingly adjectival. Rhetoric seems, from a theoretical standpoint, to be all things to all men, and we offer here only a little suggestion regarding one possibility of interpretation which we think has been overlooked. However, if what we say about Wolfe's rhetoric is true, we can no longer talk about "mere" rhetoric again. Even at its shallowest, most hollow worst, rhetoric is an instrument capable of a magnificence: as we use it, it may be, but rhetoric itself is never "mere." At its finest, as in the writings of Thomas Wolfe, rhetoric reveals the privileged moment in which human consciousness discovers its passion and power, its capacity to bind up the wound reality inflicts upon those who discover it, and in discovering it, transcend it.

21 Albert Camus, *The Myth of Sisyphus and Other Essays* (New York, 1955), p. 43. Note that we are taking this statement out of its context in the essay, considering its meaning for our present discussion quite apart from Camus' interpretation of Edmund Husserl's phenomenology—an interpretation we cannot follow.

PART FIVE

THE CRITICS SPEAK

Genius Is Not Enough*

BERNARD DEVOTO. For biographical data see *The World of Fiction* (p. 72). This essay-review of *The Story of a Novel* was published in the *Saturday Review of Literature*, April 25, 1936, while DeVoto was editor of the magazine. It is the most famous (and for many, including Wolfe, infamous) essay ever written about Wolfe, who himself felt its sting sharply.

Some months age [ago] *The Saturday Review* serialized Mr. Thomas Wolfe's account of the conception, gestation and as yet uncompleted delivery of his Novel, and Scribners' are now publishing the three articles as a book. It is one of the most appealing books of our time. No one who reads it can doubt Mr. Wolfe's complete dedication to his job or regard with anything but respect his attempt to describe the dark and nameless fury of the million-footed life swarming in his dark and unknown soul. So honest or so exhaustive an effort at self-analysis in the interest of esthetics has seldom been made in the history of American literature, and *The Story of a Novel* is likely to have a long life as a source-book for students of literature and for psychologists as well. But also it brings into the public domain material that has been hitherto outside the privilege of criticism. Our first essay must be to examine it in relation to Mr. Wolfe's novels, to see what continuities and determinants it may reveal, and to inquire into their bearing on the art of fiction.

Let us begin with one of many aspects of Mr. Wolfe's [324/325] novels that impress the reader, the frequent recurrence of material to which one must apply the adjective placental. (The birth metaphors are imposed by Mr. Wolfe himself. In *The Story of a Novel* he finds himself big with first a thunder-cloud and then a river. The symbolism of waters is obviously important to him, and the title of his latest novel is to be that of the series as a whole.) A great part of *Look Homeward, Angel* was just the routine first-novel of the period which many novelists had published and many others had suppressed, the story of a sensitive and rebellious adolescent who was headed toward the writing of novels. The rest of it was not so easily catalogued. Parts of it showed intuition, understanding and ecstasy, and an ability to realize all three in character and scene, whose equal it would have been hard to point out anywhere in the fiction of the time. These looked like great talent, and in such passages as the lunchroom scene in the dawn that Mr. Wolfe called nacreous some fifty times, they seemed to exist on both a higher and a deeper level of realization than any of Mr. Wolfe's contemporaries had attained. But also there were parts that looked very dubious indeed—long, whirling discharges of words, unabsorbed in the novel, unrelated to the proper business of fiction, badly if not altogether unacceptably written, raw gobs of emotion, aimless and quite meaningless jabber, claptrap, belches, grunts and Tarzan-like screams. Their rawness, their unshaped quality must be insisted upon: it was as if the birth of the novel had been accom-

* Bernard DeVoto, "Genius Is Not Enough," *Forays and Rebuttals* (Boston: Little, Brown and Company, 1936), pp. 324-333. Reprinted by permission of Mrs. Bernard DeVoto, owner of copyright.

panied by a lot of the material that had nourished its gestation. The material which nature and most novelists discard when its use has been served. It looked like one of two things, there was no telling which. It looked like the self-consciously literary posturing of a novelist too young and too naïve to have learned his trade. Or, from another point of view, it [325/ 326] looked like a document in psychic disintegration. And one of the most important questions in contemporary literature was: would the proportion of fiction to placenta increase or decrease in Mr. Wolfe's next book?

It decreased. If fiction of the quality of that lunchroom scene made up about one-fifth of *Look Homeward, Angel,* it constituted, in *Of Time and the River,* hardly more than a tenth. The placental material had enormously grown and, what was even more ominous, it now had a rationalization. It was as unshaped as before, but it had now been retroactively associated with the dark and nameless heaving of the voiceless and unknown womb of Time, and with the unknown and voiceless fury of the dark and lovely and lost America. There were still passages where Mr. Wolfe was a novelist not only better than most of his contemporaries but altogether out of their class. But they were pushed farther apart and even diluted when they occurred by this dark substance which may have been nameless but was certainly far from voiceless.

Certain other aspects of the new book seemed revealing. For one thing, there was a shocking contempt of the medium. Some passages were not completely translated from the "I" in which they had apparently been written to the "he" of Eugene Gant. Other passages alluded to incidents which had probably appeared in an earlier draft but could not be found in the final one. Others contradictorily reported scenes which had already appeared, and at least once a passage that had seen service already was reënlisted for a second hitch in a quite different context, apparently with

no recollection that it had been used before.

Again, a state of mind that had been appropriate to the puberty of Eugene seemed inappropriate as the boy grew older, and might therefore be significant. I mean the giantism [326/327] of the characters. Eugene himself, in *Of Time and the River,* was clearly a borderline manic-depressive: he exhibited the classic cycle in his alternation between "fury" and "despair" and the classic accompaniment of obsessional neurosis in the compulsions he was under to read all the books in the world, see all the people in Boston, observe all the lives of the man-swarm and list all the names and places in America. That was simple enough, but practically every other character in the book also suffered from fury and compulsions, and, what was more suggestive, they were all twenty feet tall, spoke with the voice of trumpets and the thunder, ate like Pantagruel, wept like Niobe, laughed like Falstaff and bellowed like the bulls of Bashan. The significant thing was that we were seeing them all through Eugene's eyes. To a child all adults are giants: their voices are thunderous, their actions are portentous and grotesquely magnified, and all their exhibited emotions are seismic. It looked as if part of Eugene's condition was an infantile regression.

This appearance was reinforced by what seemed to be another stigma of infantilism: that all the experiences in *Of Time and the River* were on the same level and had the same value. When Mr. Gant died (of enough cancer to have exterminated an army corps), the reader accepted the accompanying frenzy as proper to the death of a man's father—which is one of the most important events in anyone's life. But when the same frenzy accompanied nearly everything else in the book—a ride on a railroad train, a literary tea-fight, a midnight lunch in the kitchen, a quarrel between friends, a walk at night, the rejection of a play, an automobile trip, a seduction that misfired, the discovery of

Eugene's true love—one could only decide that something was dreadfully wrong. If the death of a father comes out even with a ham-on-rye, then the art of fiction is cockeyed. [**327/328**]

Well, *The Story of a Novel* puts an end to speculation and supplies some unexpected but very welcome light. To think of these matters as contempt of the medium, regression and infantilism is to be too complex and subtle. The truth shows up in two much simpler facts: that Mr. Wolfe is still astonishingly immature, and that he has mastered neither the psychic material out of which a novel is made nor the technique of writing fiction. He does not seem aware of the first fact, but he acknowledges the second with a frankness and an understanding that are the finest promise to date for his future books. How far either defect is reparable it is idle to speculate. But at least Mr. Wolfe realizes that he is, as yet, by no means a complete novelist.

The most flagrant evidence of his incompleteness is the fact that, so far, one indispensable part of the artist has existed not in Mr. Wolfe but in Maxwell Perkins. Such organizing faculty and such critical intelligence as have been applied to the book have come not from inside the artist, not from the artist's feeling for form and esthetic integrity, but from the office of Charles Scribner's Sons. For five years the artist pours out words "like burning lava from a volcano"—with little or no idea what their purpose is, which book they belong in, what the relation of part to part is, what is organic and what irrelevant, or what emphasis or coloration in the completed work of art is being served by the job at hand. Then Mr. Perkins decides these questions—from without, and by a process to which rumor applies the word "assembly." But works of art cannot be assembled like a carburetor—they must be grown like a plant, or in Mr. Wolfe's favorite simile like an embryo. The artist writes a hundred thousand words about a train: Mr. Perkins decides that the train is worth only five thousand words. But

such [**328/329**] a decision as this is properly not within Mr. Perkins's power; it must be made by the highly conscious self-criticism of the artist in relation to the pulse of the book itself. Worse still, the artist goes on writing till Mr. Perkins tells him that the novel is finished. But the end of a novel is, properly, dictated by the internal pressure, osmosis, metabolism—what you will—of the novel itself, of which only the novelist can have a first-hand knowledge. There comes a point where the necessities of the book are satisfied, where its organic processes have reached completion. It is hard to see how awareness of that point can manifest itself at an editor's desk—and harder still to trust the integrity of a work of art in which not the artist but the publisher has determined where the true ends and the false begins.

All this is made more ominous by Mr. Wolfe's almost incredibly youthful attitude toward revision. No novel is written till it is revised—the process is organic, it is one of the processes of art. It is, furthermore, the process above all others that requires objectivity, a feeling for form, a knowledge of what the necessities of the book are, a determination that those necessities shall outweigh and dominate everything else. It is, if not the highest functioning of the artistic intelligence, at least a fundamental and culminating one. But the process appears to Mr. Wolfe not one which will free his book from falsity, irrelevance and its private encumbrances, not one which will justify and so exalt the artist—but one that makes his spirit quiver "at the bloody execution" and his soul recoil "from the carnage of so many lovely things." But superfluous and mistaken things are lovely to only a very young writer, and the excision of them is bloody carnage only if the artist has not learned to subdue his ego in favor of his book. And the same juvenility [**329/330**] makes him prowl "the streets of Paris like a maddened animal" because—for God's sake!—the reviewers may not like the job.

The placental passages are now ex

plained. They consist of psychic material which the novelist has proved unable to shape into fiction. The failure may be due either to immature understanding or to insufficient technical skill: probably both causes operate here and cannot be separated. The principle is very simple. When Mr. Wolfe gives us his doctors, undertakers and newspapermen talking in a lunchroom at dawn, he does his job—magnificently. There they are, and the reader revels in the dynamic presentation of human beings, and in something else as well that should have the greatest possible significance for Mr. Wolfe. For while the doctors and undertakers are chaffing one another, the reader gets that feeling of the glamour and mystery of American life which Mr. Wolfe elsewhere unsuccessfully labors to evoke in thousands of rhapsodic words. The novelist makes his point in the lives of his characters, not in tidal surges of rhetoric.

Is America lost, lonely, nameless and unknown? Maybe, and maybe not. But if it is, the conditions of the novelist's medium require him to make it lost and lonely in the lives of his characters, not in blank verse bombast and apocalyptic delirium. You cannot represent America by hurling adjectives at it. Do "the rats of death and age and dark oblivion feed forever at the roots of sleep"? It sounds like a high school valedictory, but if in fact they do, then the novelist is constrained to show them feeding so by means of what his characters do and say and feel in relation to one another, and not by chasing the ghosts of Whitman and Ezekiel through fifty pages of disembodied emotion. Such emotion is certainly the material that fiction works with, but until [330/331] it is embodied in character and scene it is not fiction—it is only logorrhea. A poem should not mean but be, Mr. MacLeish tells us, and poetry is always proving that fundamental. In a homelier aphorism Mr. Cohan has expressed the same imperative of the drama: "Don't tell 'em, show 'em." In the art of fiction the *thing* is not only an imperative, it is a primary condition. A novel *is*—it

cannot be asserted, ranted or even detonated. A novelist represents life. When he does anything else, no matter how beautiful or furious or ecstatic the way in which he does it, he is not writing fiction. Mr. Wolfe can write fiction—has written some of the finest fiction of our day. But a great part of what he writes is not fiction at all; it is only material with which the novelist has struggled but which has defeated him. The most important question in American fiction to-day, probably, is whether he can win that encounter in his next book. It may be that *The October Fair* and *The Hills Beyond Pentland* will show him winning it, but one remembers the dilution from *Look Homeward, Angel* to *Of Time and the River* and is apprehensive. If he does win it, he must do so inside himself; Mr. Perkins and the assembly-line at Scribners' can do nothing to help him.

That struggle also has another aspect. A novelist utilizes the mechanism of fantasy for the creation of a novel, and there are three kinds of fantasy with which he works. One of them is unconscious fantasy, about which Dr. Kubie was writing in these columns something over a year ago. A novelist is wholly subject to its emphases and can do nothing whatever about them—though when Mr. Wolfe says that the center of all living is reconciliation with one's father he comes close to revealing its pattern in him. There remain two kinds of fantasy which every novelist employs—but which everyone employs in a different ratio. Call them [331/332] identification and projection, call them automatic and directed, call them proliferating and objectified—the names do not matter. The novelist surrenders himself to the first kind, but dominates and directs the second kind. In the first kind he says "I am Napoleon" and examines himself to see how he feels. In the second kind, he wonders how Napoleon feels, and instead of identifying himself with him, he tries to discover Napoleon's necessities. If he is excessively endowed with the first kind of fantasy, he is likely to be a genius. But if he learns to utilize the second kind in the manifold interrelationships of a novel he is certain to be an artist. Whatever Mr. Wolfe's future in the wider and looser interest of Literature, his future in the far more rigorous interest of fiction just about comes down to the question of whether he can increase his facility at the second kind of fantasy. People would stop idiotically calling him autobiographical, if he gave us less identification and more understanding. And we could do with a lot less genius, if we got a little more artist.

For the truth is that Mr. Wolfe is presented to us, and to himself, as a genius. There is no more dissent from that judgment in his thinking about himself than in Scribners' publicity. And, what is more, a genius of the good old-fashioned romantic kind—possessed by a demon, driven by the gales of his own fury, helpless before the lava-flood of his own passion, selected and set apart for greatness, his lips touched by a live coal, consequently unable to exercise any control over what he does and in fact likely to be damaged or diminished by any effort at control. Chaos is everything, if you have enough of it in you to make a world. Yes, but what if you don't make a world—what if you just make a noise? There was chaos in Stephen Dedalus's soul, but he thought of that soul not as sufficient in itself but [**332/333**] merely as a smithy wherein he might forge his novel. And listen to Mr. Thomas Mann: "When I think of the masterpiece of the twentieth century, I have an idea of something that differs essentially and, in my opinion, with profit from the Wagnerian masterpiece— something exceptionally logical, clear, and well developed in form, something at once austere and serene, with no less intensity of will than his, but of cooler, nobler, even healthier spirituality, something that seeks its greatness not in the colossal, the baroque, and its beauty not in intoxication." Something, in other words, with inescapable form, something which exists as the imposition of order on chaos, something that *is,* not is merely asserted.

One can only respect Mr. Wolfe for his determination to realize himself on the highest level and to be satisfied with nothing short of greatness. But, however useful genius may be in the writing of novels, it is not enough in itself—it never has been enough, in any art, and it never will be. At the very least it must be supported by an ability to impart shape to material, simple competence in the use of tools. Until Mr. Wolfe develops more craftsmanship, he will not be the important novelist he is now widely accepted as being. In order to be a great novelist he must also mature his emotions till he can see more profoundly into character than he now does, and he must learn to put a corset on his prose. Once more: his own smithy is the only possible place for these developments—they cannot occur in the office of any editor whom he will ever know.

[Afterword]*

BERNARD DE VOTO in 1950 made this comment on the responses to "Genius Is Not Enough." For biographical data see *The World of Fiction* (p. 72).

[3] Here I must make a personal statement. In the *Saturday Review* for April 25, 1936, I published a 2500-word article called "Genius Is Not Enough." It was a review of Wolfe's *The Story of a Novel*. Before that I had devoted a paragraph to him in a review of James Boyd's *Roll River*, which uses certain symbols that are also used in *Of Time And The River*. I have not alluded to him more than cursorily in any other context. I have refrained from writing more because it is firmly established in literary folklore, on the basis of a single review, that I spent most of my time for years attacking Wolfe. The notion is now embedded in college textbooks, which speak of my "relentless pursuit" of him. Thirteen years is a gratifying life for a book review but the folklore has estopped me from discussing Wolfe's books when they were germane to comments I was making on literary subjects. They are germane to some of the subjects I discuss here and this seems a proper time to call the attention of students to the facts. [85]

* Bernard DeVoto, from *The World of Fiction* (Boston: Houghton Mifflin Company, 1950), p. 85, note 3. Reprinted by permission of and arrangement with Houghton Mifflin Company, the authorized publishers.

The Sorrows of Thomas Wolfe*

JOHN PEALE BISHOP (1892-1944) was an American poet, novelist, and critic. His short novel *Many Thousands Gone* won the first $5,000 *Scribner's Magazine* Short Novel Contest, and Wolfe's *A Portrait of Bascom Hawke* was co-winner of the second. This essay, originally published in the *Kenyon Review* in 1939, was written on the occasion of Wolfe's death.

. . . .

His aim was to set down America as far as it can belong to the experience of one man. Wolfe came early on what was for him the one available truth about this continent—that it was contained in himself. There was no America which could not be made out—mountains, rivers, trains, cities, people—in the memory of an American. If the contours were misty, then they must be made clear. It was in flight from a certain experience of America, as unhappy as it had been apparently sterile—it was in Paris, in an alien land, that Wolfe first understood with hate and with love the horror and the wonder of his native country. He had crossed the seas from the West to East only to come upon the North Carolina hills where he had been born. "I found out," he says, "during those years that the way to discover one's own country was to leave it; that the way to find America was to find it in one's own heart, one's memory and one's spirit, and in a [**129/130**] foreign land. I think I may say that I discovered America during those years abroad out of my very need of her."

This is not an uncommon experience, but what made it rewarding in Wolfe's case was that his memory was anything but common. He could—and it is the source of what is most authentic in his talents—displace the present so completely by the past that its sights and sounds all but destroyed surrounding circumstance. He then lost the sense of time. For Wolfe, sitting at a table on a terrace in Paris, contained within himself not only the America he had known; he also held, within his body, both his parents. They were there, not only in his memory, but more portentously in the make-up of his mind. They loomed so enormous to him that their shadows fell across the Atlantic, their shade was on the café table under which he stretched his long American legs.

. . . readers of Wolfe will remember that the mother of Eugene Gant was afflicted with what is known as total recall. Her interminable narratives were the despair of her family. Wolfe could no more than Eliza Gant suppress any detail, no matter how irrelevant; indeed, it was impossible for him to feel that any detail was irrelevant to his purpose. The readers of *Look Homeward, Angel* will also remember that Eugene's father had a gift, unrivalled among his associates, of vigorous utterance. Nobody, they said, can tie a knot in the tail of the English language like old W. O. But the elder Gant's speech, for all that it can on occasion sputter into fiery intensity, more often than not runs off into a homespun rhetoric. It sounds strong, but it has very little connection with any outer reality and is meaningless, except in so far

* John Peale Bishop, from "The Sorrows of Thomas Wolfe," in *The Collected Essays of John Peale Bishop*, ed. Edmund Wilson (New York: Charles Scribner's Sons, 1948), pp. 129-137. First published in the *Kenyon Review*.

as it serves to convey his rage and frustration. We cannot avoid supposing that Wolfe drew these two characters after his own parents. At the time he began writing *Look Homeward, Angel,* he stood far enough apart from them to use the endlessness of Eliza's unheard discourses, the exaggerated violence of old Gant's objurgations, for comic effect. He makes father and mother into something at once larger and less than human. But in his own case, he could not, at least so long as he was at his writing, restrain either the course of his recollections or their outcome in words. He wrote as a man possessed. Whatever was in his memory must be set down —not merely because he was Eliza's son, but because the secret end of all his writing was expiation—and [130/131] it must be set down in words to which he constantly seems to be attaching more meaning than they can properly own. It was as though he were aware that his novel would have no meaning that could not be found in the words. The meaning of a novel should be in its structure. But in Wolfe's novel, as far as it has gone, it is impossible to discover any structure at all.

. . . .

His position as an artist is very like that of Hart Crane. Crane was born in 1899, Wolfe in 1900, so that they were almost of an age. Both had what we must call genius; both conceived that genius had been given them that they might celebrate, the one in poetry, the other in prose, the greatness of their country. But Wolfe no more than Crane was able to give any other coherence to his work than that which comes from the personal quality of his writing. And he found, as Crane did before him, that the America he longed to celebrate did not exist. He could record, and none better, its sights, its sounds and its odors, as they can be caught in a moment of time; he could try, as the poet of *The Bridge* did, to absorb that moment and endow it with the permanence of a myth. But he could not create a continuous America. He could not, for all that he was prepared to cover one hundred and fifty of its years, conceive its history. He can record what comes to his sensibility, but he cannot give us the continuity of experience. Everything for Wolfe is in the moment; he can so try to impress us with the immensity of the moment that [131/132] it will take on some sort of transcendental meaning. But what that meaning is escapes him, as it does us. And once it has passed from his mind, he can do nothing but recall another moment, which as it descends into his memory seems always about to deliver itself, by a miracle, of some tremendous import.

Both Crane and Wolfe belonged to a world that is indeed living from moment to moment. And it is because they voice its breakdown in the consciousness of continuity that they have significance for it.

. . . .

It can be said of Wolfe, as Allen Tate has said of Hart Crane, that he was playing a game in which any move was possible, because [132/133] none was compulsory. There is no idea which would serve as discipline to the event. For what Wolfe tells us was the idea that furiously pursued him during the composition of *Of Time and the River,* the search for a father, can scarcely be said to appear in the novel, or else it is so incidentally that it seems to no purpose. It does not certainly, as the same search on the part of Stephen Dedalus does in *Ulysses,* prepare a point toward which the whole narrative moves. There was nothing indeed in Wolfe's upbringing to make discipline acceptable to him. He acts always as though his own capacity for feeling, for anguished hope and continual frustration, was what made him superior, as no doubt, along with his romantic propensity for expression, it was. But he was wrong in assuming that those who accept any form of discipline are therefore lacking in vigor. He apparently did not understand that there are those who might say with Yeats, "I could recover if I shrieked my heart's agony," and yet like him are dumb "from human dignity." And his failure to understand was due to no fault of the intelligence, but to lack of love. The Gant family always strikes us, with its howls of rage, its loud hah-hahs of hate and derision, as something less than human. And Eugene is a Gant. While in his case we are ready to admit that genius is a law unto itself, we have every right to demand that it discover its own law.

Again like Crane, Wolfe failed to see that at the present time so extreme a manifestation of individualism could not but be morbid. Both came too late into a world too mechanic; they lacked a wilderness and constantly tried to create one as wild as their hearts. It was all very well for them, since both were in the way of being poets, to start out to proclaim the grandeur of America. Such a task seemed superb. But both were led at last, on proud romantic feet, to Brooklyn. And what they found there they abhorred.

They represent, each in his way, a culmination of the romantic spirit in America. There was in both a tremendous desire to impose the will on experience. Wolfe had no uncommon will. And Crane's was strong enough to lead him deliberately to death by drowning. For Wolfe the rewards of experience were always such that he was turned back upon himself. Isolated in his sensations, there was no way out. He continually sought for a door, and there was really none, or only one, the door of death. [**133/134**]

III

The intellectual labor of the artist is properly confined to the perception of relations. The conscience of the craftsman must see that these relations are so presented that, in spite of all complications, they are ultimately clear. It is one of the conditions of art that they cannot be abstractly stated, but must be presented to the senses.

. . . .

He sees from a train a boy trying to decide to go after a girl; wandering the streets of New York, he sees death come to four men; through one of his students at the university, he comes in contact with an old Jewess wailing a son dead for a year. Each of these moments is completely done; most of them, indeed, overwrought. From the country seen from a train he derives "a wild and solemn joy [**134/135**] —the sense of nameless hope, impossible desire, and man's tragic brevity." He reacts to most circumstances, it must seem to us, excessively. But to men and women he does not really answer. The old Jewess's grief fills him "with horror, anger, a sense of cruelty, disgust, and pity." The passion aroused returns to himself. And it is precisely because his passions cannot attain their object, and in one person know peace, that he turns in rage and desire toward the millions. There is in Eugene every emotion you wish but one; there is no love.

The most striking passages in Wolfe's novels always represent these moments of comprehension. For a moment, but a moment only, there is a sudden release of compassion, when some aspect of suffering and bewildered humanity is seized, when the other's emotion is in a timeless completion known. Then the moment passes, and compassion fails. For Eugene Gant, the only satisfactory relationship with another human creature is one which can have no continuity. For the boy at the street corner, seen in the indecision of youthful lust, he has only understanding and pity; the train from which he looks moves on and nothing more is required of Eugene. But if he should approach that same boy on the street, if he should come close enough to overhear him, he would hear only the defilement of language, words which would awaken in him only hate and disgust. He would himself become lonely, strange and cruel. For emotions such as these, unless they can be used with the responsibility of the artist, must remain a torment to the man.

The only human relationship which endures is that of the child to his family. And that is inescapable: once having been, it cannot cease to be. His father is still his father, though dying; and his brother Ben, though dead, remains his brother. He loves and he hates and knows why no more than the poet he quotes. What he does know is that love has been forbidden him. [135/136]

. . . .

In his father's yard, among the tombstones, has stood for years a marble angel. Old Gant curses it, all hope he thinks lost that he will ever get his money back for it. It stands a magnificent reminder of the time when as a boy, with winged ambition, he had wanted to be not merely a stonecutter but a sculptor. Then, unexpectedly a customer comes for it. The one symbol of the divine in the workshop is sold to adorn the grave of a prostitute; what the boy might have been the man lets go for such a purpose. It cannot be said that Thomas Wolfe ever sold his angel. But the faults of the artist are all of them [136/137] traceable to the failures of the man. He achieved probably the utmost intensity of which incoherent writing is capable; he proved that an art founded solely on the individual, however strong his will, however vivid his sensations, cannot be sound, or whole, or even passionate, in a world such as ours, in which "the integrity of the individual consciousness has been broken down." How far it has broken down, I do not believe he ever knew, yet all that he did is made of its fragments.

Thomas Wolfe: Discovery of Brotherhood*

JOSEPH WARREN BEACH (1880-1957) taught English at the University of Minnesota for almost half a century, retiring in 1948 as professor and chairman of the department. He was an American pioneer in the serious and critical examination of recent fiction. Among his major works are The Method of Henry James, The Twentieth Century Novel: Studies in Technique, and American Fiction 1920-1940, a study of eight American novelists, from which the following selection is drawn.

. . . .

To begin with what is, after all, the main business of a novelist, he has an undoubted genius for the creation of characters and setting them in scenes that bring out their quality. There is in these four books the matter for dozens of novels. There are literally dozens of characters who, by their vivid colorfulness, their individuality, their drollness and eccentricity, make one think of Dickens, and who, by their fierce vitality, their tragic perverseness, the insuppressible force of life that is in them, go beyond Dickens and make one think of Shakespeare or Ben Jonson. They are all, it seems, extraordinary; and yet we believe in them, not as we believe in the creations of romance, but as we believe in verified freaks of nature. And they are not freaks. For we have seen their like; we recognize the motives and conditions that made them what they are. And if they carry their passions and peculiarities to fabulous lengths, we cannot doubt the truth of the words they utter, the special things they do which no one [206/207] would think of inventing, and which carry the very accent of individual truth.

. . . .

No two of his characters are to be confused; no two of them speak alike, unless they are anonymous muckers of Brooklyn or Manhattan. The speech is differentiated by class and individual, with a thousand specialties of tone and idiom and dialect. There is the racy language in which Aunt Maw tells [207/208] her stories of Zebulon County before the Civil War. There is the tone of the Irish boarding house in Boston; the tone of Old Wakefield defending the Grand Army Post against the upstart impudence of the American Legion; the tone of Daisy Purvis suggesting a change of dishes for breakfast or lamenting that 'is Grace, the Duke of Basingstoke, has been reduced by oppressive taxes to sell his estate in Gloucestershire, leaving him only his place in Devonshire, his place in Yawkshire, and his hunting preserve in Scotland. . . .

All of Wolfe's characters are remarkable—more than life-size—gargantuan in appetite, prodigious in suffering, furious in their passions, gigantic in physical stature, extreme and unmeasured in all things. It is partly the vigor of his writing that gives us this sense of dealing with a race of Brobdingnags—the way he plasters them with adjectives and superlatives. But if we are inclined to think it is verbal exaggeration, he confounds us with facts, with actual circumstance and idiosyncrasy, which bear him out in his extravagance.

* Joseph Warren Beach, from "Thomas Wolfe: Discovery of Brotherhood" (Chapter 9), *American Fiction 1920-1940* (New York: The Macmillan Company, 1941), pp. 197-215. Republished, New York: Russell and Russell, Inc., 1960. Reprinted with the permission of Russell and Russell, Inc.

And above all it is by their speech that his account of them is borne out. This has the indubitable ring of truth about it. This is not the invention of melodrama, but the actual speech of men and women. And it renders convincingly the sense men have of the intensity of their own feelings and the unparalleled greatness of their sufferings and wrongs. The torrent of complaint to which George's [Eugene's] sister Helen gives vent on the station platform— every burden is laid upon her, and there is no peace to be had, no peace to be had in the world—this corresponds exactly to the lonely obsession of her sleepless nights, with their endless repetitions of fear and anguish. No one has rendered better than Wolfe the pitiless candor of speech between kindred and intimates when unrestrained by the code of reason and politeness—the violent recriminations [208/209] and passionate self-justifications, the savage invective, the blind anger in which things are said which can never be taken back and scars inflicted that can never be healed. The quarrels between Eugene and Eliza Gant, between Eliza and her children, between George Webber and Esther Jack, are among the most convincing scenes of fiction.

And not less convincing are the moments of peace and assuagement, of wisdom and vision, that drop mysteriously upon them when their passions are spent and their nerves discharged and voided of their evil humors. . . .

One thing that saves the work of Wolfe from being depressing is his enormous gusto—the satisfaction he takes in every aspect of the human spectacle, in every appeal to the senses and the appetites. Zola or Huysmans cannot match him for discrimination and assiduous collection of smells. His specialty is the smells of childhood—good smells and bad, the smells of vegetation and food and industrial products—the smells that render for the child the qualities of things and bring him the most vivid sense of his vitality, his livingness—the smells associated with emotion and memory, nostalgic smells recalling things long past or promising fulfillments in the future—shameful and humiliating smells—the enchanting odor of woodsmoke and of burning leaves—the scents of spring and the parched odors of summer and the passionate invigorating smells of autumn, of cooling earth and mountain winds and sodden leaves. Rabelais cannot match him for celebration of the joys of the palate and the joys of the eye in [209/210] contemplating things to eat.

In this appeal to the senses, it is not so much the thing itself as the idea of the thing that intrigues him. It is the thing as characteristic, as capable of being distinguished and being put in sounding and savory words. It is the precious thing as worthy of man's estate, the proper furniture of his abode, his due perquisite as a spiritual being and lord of the universe. And this applies, *a fortiori,* to landscapes and seasons, the beauty of nature and the physiognomy of the earth, all more lavishly presented than in any other contemporary novelist and in a vastly more extravagant vein of poetry. No one has written more eloquently of mountains, of summer sunrise in a garden, of French cities and the English countryside, and of the "grand and casual landscapes of America." No one has done greater justice to the sleepy back streets of small towns, the dreary lengths of lamplit city streets in winter, and to all the riot and intoxication, all the splendor and misery, of Manhattan and its manswarm. No one has better rendered the passion and romance of travel by train, the power and mystery of locomotives, the changing aspects of the country as you pass from one region to another, as from the glamorous and dreamy South into the magnetic and prevailing North. Wolfe's heroines love to lie awake all night in their pullman berths with curtains raised, spying out the marrowy and shameful secrets of towns as the train pauses at the station, thrilling with the mysteries of human nature in its furtive and nocturnal phases.

Nothing human is alien to him, and it

is ever the emotional essence, the quality of the living experience, both as [210/211] it is seen from without and as it is felt within, which he is eager to catch in the net of words. Above all, it is the intangibles of inner experience—the loneliness and wordless longing of men, the pathos and grandeur of the spirit, the long, long thoughts of youth, the beating of strong wings against the bars of our temporal cage. And then there are the long and wide views of the manswarm in its crowded haunts, across the continent and down the centuries, the sounding of the wells of memory, the visions of lost time and of the ever-flowing river of humanity.

Such are the themes on which he spends himself with tireless passion, directing upon them a furious and unremitting battery of words drawn from the literary arsenals of all the world. I have compared the structural form of his writing to the music of Wagner, Strauss and Tschaikowsky. These three composers come naturally to mind in connection with Wolfe, because in his verbal style he has much the same qualities of romantic declamation and exaggeration as they have in their music. I have sometimes referred to his writing as Southern rhetoric on the rampage. And I think it is not too fanciful to associate Wolfe's inclination to extravagant and ornamental writing with something in the tradition of Southern culture which one finds in authors like Edgar Poe and William Faulkner. The defeated and impoverished South is acutely conscious of its gentility and tarnished elegance, and often strives to compensate with these for what it lacks in fortune and efficiency. It sometimes makes one think of a poor countryman of proud lineage trying to dazzle his prosperous city cousin with graces and refinements never learned in store or bank. Both Wolfe and Faulkner have brought to the contemporary novel an outmoded romanticism of feeling and fancy. And in their styles one feels that they have raked the attics for cast-off finery.

Wolfe uses three or four times the requisite number of words for anything he wants to say. He makes the most prodi- [211/212] gal use of adjectives, and not merely simple adjectives of description, referring to specific qualities like color, texture, temperature; but still more those adjectives that are intended solely to enlarge and exalt the subject in the realm of emotion. Everything is superlative, gigantic, unique, mysterious, magical, impossible, unutterable, intolerable, and of an extreme degree of intensity, whether of beauty or terror. The adjectives and phrases go regularly in pairs, or in long tumultuous series, with a high percentage of sonorous Latin words and words abstract and vague in connotation. It is an inflated style, in which everything is blown up to many times its natural size. It is a drunkenness of words. There is an excessive repetition of emotional words, as if the author were reciting an incantation, or trying to put the reader under a hypnotic spell.

. . . .

It is a style often tawdry and sophomoric, not even keeping to the natural rhythms of prose, but swollen into pentameters—flaunting the finery of Milton or Byron.

Or in the black dark of some forgotten winter's morning,/child of the storm and brother to the dark,/alone and wild and secret [212/213] in the night/as he leaned down against the wind's strong wall/towards Niggertown,/blocking his folded papers as he went/. . . . Deep as the tides of time and memory,/deep as the tides of sleep the river runs/. . . and presently, just for a few brief moments as it swept along/below the magic and familiar hill,/he caught a vision of the great white house/set proudly far away up on the hill/and screened with noble trees. . . ./Even while he stared within his mother's flesh,/she was an adolescent girl, orphaned of love,/knowledged in grief and loss and bitterness,/and strong in hopeful fortitude. . . . We reach for life with all these traps and nets of words,/our frenzy mounts up with our impotence,/we try to keep and hold some single thing/with all this fecund barrenness of print,/and the sum of it all is a few blown papers in the wind.

This lapse into blank verse—rolling

iambs ranged in fives—became with Wolfe a habit, a kind of vice. I do not suppose it was a conscious trick, and that he worked it like an organ stop. He simply fell into this strain whenever he felt the mounting sense of the poetry of his thought. I am not sure that I know just why this mixing of verse rhythms with prose is so offensive to an ear tuned either to fine poetry or to fine prose. I know of only one first-class prose writer who is guilty of the practice. Thomas De Quincey sometimes indulges in it in his most sentimental moods. And even with De Quincey it is a blemish. Wolfe has been much influenced by De Quincey, as anyone can see who will compare, say, the peroration of his sketch, "Death the Proud Brother" (in the volume, *From Death to Morning*), with various passages in De Quincey's *Confessions, The English Mail Coach,* and his chapter called "The Affliction of Childhood." There are the same elaborate apostrophes to abstractions like Death and Sleep, the same extended parallelism and musical repetition of phrases, and the same passages in meter. Or rather not the same. For Wolfe has not De Quincey's ear for the niceties of rhythm and sound. He is much further from the classical sources of De Quincey's labored eloquence. And what in [213/214] De Quincey is a venial offense often in Wolfe comes very near to being a mortal sin.

I do not think the purist's objection to the confusion of prose and verse is merely conventional or pedantic. To begin with, there is the incongruity growing out of conflicting ranges of association. The use of meter in prose writing is like wearing a boiled shirt with tennis shorts or sporting a sweatshirt at a formal dinner. And then there is the tendency to pad the phrase in order to round out the pentameter, serving to reinforce the already too strong drive toward lushness and redundancy. With that there is the disposition to play up emotion at the cost of sense, landing our writer in sentimental moonshine. There is the temptation to windiness and fustian. There is danger that the pseudo-poetry will drug the senses and blunt one's feeling for the subtle and varied rhythms of prose. Altogether it is a hazardous and dubious indulgence.

However, I do not wish to lay too much stress on this matter nor browbeat any reader who may happen to enjoy what so upsets me. I do not mean to say that, on the whole, this writing does not carry one along with it. There is in Wolfe a power of feeling and imagination that overrides a hundred faults. And in any case, the heart of man is naturally at home with bigness and inflation; the heart of man is windy and romantic, doting on words that flatter and bamboozle.

It is a mad and frenzied style. And the hero of these pages is a mad and frenzied man. He tells us so himself a hundred times, and often we wonder whether he is not telling the literal truth about Thomas Wolfe. There is more than a hint of paranoia in the behavior of Eugene Gant and George Webber; and we wonder whether, if Wolfe had lived, these symptoms might have appeared in aggravated form. At least, we did so wonder until the final book appeared, with its assurance that sanity at length had gained the upper hand. The emotional unbalance of adolescence was unduly prolonged [214/215] into the period of manhood. But with success in his vast undertakings, the fever abated and something like calmness supervened. And with greater calmness there was a notable abatement of lyrical frenzy in the style.

But even in the earlier volumes, our judgment of the work was not too heavily affected by the madness of its manner. That it was far from a model of classic reason and order we must admit. But that it was thereby less human and representative—no. Madness is but the final term of the contradictions and propensities common to us all. Madness is the breaking point of human nature driven to distraction between its ideals and its limitations. It is in a sense the most human of our states of mind, for it is the gauge of our discontent with reality. This is a romantic point of view, and Wolfe is the most romantic of realists. That is why, to many readers, he will seem the most satisfying of the eight authors of our group. [The others are Dos Passos, Hemingway, Faulkner, Caldwell, Farrell, Marquand, and Steinbeck.] He has more to say than any of them on what man is like in his heart.

We may be glad indeed that in *You Can't Go Home Again* Wolfe came out of his period of *Sturm und Drang*. But it would have been matter for regret if he had never passed through that period nor left his cloudy luminous record of it. It is a pity that we can look for nothing more from his fervid and magical pen. But we have just begun to enjoy what he left us when he died. We have scarcely begun to assimilate it. He is still very much a writer of the moment. And it will be long before he becomes that thing of the past, a specimen in the literary museum.

The Vitalist Trend and Thomas Wolfe*

BELLA KUSSY (1914-) has changed her field of interest from literature to philosophy since writing this essay. She holds the Ph.D. in philosophy from New York University and is the author, under her married name Bella K. Milmed, of *Kant and Current Philosophical Issues*. "The Vitalist Trend and Thomas Wolfe" grew out of her study of the social philosophy of Carlyle and Nietzsche and the political philosophy of the Nazi state, to some manifestations of which she makes reference in the final paragraph. She is married to Leon S. Milmed.

The obvious change in the character of Thomas Wolfe's writing, a change which began to appear in THE WEB AND THE ROCK and became fully apparent in the still later work, has usually been discussed as a purely literary one, a transition to an ever-increasing objectivity which at last culminates in the fragment of THE HILLS BEYOND. Actually, the change is a much deeper one, a complete transformation of basic temperamental attitude; and not the least significant of its aspects is social and political.

The basis of Wolfe's earlier work, the source from which all its essential characteristics spring, can best be identified as vitalism. It is an attitude which does not, in Wolfe, express itself in social or political terms. Only in YOU CAN'T GO HOME AGAIN, the book in which the transition to "objectivity" is fully accomplished, are some social and political ideas and material introduced. Only after a long recapitulation in which Wolfe rejects much that had been central in his life and work —his introversion and egotism, his preoccupation with the past, some vaguely defined element in German tradition that had been irresistibly fascinating to him— do we find that impressive "Credo" in which a magnificent, almost incredible,

optimism and an even more magnificent power of expression combine in a superb affirmation of democratic faith. Yet even this negative correlation may indicate that Wolfe's vitalism has some inherent political significance; and the narrative itself seems to associate Wolfe's transformation very closely with George Webber's visit to Nazi Germany.

This association may perhaps become clear if we consider the social implications of vitalism where they are most clearly and directly expressed; not in Wolfe, but in a series of writers of a similar tendency who are explicitly political—in Whitman, in [306/307] Nietzsche, and finally in the Nazis. If this line of development proves to be the natural one for vitalism, Germany under the Nazis must have been to Wolfe a revelation of the disastrous consequences of that approach which had been his own.

I

In speaking of vitalism in literature and politics, I am using that rather abstract term as a convenient shorthand symbol for the approach and motivation whose basic feature is emphasis on life as an all-pervasive force and especially as the supreme value. I mean the expression in

* Bella Kussy, "The Vitalist Trend and Thomas Wolfe," *Sewanee Review*, L (July-September, 1942), 306-324. Reprinted by permission of *The Sewanee Review* and Mrs. Leon S. Milmed.

literature and in politics, more through feeling and temperament than through theoretical application, of the recognized vitalist tradition in philosophy, as found, for example, in Nietzsche or Bergson. And the "life" of which we speak in this connection is intensive life, life with all its distinctive characteristics emphasized, not a mere minimum of animate existence. As Nietzsche puts it, it is life as "will to power," not as mere "struggle for existence." There is an inherent tendency to run over into an unrestrained dynamism, in which "life" becomes a force of violent and terrific intensity.

Wolfe's characters, for instance, are preeminently alive, not in the realistic sense of being "true to life" so much as in the vitalistic sense of throbbing and overflowing and bursting with dynamic energy. It is this characteristic of the members of the Gant family, at once so widely varied and so closely akin, which constitutes their kinship and their explanation. And as for Eugene Gant, or George Webber, or Thomas Wolfe, the expression of this same vitality in his novels, and the attitudes which it arouses, are precisely the points which are of interest as characteristic of vitalism in general, and of its most dynamic forms in particular, in literature and elsewhere.

The world of Thomas Wolfe is a vital, animate world. Whether or not this is true for him in any philosophical sense (and there is no indication that he ever thought about the matter at all in this sense), at least in an imaginative sense Wolfe and the reader of his novels find themselves in a living cosmos, and especially on a living and breathing earth which "broods round them . . . with its secret and mysterious presences." And in this world all ex- [307/308] perience is tremendously animated and exaggerated; for every sight and sound and smell, every new scene and new face, every thought and every feeling, is part of the overwhelming experience of living and full of the energy and importance of living. This is the source of that sensory vividness which is so acute in Wolfe's writing that it becomes transformed into an intense emotional excitement.

In this all-embracing exaggeration and animation, distinctions in importance or value naturally tend to be lost. We are in a world in which all life is important and valuable, and in which all things are full of life. We are caught up in a sweeping confusion of values, an exuberant amoral lumping together of "the whole packed glory of the earth," the whole multitude of "men and women who had worked, fought, drunk, loved, whored, striven, and died." The most rudimentary forms of exaggeration, sheer size and quantity, themselves become values.

The consuming desire for quantity, arising from the overflow of vital energy, obviously cannot be satisfied with any fixed quantity, however large. There is always more to be had; and indeed more must be had, since there is a limitless flow of energy for which an object must be found. Eugene Gant, while performing the Herculean feat—incredible, if true—of reading two hundred thousand books in ten years, is tormented by the thought of all the books he has not read; yet he reads, says Wolfe, not because he is bookish, but because he is consumed by a craving "to know all, have all, be all," a "hunger that grows from everything it feeds upon." Growth, expansion, assimilation, the fundamental characteristics of life, become dynamic driving forces of infinite intensity.

These driving forces are elemental and primitive, expanding outward into the world but rooted deep in the sub-human origins of life. Wolfe's work is full of a sensual primitivism animated and glorified by expansive vitality. There is an abundance of sensuality in the literal sense, sheer physical enjoyment—a stupendous delight in food, for instance, and in sexual experience. But more important is the fact that all this is more at times than mere physical enjoyment. Often it takes on the aspect of an almost mystic primitivism, finding its essential expression in the continually recurring "goat-cry" of Eugene Gant and George [308/309] Webber alike, that "centaur-cry of man or beast," that concentration of the "savage and unutterable" within him in a "bestial cry of fury, pain, and ecstasy." It is the same impulse that appears in a more sinister form in the inarticulate yells of the near-idiot Luke.

The somewhat sinister and destructive note which intrudes here is not foreign to vitalism, but essential to it. For many of those forces which undermine and destroy life are themselves part of life and full of vital energy. It is vital energy itself, driven to an abnormal intensity, that creates the sympathy of the Gants with lunacy; that fills them with the "mad devil's hunger all men have in them" for storm, darkness, speed; that rises to a "demoniac ecstasy" before the "green corrupted hell-face of malignant death." It is in this spirit that "War is not death for a young man; war is life," with all the horrible implications of that statement. A destructive dynamism emerges.

For there are two kinds of death, from a vitalistic point of view such as Wolfe's, and only one of them is horrible. That one is "death-in-life," as Wolfe repeatedly phrases it—absence of vitality, the root of all that is really evil and unpardonable. Sharply contrasted with this kind of suspended animation we have the actual death of the elder Gant, who puts up so magnificent a fight, and dies with so vast a cataclysm of his huge physical frame, that the predominant impression with which we are left is not one of the final inanimateness but rather one of the tremendous vitality with which he dies. His death itself becomes the last of his colossal vital experiences.

In fact, it is only in these terms that vitalism, the glorification of life, can reconcile itself with death at all. Eugene Gant, horrified at first by a spot on his skin which he considers a blemish on his physical vitality, acquires a "deeper and darker knowledge" which tells him that all the "subtle and beautiful in human life" is "touched with a divine p[e] ness." Thus is justified in vitalis[t] that abnormal intensity and excess of lit[e] which becomes destruction of life, and that susceptibility to the fascination of death and destruction which appears in the short story DEATH THE PROUD BROTHER, with its series of almost ecstatic descriptions of violent deaths on city streets, or in the [309/310] account of the lynching of Jim Prosser. The fascination of death becomes equal to and part of the fascination of life.

II

The novels of Thomas Wolfe, then, epitomize all that we mean by vitalism in literature. In turning to the political significance of vitalism, we may seem to be taking an unwarranted leap, largely because there is no explicit political element in Wolfe's work up to YOU CAN'T GO HOME AGAIN, where indeed that element is vague enough. But the vitalistic approach which we have been discussing is a basic and distinctive philosophy of life, whether conscious or unconscious; and it has implications, whether conscious or unconscious, for every field of human thought and action. To understand what happens when Wolfe does begin to think about social problems, since he himself does not explain it clearly or fully and—for all the reader knows—was probably unable to do so, we must first turn to other writers whose work embodies the same vitalistic approach.

The writer who comes immediately to mind as most similar to Wolfe in impulsion and approach is Walt Whitman. For him, as for Wolfe, the source, the driving energy, and the supreme value are "Life immense in passion, pulse, and power." For him even more explicitly than for Wolfe, the universe in which we live is itself alive and bursting with vital energy— "the procreant urge of the world." For him, too, every detail of experience embodies this same dynamic intensity. And since "a leaf of grass is no less than the journey-work of stars," we arrive, in Whitman, as in Wolfe, at a vast confusion of values, a universal "reception, not preference nor denial," in which wisdom is reduced to "the certainty of the reality and immortality of things, and the excellence of things."

Out of Whitman's dynamic aliveness and all-embracing enthusiasm, as out of Wolfe's, comes an unrestrained, expansive urge "To see no possession but you may possess it." And Whitman's expansive urge, like Wolfe's, is rooted in a primitivism of which the vitalistic confusion of values is both cause and effect—a longing "To confront night, storm, hunger . . . as the animals do," a sweeping away of rationality and civilization in the "barbaric [310/311] yawp" which is a variant of Wolfe's "goat-cry." Wolfe indeed borrows Whitman's phrase for his final description of his own early writing. And the essence of mystic primitivism, the epitome of that inextricable blend of sensuality and sentimentality, is found in the whole concept and expression of *The Body Electric*.

Whitman's vitalism, integrated as it is in the extraordinarily sane and healthy outdoor atmosphere which pervades most of his work, rarely bursts out with the vehement dynamism characteristic of Wolfe. Yet even in Whitman we find outbursts of the same sinister fascination of death and destruction that we find in Wolfe, and arising from the same sources. His most lyrical poems are about death; and in one of them, *Out of the Cradle Endlessly Rocking,* he develops the concept of death as the source of all poetry, along the lines of the "divine pearl-sickness" revealed to Eugene Gant as more beautiful than health. "And as to you Life"—so Whitman apostrophizes that "Life" which is the theme and motive force of all his poetry—"I reckon you are the leavings of many deaths." For him as for Wolfe, death seen in this vitalist ecstasy is an integral part of life; in fact, it is a particularly intensive phase of life.

What makes all this extremely interesting, and ultimately enlightening for the reader of Wolfe's novels, is the fact that Whitman, unlike Wolfe, is very much a political poet. He considered himself and has been considered by others the poet of democracy *par excellence*. And this estimate is unmistakably true. He abounds with a real democratic spirit when he sees

You workwomen and workmen of these States
    having your own divine and strong life,
and all else giving place to men and women
    like you,

and comes down to the real "password primeval" or democracy when he declares "By God! I will accept nothing which all cannot have their counterparts of on the same terms."

Yet, latent in Whitman's conception and expression of democracy, we may discover unstable elements and even potentially anti-democratic elements, some of them mutually contradictory, all of them rooted deep in the vitalistic basis of his poetry. We find, for instance, that his glorification of the common man is usually based not on a sense of value but on his characteristic [311/312] confusion of values, not on a recognition of the worth of human personality but on an indiscriminate lumping together of the good and the evil in human life as in the world at large. He builds up his vision of vital human energy from "all the menials of the earth, laboring," through "the blind, the deaf and dumb, idiots, hunchbacks, lunatics," to "pirates, thieves, betrayers, murderers," and even "slave-makers of the earth," and ends with "I salute all the inhabitants of the earth!" And all these merge in that "divine average" which may become a dangerous concept in which all individuality and all distinctions of value are lost.

On the other hand, even more predominant in Whitman is an individualism which goes to such lengths as to become implicitly anti-social. The whole of the *Song of Myself* is, of course, the most obvious example of the glorification of "Walt Whitman, a cosmos," who announces that he will celebrate himself only because "every atom belonging to me as good belongs to you," but who actually is driven along by vitalistic expansiveness to become "loosed of limits," his "own master, total and absolute," implicitly infringing on the rights of others in an interdependent world.

Whitman himself was fully aware of the dilemma involved in his resolve to glorify the

> ... simple separate person,
> Yet utter the word Democratic, the word En-Masse.

In DEMOCRATIC VISTAS he returns to this dilemma again and again. Occasionally, too, there is a hint at a solution. Through "companionship thick as trees along the rivers of America," through "the manly love of comrades," the opposite dangers of absorption in the mass and of an atomic and perhaps domineering individualism are overcome, and the social and personal values combined in a living democracy.

But the world in which this relationship is entirely spontaneous, self-sufficient, and socially adequate is a very simple world indeed. It is a widespread, outdoor world, as Whitman himself often points out; a world in which strangers speak to each other in passing, with hearty and casual goodwill. Indeed, the very essence of Whitman's concept of comradeship is to be found in the many glimpses he gives us of himself exchanging greet- [312/313] ings with fishermen and truck-drivers and all sorts of passers-by as he tramps down the road. This is a kind of intercourse involving a certain amount of distance between individuals; it is possible primarily between those who meet but also pass by. These people are forced neither to work together nor to compete with each other, but merely to share in the common life and resources of a wide open world with room for expanding vitality on the part of each individual. For this world was not only a simple one but an expanding one, geographically and industrially.

III

What would happen to the vitalistic approach in an older, more sophisticated, more crowded world? Whitman himself caught a glimpse of "that problem, the labor question, beginning to open like a yawning gulf" which he could not fathom. For one answer, we may turn to a European vitalist. Friedrich Nietzsche is interesting at this point because he not only was more sophisticated intellectually than Whitman but lived in a more sophisticated society, under more advanced economic conditions than those of nineteenth century America. He is a clearer example of pure vitalism as applied to social problems than Bergson, whose democratic political theory is founded on the most dualistic and least vitalistic aspect of his philosophy, or than George Bernard Shaw, whose socialist economic theory is derived from sources completely extraneous to his vitalism and often comes into most bizarre combination with it.

In Nietzsche again, as in Whitman and Wolfe, we find a thoroughly animate and dynamic world, more clearly defined than theirs because more philosophically conceived. This world is animated by a "will to power" whose nature can best be understood through the "tonic passions which enhance the energy of the feeling of life," the same energy which drives each member of the Gant family to his own excesses, the same feeling of "Life immense in passion, pulse, and power" of which Whitman writes. The will to power is "a wish to overpower, a wish to overthrow," to expand, to absorb and dominate all things, Eugene Gant's will to "know all, have all, be all."

It is a primitive and irrational drive, too, and more conscious- [313/314] ly so than in Wolfe or Whitman; and to find it most simply and clearly manifested in human life Nietzsche looks to the barbaric, primitive races. He sees it as the impulse and energy which drove the "blond beasts of prey" who first conquered the weak races and became the founders of society; and even Nietzsche's "philosophers of the future" are queerly shot through with the "blond beast" strain, filled with that "preference for questionable and terrible things" which for Nietzsche is a "symptom of strength." To live intensely is to expand, and so to destroy.

In Nietzsche we find vitalistic individualism, too, much more definitely and consciously expressed than in Whitman. Each man, he says, must follow the individual "will to power" that is in him, the inner drive by which he lives and grows. "There is no such thing," however, "as an egoism which keeps within its bounds"; and the ego of the superior individual, vitally expansive to an exceptional degree, is strong enough to impose its standards on others. It is the great individuals who create institutions and eras.

In Nietzsche's formulation, however, even of these attitudes in which he so closely parallels Whitman and Wolfe, a decided difference of tone and emphasis is evident. The animate world becomes a world of an infinite number of animate units of energy, each struggling for domination over all. Vital expansiveness, outcroppings of primitivism, susceptibility to the fascination of death and destruction as vital experiences, all become intensified and crystallized in a particular emphasis on conflict, force, and ruthlessness. Spontaneous individualism has become a conscious ethics based on the will to power of the individual. Here, in this violent and specifically formulated dynamism, are direct reflections of a more thoroughly industrialized economy in which competition is more destructive, and of a far more conventional society with which a positive individualism finds itself automatically in bitter conflict.

For these reasons, too, Nietzsche develops out of the vitalistic confusion of values, which we have noted in Whitman and Wolfe, a new set of highly dynamic values indigenous to vitalism. Although life and the will to power are the essence of all things, in some cases they are strong and growing, while in others they are weak and declining. Thus "all that makes for strength" is [314/315] valuable, while "all that makes for weakness" is objectionable. On this basis, the indiscriminate delight in all things and all men which is fundamental in Whitman's glowing democracy is replaced by something radically different—glorification of strong, vital, dynamic men and contempt for weak, decadent ones.

Whitman's enthusiasm and feeling of fellowship extend to all classes as well as to all types of men. In Nietzsche's world, social classes were already pitted against each other to such an extent that such all-round enthusiasm would be unlikely. Nietzsche's ideal is definitely that of a class society; and though the classes which he envisages are not necessarily divided precisely along economic lines, and certainly not for economic reasons, he has a particular contempt for the working class and tends to identify it with the weak, the "botched and bungled," since the strong are able, in his view, to raise themselves above the mass. And there are two kinds of morality, one for the masters, the strong individuals who must exercise their strength, and the other for the slaves, the weak ones who must exercise the social or "herd" virtues to protect themselves against the strong. Just what the vital, superior man is to do with the herd, whether to rule, shun, or exterminate it, is by no means clear to Nietzsche. But when the superman is conceived as ruler, really the only practicable one of these alternatives in the modern world, Nietzsche's doctrine is obviously very close indeed to that of the Nazis.

IV

The fascist ideology as presented by Hitler in MEIN KAMPF is essentially vitalistic, full of contempt for economics in favor of a society which is a "living organism" rather than a "dead machine." The familiar concept of Lebensraum means not merely room for the population to survive, (if it did, there could be no ex planation of the efforts of all fascist countries to increase their populations while complaining of lack of room for the existing ones,) but rather room to grow and expand. Vitalistic expansiveness thus presents a poetic and dynamic ideology for aggressive imperialism. There is plenty of conscious primitivism, too, in the idea that "all the wisdom of this earth is as nothing unless served, covered, and protected by force." There is an abundance [315/316] of delight in conflict and destruction—insistence on the "right" to fight, praise of the virtues of "the nobility of the sword" as opposed to those of "the nobility of finance." And in assertions of the "eternal privilege of force and strength" and the "ruthless determination to destroy excrescences which cannot be remedied," there are distinct echoes of Nietzsche's master and slave morality.

It is this whole vitalistic impulse in Nazism, this whole expansive, primitive, destructive outburst of vital force, that Hermann Rauschning has in mind in calling his well-known book on the Nazi movement THE REVOLUTION OF NIHILISM. He speaks of a "revolutionary dynamism," with violence as its only method, which necessitates an anti-intellectual philosophy because it is itself thoroughly irrational. He goes so far as to believe that the Nazis are driven along by the irrational character of their movement into a course of pure destruction for its own sake, with no other purpose whatever. While this analysis is certainly an over-simplification, it makes clear what must be at least one important aspect of the Nazi regime. The Nazis' appeal to youth seems to Rauschning to lie in "the idea that all doctrines . . . have become out-of-date and meaningless" and in the opportunity for "a new, unknown, and dangerous life, but at all costs a life of strength and energy." Is not this in essence the life idealized in different ways by Whitman, by Nietzsche, by Thomas Wolfe? And Rauschning also emphasizes the further Nietzschean element of the existence of two groups, the "élite" or ruling group, which controls everything

and is motivated by the desire for power, and the masses, who know nothing of what is really happening and for whom the members of the élite feel only contempt. Pertinent here is the account in MEIN KAMPF of the way in which the masses must be deceived by false and clever propaganda.

There are obviously elements in Nazism which are not Nietzschean; but these are still vitalistic, and arise merely in the accommodation of theory to practice. For instance, the goal of a race of supermen in the distant future, entirely too remote and intangible for a political movement, is replaced by the glorification of a present superior individual and a present superior race. Absolute individualism, which in the political sphere would bring [316/317] all individuals into fatal conflict, is transformed into the rule of *one* absolute individual; so that from his peculiar vantage-point, at least, totalitarian dictatorship is a dynamic development of the tradition of vitalistic individualism! One of the virtues attributed to Nazism by MEIN KAMPF, in fact, is the reaffirmation of the "value of the individual" as opposed to democracy's "dead weight of numbers"; and of course the doctrine is expounded that all progress is the work of great men.

Further, in the actual present-day world the masses are a real force from any point of view; and fascism, as a political movement, not only must decide what to do with those masses whose place in the scheme of things Nietzsche never could decide, but must use them as the base of its power. They cannot be permitted to rule, but they can get their experience of power vicariously, through the state. Incorporated and submerged in it, their own individuality suppressed by it, they are made to feel that they are part of its life and share in its dynamic drive. And its life and dynamic drive are preëminently those of the vital, expansive individual of vitalist tradition. Its relation to other states is preëminently that of this individual to other individuals. Nietzsche himself once anticipates such a possibility, declaring that the society of supermen will "do all that toward other bodies which the individuals within it refrain from doing to each other." Nietzsche, however, had no conception of that dynamic force of mass psychology which fascism uses for this purpose, at once giving it a pseudo-metaphysical justification and harnessing it to a powerful and rigidly controlled government machine, by the introduction of the concept, idealistic rather than vitalistic in origin, of the totalitarian state.

This means that if we start our political thinking in terms of primitive, expansive, often destructive vital energies, and try in these terms to relate the vital energies of individuals to each other and to the group, we shall find that at least under present-day conditions we must introduce the idea of the totalitarian state. Paradoxically, this concept becomes the successor of Whitman's thoroughly democratic concept of fraternity, which defines these same relations, on the same vitalistic basis, in terms of a less advanced society. And so we see where the vitalistic approach, in spite of its innocent aspect in a simple frontier setting [**317/318**] like Whitman's and its attractive aspect in a purely literary application like Wolfe's, really leads politically.

V

Now we are ready to ask where it really leads Thomas Wolfe. Considered in isolation and somewhat superficially, none of his books except YOU CAN'T GO HOME AGAIN has seemed to contain any political material. But in the light of the political trends which we have seen, both in similarly vitalistic writers and in the ideology of fascism itself, many elements in Wolfe's attitude which are not explicitly political take on a political significance. The same dynamic impetus for life stepped up to a maximum degree of intensity, of expansion, and of destruction which we have found in Wolfe, we have found also in the psychological and ideological side of

Nazism. Some of Wolfe's most characteristic and indeed most compelling dithyrambs reveal this identity most clearly. For example:

Who has been mad with fury in his youth, given no rest or peace or certitude by fury, driven across the earth by fury . . .
    . . . it is a spirit wild and dark and uncontrollable . . . it is in the saddle now, horsed upon our lives, . . . the mad and cruel tyrant who goads us forever down the blind and brutal tunnel of kaleidoscopic days at the end of which is nothing but the blind mouth of the pit and darkness and no more.

Nothing could be more expressive, on a subjective plane, of at least a phase of the spirit of that "revolution of nihilism" which is likewise "driven across the earth by fury." The identity of imaginative impression is at least as great as the point by point identity of content which we have been tracing.

Now, too, we can see as a fundamentally vitalistic and potentially political trend an individualism which seems, when we consider Wolfe alone, to have little connection with either vitalism or politics. Eugene Gant's childhood dreams of some brilliant future "victory," developing into the violent craving of both of Wolfe's heroes for fame, are significant. Still more significant is a continual emphasis on the need to be independent of all ties and all influences, the need to break away from fam- [**318/319**] ily and home, to break up friendships and love affairs and all relationships which encroach on absolute individuality. It is a conscious struggle for a kind of self-sufficiency which comes quite naturally to Whitman; but in Wolfe it takes on a morbidity unknown to Whitman but inevitable for such individualism in a world where it can no longer be spontaneous or practicable. Whitman never felt "lost," never considered himself a "stranger" or was so considered by others; on the contrary, all actual strangers were his friends. In Wolfe's world, as in Nietzsche's, the distance between individuals, literally as well as figuratively, has diminished; and, if they are to remain absolute individualists, the antagonism between them must increase.

And Wolfe's resentment of the interrelated society of which he is a part in spite of himself, his antagonism toward the other people from whom he cannot escape, approaches a Nietzschean contempt for the masses. A case in point is the nature of his horror of the standardized office building and apartment house architecture of New York as "a new and accursed substance. . . designed not for the use of men but for the blind proliferations of the manswarm, to accommodate the greatest number in the smallest space . . . all the nameless, faceless, mindless manswarm atoms of the earth." Another case in point is Eugene Gant's loathing of the students whom he teaches, his "sense of drowning daily in the manswarm," his daily waging of "the struggle of man against the multitude." This struggle is to him that of life against a hostile environment, of expansive egotism against society, of the vitally superior individual against the vast, valueless mass of beings without vitality.

If we compare Wolfe's loathing of the "manswarm" of the metropolitan college with his reaction to another mass of people, the crowd in the Munich beer hall, singing and swaying together with a rhythmic motion, we find a striking contrast. In these he feels a vital force so dynamic and compelling "that they must smash whatever they come against." They make him feel "as if he had dreamed and awakened in a strange, barbaric forest to find a ring of savage, barbaric faces bent down above him . . . upon their mighty spear-staves." This crowd is transformed into something sinister, but how vital and glamorous! George Webber is frozen with fear, but how thrilling a fear! For this [**319/320**] mob is no mere agglomeration of average human beings thrown together by circumstances and living undistinguished lives, but a fusion of such individuals into a collective living entity of tremendous vital power, at once sensually and mystically primitive, full of the latent menace and

"fury" of vital power as Wolfe conceives and feels it. It is a group acting as an intensely vital and potentially expansive and destructive individual, but with a mass force of which no single individual could be capable.

At the beginning of his visit to Germany in the latter part of YOU CAN'T GO HOME AGAIN, Wolfe is still enthralled by this phenomenon. He is thrilled by the collective vitality of the huge crowds at the Olympic games, by "something like a wind across a field of grass . . . shaken through that crowd" when the Führer comes. Indeed, the irresistible appeal of Germany in general for him seems to be an all-round vitalistic one, and his imaginative descriptions of Germany are in terms with vaguely vitalistic connotations. "An unfathomed domain of unknown inheritance," he calls it; or again, "wizard Faust, old father of the ancient and swarm-haunted mind of man, . . . dark Helen burning in our blood, . . . dark land, old ancient earth . . ." source of mysterious, primitive, sinister, and enthralling vitality. And more and more the sinister side of all this becomes uppermost in his mind, as he absorbs this atmosphere more fully, and as at the same time he gains more knowledge of the social and political life of the country as it exists today. Especially in the tense crowd gathered around the hapless refugees caught by the police, he feels "the tragedy of man's cruelty and his lust for pain—the tragic weakness which corrupts him, which he loathes, but which he cannot cure," the same fascination of destruction and death that he has felt at home in the crowds surrounding the dead or dying victim of an automobile accident or a lynching. But now he does not share this fascination as we have seen him share it earlier. He feels in the hold of this fascination on men a life, a dynamism, that is self-destructive; no longer a great energy alone, but a great morbidity, a miasmic poison which in Germany under the Nazis he finds permeating everything.

And now Wolfe considers all the evils

which he has seen there, the race doctrine, the worship of force, the anti-intellectual suppression of truth in favor of myth; and he relates them all to the [320/321] kind of vitalistic primitivism which we have noted throughout his own work. He sees in them all a form of the "fierce and animal tribalism" of the primitive Teutons who destroyed Rome; not, however, something necessarily or exclusively German, but rather a "primitive spirit of greed and lust and force" which is "a terrible part of the universal heritage of man." Wolfe, moreover, recognizes and rejects the same atavistic urges in himself, the lure of "that dark, ancestral cave" which "forever pulls one back." It is to this primitive, sub-rational, almost sub-human childhood of the race that humanity "can't go home again" without dire consequences.

Wolfe recognizes and rejects also that individualism which in himself has been rooted in such primitivism, resolving to turn his attention from himself and from man's elemental past "outward . . . toward the rich and life-giving soil of a new freedom in the wide world of all humanity." In other words, not life but humanity will be the supreme value for him. In Germany under the Nazis he has seen the ultimate political and social effects of that vitalism which has been the supreme impetus and characteristic of his own life and work. Still susceptible to its fascination and power, still conscious of it as basic and essential and all-pervasive in his own life, he sees that he must either accept its social consequences or reject it completely; and he has enough humanity and resolution in him to do the latter.

What this rejection means in Wolfe's development is incalculable. It means a renunciation not of opinions, which are comparatively easy to change, but of instincts, of temperamental attitudes and reactions, virtually of his entire personality. Because this change leaves Wolfe in so complete a vacuum, and also because the suppression of critical intelligence has come to represent to him one of the greatest evils of that vitalism against which he

is here reacting, he is compelled for the first time, in YOU CAN'T GO HOME AGAIN, to use his brain, to analyze the society in which he lives and to try to understand it through the exercise of critical intelligence. And tragically enough, we find that his powers of critical intelligence do not amount to much. His criticism is obvious and superficial throughout. He creates a sharp and brilliant picture of the shallowness and unreality of the life and attitudes of the sophisticated New York intellectuals. [321/322] He portrays somewhat less impressively the great contrast between existing extremes of wealth and poverty, the vast amount of toil by vast numbers of people necessary to produce the brilliant life of the fortunate few; and he hints that this situation is undesirable. Its causes he conceives in terms of vague platitudes—materialism and greed, old forms of society which "are dying and must die," a social enemy which is "sleek and fat"—"rich and powerful." Even the magnificent "Credo" gives us only a stirring and indomitable faith in nothing more precise than an amorphous "future," an undefined "truth," a "true discovery of our democracy" which is "still before us."

Nor does what we have of THE HILLS BEYOND embody any significant advance. Wolfe's new democratic "social consciousness" makes itself felt in incidental comments and digressions, but the one social theme which seems to be an integral part of the work, the decadence of the South, its tendency to escape from reality to an imaginary Civil War and pre-Civil War past, has already been presented—and presented more impressively, though less precisely and analytically—in all his earlier work.

An[d] now it is clear, too, why YOU CAN'T GO HOME AGAIN, (not to mention too emphatically THE HILLS BEYOND which is too fragmentary to be judged fairly), is not nearly so good a novel from a purely aesthetic point of view as LOOK HOMEWARD ANGEL or OF TIME AND TH RIVER. There is an impression of discor tinuity, explainable only in part by the existence of gaps which Wolfe would have filled in if he had lived; for actually the earlier novels may be found, upon analysis of the mere subject matter, to consist of almost equally disjointed episodes. But there was an overwhelming cumulative momentum which swept these episodes into one continuous stream; and this momentum is lacking in the later work. A discontinuity not only of form but of meaning must have been evident even to Wolfe himself, since he found it necessary to recapitulate and interpret his story at the end. Wolfe's style, which critics praised for its new "objectivity" in YOU CAN'T GO HOME AGAIN, has finally, in THE HILLS BEYOND, become objective to the point of flat, lifeless dullness. When we compare the brief, commonplace, description of the arrival of the first railroad train at Lybia [Libya] Hill, for instance, with the cataclysmic impact of just any ordinary train [**322/323**] in OF TIME AND THE RIVER, we find that what has been lost is not merely "subjectivity," but movement and color, individuality and magnificence.

For Wolfe's earlier way of writing was not a mere literary tool. It was an outgrowth, or rather an application, of his entire temperament and basic attitude, and the momentum and magnificence of his writing were the momentum and magnificence of that *élan vital* which he found himself compelled to renounce. And for this he has no compensation. Just as Wolfe had not the kind of intellect that could powerfully analyze the present or envisage a future for society, so he had not the kind of literary art that could compensate for loss of momentum by structure or for loss of color and movement of style by anything more than objectivity. And objectivity in itself is a mere negative quality unless it leads to something—to keener vision, clearer knowledge, more scrupulous and significant truth. Since Wolfe was unable to attain these ends, except perhaps to the extent of a confused awareness of them, it is hardly accurate to say that he "found himself" by attaining objectivity at the expense of all that had been himself.

VI

That means that an aesthetic question of far-reaching significance has been raised. If the whole vitalistic approach must be rejected on social grounds, is there any substitute that an artistic temperament of the kind adapted to it can produce? Wolfe, as the first vitalistic artist to see the social consequences of his vitalism and to reject it, might have answered this question. He was making a heroic attempt, but no one knows whether he would ever have succeeded. Before he died, he had not succeeded, and there are no indications in his very latest fragment that he was moving in the direction of success.

There is also an important current political implication. What of the daily more insistent and numerous demands for an end to "scepticism" (or critical analysis), for a new "dynamic" philosophy, for a "re-vitalized democracy" which above all can "act"—or even expand and dominate? What of the outcry against all "isms"—that is, against all coherent theories (as well as pseudo-theories) and so in favor of the recrudescence of primitive irra- [**323/324**]tionality? What could be closer to the Nazi idea, as formulated by Rauschning, "that all doctrines . . . have become out-of-date and meaningless"? Many of these appeals may be attractive, with a touch of the same attractiveness that appears in the tremendous dynamic vitality of a Wolfe novel. But Thomas Wolfe's experience of these trends in himself and of their consequences in society may lead us to believe that democracy needs not to be re-vitalized but to be re-humanized, not to be driven by the blind momentum of mere life and force but to be directed by a conscious purpose of providing for the wants of human beings. For if individuals can no longer, as in Whitman's day, be so spread out that they can live separately, perhaps they can be so organized that they can live together.

Thomas Wolfe and the American Dream*

EDGAR JOHNSON (1901-   ) is chairman of the Department of English at the City College of New York. He is best known for his two-volume biographical and critical study, *Charles Dickens: His Tragedy and Triumph.* The following essay is the introduction to a selection from *You Can't Go Home Again* in Professor Johnson's anthology, *A Treasury of Satire.*

In the great and many-sided talent that was Thomas Wolfe's, the sound of satire was but one of many orchestral tones. Lyrical, dramatic, tragic, uproarious, Gargantuan, and overwhelming, he built his novels into tremendous symphonic structures, pouring his emotions out in a huge glut and torrent that fill page after singing page with rejoicing, lamentation, gusto, fury, and despair. No genre is big enough for his enormous grasp; he breaks all molds. Entangled and tortured in self-examination almost to narcissism, he paints Eugene Gant and Monk Webber in turn, both violent and unescapable projections of himself. And yet no writer so persistently introspective has a broader canvas of social observation or paints so many people in bold and penetrating strokes. His delineation of them ranges all the way from fierce travesty to tender and tragic sympathy. His tone, although always characteristically flowing and abundant, runs the gamut from harsh naturalism to those great dithyrambic incantations in which he celebrates trains plunging across the country through the night, curling down the sides of mountains and into dark valleys, racing past the lights of lonely farms and roaring through the empty streets of towns. [**741/742**] Ultimately he is both lyric and epic, vibrant and drenched as no other writer save Walt Whitman with the life and spirit of America itself.

But beneath this soaring melody, satire is a ground tone which we hear sounding more and more persistently until in Wolfe's final period it becomes dominant. Wolfe's career thus becomes further evidence of how characteristic a mode of expression satire is for our time, and of its being no accident that so many major voices among our novelists have a powerful strain of satire in their work. Wolfe himself writes, "Satiric exaggeration belongs to the nature of life, and particularly American life." How could any sensitive American live through this last half century during which America ceased to be a provincial outpost of Europe and became a world power and a world center without feeling that there was something extravagant in the contour of American destiny? How could anyone pass from the primitiveness of spiritual background that Wolfe knew in his childhood to the glittering subtlety of urban culture without feeling that there was something fantastic about the pattern of modern life? How could anyone look beneath the gleaming surface of all this power and success, and not see how much was contradictory, false, hollow, and cruel? No wonder, then, that "the satiric note grows steadily stronger" in Wolfe, as Maxwell Geismar says, "until his last volume contains such devastating

* Edgar Johnson, "Thomas Wolfe and the American Dream," *A Treasury of Satire,* ed. Edgar Johnson (New York: Simon and Schuster, 1945), pp. 741-745. Copyright 1945 by Edgar Johnson. By permission of Simon and Schuster, Inc.

critiques of American society."

Wolfe's power as a satirist depends largely upon his command over invective and burlesque. His irony is apt to be that of a young giant who has no idea of his strength and who imagines he is being delicate and restrained when he is flattening something beyond recognition; it alternates between a clumsy callowness and a battering with blows as of Thor's hammer. Indeed, Wolfe is comically like the hero in one of A. P. Herbert's poems, who

> could not walk into a room
> Without ejaculating, "Boom!"

But these very qualities, which make him a heavy-handed ironist, help to magnify his fanfaronades of abuse and his wild parodies into a kind of gigantic and overpowering horseplay. [742/743]

. . . .

The satire in Wolfe's first novel, Look Homeward, Angel, is almost purely personal, centered upon the members of Eugene Gant's family. We have the roaring bombast and rhetoric of old Gant's Elizabethan rodomontade; the insensate miserly string-collecting and bottle-saving of Eugene's mother Eliza; Steve's combination of bullying swagger and foul-breathed whining; Helen's furious energy, her wild "K-k-k-k" of laughter over some parody of their mother ("Law me, child. H-m! Yes. It's good soup"), and her dark slave-driven hysteria. We have Luke's crazy chortling, his Rabelaisian humor, and his stammering need for popularity; Ben's lean, gray bitterness, and his sideways appeal to some dark angel: "Oh, my God! Will you listen to that now?" And we have Eugene's agonized outburst against Eliza's lurid penny-pinching: "Mama, mama, in God's name what is it? What do you want? Are you going to strangle and drown us all? Don't you own enough? Do you want more string? Do you want more bottles? . . . Do you want the town? What is it?"

In Of Time and the River the satiric perception grows and blossoms into those wonderful pages describing Professor Hatcher and the students in his celebrated course in the drama, the Murphys and the lower-middle-class Boston Irish, and the terrors, jealousies, and hatreds of teaching in the great urban university. Personal satire is continued in the portrait of Bascom Pentland and Eugene's antics with the Simpsons, mother and daughter, but it is becoming submerged in satire of more widespread significance. Wolfe's insight into the members of the drama course is profound and pitiful.

"They belonged to that huge tribe of all the damned and lost who feel that everything is going to be all right with them if they can only take a trip, or learn a rule, or meet a person. They belonged to that futile, desolate, and forsaken horde who felt that all will be well with their lives, that all the power they lack themselves will be supplied . . . if only they eat bran for breakfast, secure an introduction to a celebrated actress, get a [743/744] reading for their manuscript by a friend of Sinclair Lewis, or win admission to Professor Hatcher's celebrated class of dramatists."

Apprentices in the academic world can bear witness to the terrible truth with which Wolfe portrays its hidden struggles: "They wasted and grew sick with hate and poison because another man received promotion, because another man had his poem printed, because another man had eaten food and swallowed drink . . . and they whispered with trembling lips: 'Has he spoken to you yet?' 'Has he said anything to you yet about next year?' 'Are you coming back next year?' 'Did he say anything to you about me next year?' "

The implications of such scenes go far deeper than uncovering how pitiful is the pretense of scholarly detachment and academic calm. These poor miserable collegiate hacks show in a more poignant form the fear-haunted insecurity that Sinclair Lewis hinted beneath the placid surface of Zenith's plump middle class, and that Wolfe was to reveal even more feverishly in the infernal competitive tension of the Federal Weight, Scales, and Com-

puting Company, with its dreadful
Heaven of "the Hundred Club," its Hell
of being "no longer with the Company,"
and its desperate orgiastic "Week of Play."
The glittering shell of the world cracks
beneath such hammer blows, and reveals
the dark things beneath.

Throughout both The Web and the
Rock and You Can't Go Home Again are
scattered satiric diatribes on all the literary, artistic, and social movements and
crazes that have agitated the surface of our
cultural life: ivory-tower aestheticism, de-
bunking, primitivism, expressionism, psychoanalysis, the new humanism, Southern
agrarianism, retreat to the farm, highbrow
communism. But even more significant
are the chapters in You Can't Go Home
Again devoted to painting the madness of
the twenties, Libya Hill feverish with speculation, the obscene outrages of high-
pressure salesmanship, the dying orgies of
the bull market. There is something almost prophetically terrifying in Wolfe's
denunciations of a callously luxurious
world of wealth and fashion holding its
gorgeous revels in lofty Babylonian gardens and applauding Mr. Piggy Logan's
circus while its own foundations tremble:

"The highest intelligences of the time
—the very subtlest of the chosen few—
were bored with many things. . . .
They were bored with going abroad, and
they were bored with staying at home. They
were bored with the great poets of the
world whose great poems they had never
read. They were bored with hunger in
the streets, with the men who were killed,
with the [744/745] children who starved,
and with the injustice, cruelty, and oppression all around them . . . They were
bored with living, they were bored with
dying, but—they were not bored that year
with Mr. Piggy Logan and his circus of
wire dolls."

And meanwhile this symbolically entitled "House That Jack Built," seeming so
powerful, as if founded upon a rock, shiv-
ers mysteriously at intervals to subterranean agitations, and cavernous noises
come up from the depths of the earth.
These rumblings of doom are not merely
a knell for a system Wolfe has at last en-
compassed and condemned. They are pro-
phetic, as well, of his larger hope for the
American promise of generosity and freedom: "I think these forms are dying, and
must die, just as I know that America and
the people in it are deathless, undiscov-
ered, and immortal, and must live.

"I think the true discovery of America
is before us. I think the true fulfillment of
our spirit, of our people, of our mighty
and immortal land is yet to come. I think
the true discovery of our own democracy
is still before us. And I think that all these
things are as certain as the morning, as inevitable as noon. I think I speak for most
men living when I say that our America is
Here, is Now, and beckons on before us,
and that this glorious assurance is not only
our living hope, but our dream to be accomplished."

Thomas Wolfe's Discovery of America*

EDWIN BERRY BURGUM (1894-   ) taught English at New York University for many years. He has been editor of *Science and Society* and has written a number of essays examining the modern novel in terms of its social implications. The following selection is from one of these essays published in his collection, *The Novel and the World's Dilemma*. It originally appeared in the *Virginia Quarterly Review* in 1946.

The career of Thomas Wolfe is the spectacle of a novelist who began with the sole concern to transfer to others his fascination with his own family as material for fiction, who turned thereafter in the same simplicity of intention to his own relations with persons outside his family, but who found pouring into these relationships all the disorders of the contemporary world until at the end he was forced to attempt their solution in a letter to his editor on his social views, in which his work as a writer culminated and, it may be said, his life concluded.

The bridge between the personal and the social was Wolfe's discovery that his own personality was a microcosm of the state of society. It was not quite a conscious discovery. He was not only the least intellectual of novelists; he was altogether incapable of writing well unless deeply moved by the personal contact. The transformation in his case was, therefore, a gradual and an almost automatic broadening of his interests until he had passed from one of the most subjective of novelists at the beginning, to one of the most objective at the end. Having exhausted his relationship with his family (which was virtually a part of himself), and then his relationships with friends and lovers, as he groped in his isolation for new ties he discovered [302/303] his fellow men.

Through the projection of sympathy alone, and not any actual awareness of the parallel, his imagination turned to the social scene. But his new attitude of sympathy for human misery in general took the form of his break with his one remaining friend.

Perhaps also, for his readers as well as himself, consciousness of these facts has been clouded by the spirit of gusto that seemed to dominate his first book, *Look Homeward, Angel.* We have gained a mind set from first contact with that book which we have carried over into his later books. Different readers have reached this state of mind in different ways. But we have all made some extravagant emotional response to some extravagant emotional assault this book has made upon us. Those who dislike extravagant emotion altogether have escaped into a distaste for the unevenness of its style, the lifeless prose of passages in which Wolfe's emotions were not involved, the adolescent rhetoric into which his emotion too often evaporated, the overwritten formlessness of the whole. Others, younger or less sophisticated, intoxicated by the gusto, accepted it at its face value. They found something epic in its exaggeration, something tonic and awesome about their participation in its emotional excess. And so they called it the transfer into fiction of the spirit of Paul

* Edwin Berry Burgum, from "Thomas Wolfe's Discovery of America," *The Novel and the World's Dilemma* (New York: Oxford University Press, 1947), pp. 302-310. Reprinted by permission of Edwin Berry Burgum.

Bunyan, forgetful of the careless ease, the robust self-assurance with which Bunyan acted; whereas in Wolfe the utterance is explosive, the strength illusory, the action destructive, as the individual seeks in vain to free his tortured spirit, madly to break through the inner conflicts that reduce him to impotence. Or they were reminded by his style of the Teutonic humor of Carlyle, its earthy vulgarity transfigured by the lightning flash of the Valkyries, though they then forgot that there is no humor in *Look Homeward, Angel,* only a hypnotic identification with the violence of despair. Or they thought of Whitman, sensing some small cry for warmth and understanding, lost in the impulsive clamor of Wolfe's egotism. But they then forgot that he **[303/304]** was a Whitman disillusioned, a Prometheus forced back into his chains.

More accurate certainly, since the imitation of his style betrayed Wolfe's awareness of the parallel, was the echo of what has been called the Rabelaisian spirit in James Joyce. But since almost everyone misinterpreted Joyce on this point, failing to sense the pessimism beneath the burly façade of humor, the comparison only strengthened the delusion about Wolfe. Nevertheless, those who liked this novel were more sound in their reactions (if not in their reasons) than those who rejected him on grounds that missed his main intention. Better than Hemingway (who represented the minority of the sophisticated), better than Dos Passos (who could only describe the appearance of things), Wolfe was the novelist of the average American youth of the postwar period, the small-town boy who confused his restlessness with ambition, who thought himself a profound optimist when actually inhibited by inner doubt, and who was sustained chiefly by an illusory identification with the grandiose.

What is taken for gusto in *Look Homeward, Angel,* then, is actually a grandiose illusion expressing itself in random and futile violence of word and action. And this dubious gusto belongs to the father

rather than the son. It is under the spell of his father's spirit that the young Gant falls, until it seems to become his own and the reader's. Later on, in the false and doubtful maturity of the son in later volumes, this imaginative identification will become real, and the son will succeed his father. For the time being, the father's spirit, once identification has been exhausted, is sublimated by the inexperience of youth into the justifiable inevitable dreams of adolescence, which reach out for the life that lies ahead in an ecstasy of escape and self-fulfilment. But even vision cannot be kept steady and uncorrupted. The youth recoils from it, looking homeward, until his leap into the future for a security he has never known degenerates into an ambiguous nostalgia. 'Oh lost, and by the wind grieved, ghost, come back again.' Specifically, the ghost is the **[304/305]** spirit of his dead brother Ben. But since only through his friendship with this brother had he known love and the security of home, the ghost symbolizes these qualities, and the plea for his return becomes a restatement of the title of the novel, a demand at one and the same time for the satisfaction of his dream in terms of his subjective needs, and its satisfaction in the objective form of a decent family life. 'Come back' means not only 'come back to me as a person,' but 'come back to secure for me what should be mine, the sense of being at home in my family and in that larger family which is Altamont.' But such a homecoming of the spirit is impossible on the level of reality. Though almost drowned out by the theme of identification with the father, a second theme finds its origin in this dilemma. Eugene's helplessness takes refuge in the substitute paternity of friendship with this older brother, though this tenuous intermittent substitution is soon broken by Ben's death. In the strong somber elegy of Ben's dying, the identification changes, and the second melody succeeds in dominating the book. Ben having died, what made home endurable has been withdrawn. But in the moving hallucination of the return of his spirit as Eugene stands in front of his father's shop at midnight, Ben counsels his younger brother more fully and more intimately than ever in life, leaving Eugene 'like a man who stands upon a hill above the town he has left, yet does not say "The town is near," but turns his eyes upon the distant soaring ranges.' For the time being the dilemma has been resolved by the restoration of adolescent optimism, and the possibility of a home is the hope of a future elsewhere.

Life there, when he gets to know it, will only repeat the same patterns. Indeed, they are already emerging in equivocal form in *Look Homeward, Angel.* The tenderness of Ben and Eugene for each other, born out of their mutual loneliness, must seep through an appearance of gruff detachment on the part of the older son and a timid inarticulate assent on the part of the younger. Their great need for each other makes this surface unimportant to them. But in other relations, the negative emo- [305/306] tion is not a façade, easily ignored, but an active ingredient corrupting the superficial optimism in which Eugene takes confidence. He is scarcely aware of how much contamination from the family pattern is already present in his dreams of the future. The town he has left is nearer than he thinks.

Ah [he says in the easy assertion of reverie after he has left Altamont], I'll tell you why you laugh; you are afraid of me because I am not like the others. You hate me because I do not belong. You see that I am finer and greater than any one you know; you cannot reach me and you hate me. That's it. The ethereal (yet manly) beauty of my features, my boyish charm (for I am Just a Boy) blended with the tragic wisdom of my eyes (as old as life and filled with the brooding tragedy of the ages), the sensitive and delicate flicker of my mouth, and my marvellous dark face blooming inward of strange loveliness like a flower—all this you want to kill because you cannot touch it. . . Ah, but she will know. . . Proudly with misty eyes, he saw her standing beside him against the rabble; the small elegant head, wound with a bracelet of bright hair, against his shoulder, and with two splendid pearls in her ears. Dearest! dearest! We stand here on a star! We are beyond them now. Behold! They shrink, they fade, they

pass—victorious, enduring, marvellous love, my dearest, we remain.*

This is the essence of his youthful vision, and his vision expresses the subjective state of his most enthusiastic audience, the youth of the early Depression years. Wolfe could no more have spoken thus frankly in actual life than the youth he represents. But this is the way they both felt, with an intensity that varied only with the differing pressures of their individual potentialities. Most of them, having less promise than Wolfe, doubtless experienced a less intense conflict, and it was easy for the observer to recognize the inertia, the lassitude, and hopelessness in which the conflict ended. But the youth himself, no more than Eugene Gant, recognized the stalemate; instead he festered in his inner [306/307] rebelliousness, supported by its justification in lack of opportunity, and willed the happy ending in fantasy when he could not in fact. His was as false an affirmation as that with which Joyce's *Ulysses* ends.

In another mood, toward the end of the book, Wolfe expressed more frankly the typical American characteristics of his hero.

He had no greater need for rebellion than have most Americans, which is none at all. He was quite content with any system which might give him comfort, security, enough money to do as he liked, and freedom to think, eat, drink, love, read, and write what he chose. . . He did not want to reform the world, or to make it a better place to live in; his whole conviction was that the world was full of pleasant places, enchanted places, if he could only go and find them. The life around him was beginning to fetter and annoy him; he wanted to escape from it. He felt sure things would be better elsewhere. He always felt sure things would be better elsewhere.*

This passage is typical even in the unconscious hypocrisy of its denial of rebelliousness. An interesting confirmation of it, at a

---

[P. 306] * Wolfe, Thomas, *Look Homeward, Angel*, New York, 1929, p. 523. By permission of Charles Scribner's Sons.
[P. 307] * Ibid. pp. 588-9.

much later date, may be found in Ralph Ingersoll's *The Battle is the Payoff*, in which he describes the American soldier in North Africa during the Second World War in almost the same terms, as always restlessly expecting happiness not where he is, but somewhere he has left behind or hopes to go to.

But I must not press too far this comparison between Wolfe and the average American boy. The differences of potentialities in them produced a difference in the degree of assertiveness. But assertiveness there was in both cases, ranging from mere querulousness or disorderly conduct to active participation in radical or reformatory measures. Where Wolfe's rebelliousness, as an example of the most active type, differed from the ordinary (where it proved perhaps that he was a production of the postwar generation rather than the Depression) was that it remained **[307/308]** purely personal at first, and uninterested in politics. As we read this first volume, if we are not intoxicated by its rhetoric, we recognize how much need to compensate for frustration and wounded feeling by an attempt at domination of other individuals lurks behind the affirmation of mutual loves just quoted. His egoism buoyantly reasserts itself, whatever the obstacles, and always in a demand for the individual contact. And it is, I believe, in this reaction of buoyancy that his unique, his specifically American contribution to the contemporary novel is to be found. The inability to make friendships, the predominance of rejection, the sense of everybody's being hostile or indifferent, I have elsewhere described as the theme of Joyce's *Ulysses* and much of our other good fiction. Most authors have been resigned to the situation they depict. The characteristic contribution of Wolfe is both that he presents characters in rebellion against their isolation and shares the optimism implied in the new positiveness of their demand.

In the portrait of his father (whom I do not pretend to be typical of an older generation), the rebellion is certainly a futile one, and the warmth of spirit which might attract a response has all but died within. His is the failure the son must avoid, obscured by the excess of the moment, substituting a grotesque and desperate sadism for the love that has passed beyond reach. Actually this parent, who has so bound his sons to himself, has very little to do with them. He proffers usually the hostility of his explosive moods, whether he is rousing them from bed in the morning with the same familiar imprecations hurled from the bottom of the stairs, or making himself in the only way he can the center of a distraught family by coming home drunk, needing eventually to be subdued and put to bed. Such conduct forms a precedent as dangerous as tempting to the son, for it is altogether without promise.

But in later novels, in which the focus shifts from father to son, and in which I have said the son takes over his father's personality, an important modification appears. The father's per- **[308/309]** sonality in the son proffers a constructive aspect. When the young novelist turns to explore his own difficult attempts at friendship, if attachments are eventually broken, it is not from perversity alone. The valid evidence of optimism in Wolfe, the justification for thinking of him as a belated successor to Whitman rather than an American version of Proust's or Joyce's despair, is that his breaking of a relationship is always bound up with an obscure kind of growth. He reacts from a friendship partly because he has discovered an imperfection in it he can no longer tolerate. He learns something from every new experience, as he passes from a provincial boyhood where a lust for money has corrupted the quality of the folk inheritance, through the social contacts of a college education in which only the voracious reading of literature counted, into restless travelling that gave him a cosmopolitan knowledge of the world. Under these circumstances, each new friendship starts on a higher level than the last, and has stimulated a superior sense of human values.

Thus, I imagine, the cold precepts of

his mother, which she never practiced, got written the more indelibly into his unconscious, precisely because (in contrast to his father's expletives) they carried so shy an emotive content. After a bitter quarrel, instigated by the father, in which for all her stubborn self-assurance she played as usual a passive role, when left alone with her son, 'Poor child! Poor child!' the mother whispered faintly. 'We must try to love one another.' Such remarks must have become convictions buried deeper than thought, buried so deep that they may seem scarcely to influence conduct at all, yet hibernating within to rise into authority once the process of living gave them any verification. Never systematized into a philosophy, set in the context of American history, they brought him against the grain of the surface into the tradition of Whitman, causing him to scorn the cant of our Puritanism and our democracy. These ideals were too precious for lip service. They remained a deeper order of compulsions than his apparent bel- **[309/310]**

ligerency, at the very basis of his personality where they could order his experiences the more and more openly as life allowed. When once we escape the irrelevant details of the particular novel and see the series together as his life's tale, we become aware of the grandeur of the forming pattern. A modern Prometheus, because he recognized he was in chains, and sought with a terrible sense of isolation to wrest himself free of them, he discovered that toward the end of his short life he was not alone. The distortions of his personality turn out to be his challenge to the forces in contemporary life opposed to the tradition of Whitman. When the shock of the Depression reveals to him that his problem is common to Americans generally, the distortions disappear; for he has gained allies in deprivation, and the mere reality of this sympathy of kinship reawakens a confidence in the principle of kinship as the fundamental and persistent directive of American life.

.   .   .   .

Thomas Wolfe*

HERBERT MULLER (1905-   ) is professor of English and government at Indiana University. He has written on contemporary fiction and the meaning of history, his best known works being *Modern Fiction* and *The Uses of the Past*. He met Wolfe in 1938; and, his critical study, from which the following selections are taken, was the first book-length American attempt to evaluate Wolfe's work.

1. ON MYTHS AND LEGENDS

.   .   .   .

Yet Wolfe stands out, and not merely as a romantic or freakish figure. Although he has been patronized as a gifted amateur or magnificent adolescent, he has also been flattered, more than any other contemporary American novelist, by comparisons to the great novelists of the past, such as Balzac, Dickens, Melville and Dostoyevsky. He would remain important for the simple reason that he created many unforgettable characters and scenes, a whole swarming world; for if this primal creative power ultimately defies analysis, it is nevertheless what distinguishes major from minor fiction. Wolfe is also important, however, because he grappled with the fundamental issues of modern life and literature. His work is not only a symptom of this age, reflecting its deep confusions and discords, but finally a significant criticism of it. If most of our leading writers have been intellectually more acute than he, more resourceful in their experimentation with new methods and materials, more brilliant in their technical achievements, none have been more honest and thorough-going in their effort to come to terms with their world. In his simplicity Wolfe forces us back to elementary principles, the first and last things that subtle,

sophisticated writers are apt to overlook. And at that his simplicity is deceptive. It is atop complexity as well as beneath it; Wolfe was fully aware of the complexities of modern life, if only because of his mad hunger to experience everything; and so he always went through them, not around them. Unlike most of his intellectual betters, he was never taken in by the fashionable simplicities of [3/4] his time—the cults of the wastelanders, the esthetes, the literary communists, the literary agrarians, the literary primitives.

Hence we might pause to get our bearings. The most illuminating perspective on Wolfe's life and work can be got, I believe, by a roundabout approach through a term that has recently become popular in literary circles—the term *myth*. We have rediscovered that a myth is not simply a pretty fancy, a charming memento of the childhood of the race, or something to be "exploded." The great myths—as of Prometheus, of Jacob and his sons, of the resurrection of Christ—symbolize the fundamental meanings of human existence, the timeless patterns or cycles of life and death, the timeless problems of love and justice. They represent, in the words of Mark Schorer, "a large, controlling image . . . which gives philosophical meaning to the facts of ordinary life, that is to say, which has organizing value for experi-

* Herbert Muller, from *Thomas Wolfe* ("The Makers of Modern Literature"; Norfolk, Conn.: New Directions, 1947), pp. 1-22, 161-189. Copyright 1947 by New Directions. Reprinted by permission of New Directions, Publishers.

ence." In other words, the myth is not a way of disguising or evading the shocking facts of life but a way of ordering and accepting them. It is an indispensable way, since the facts do not really speak for themselves.

All imaginative literature may be conceived as sophisticated mythology, or philosophy as rationalized mythology, or religious dogma as fossilized mythology. In the beginning was the word as *mythos,* the ancient, concrete story of the origin and nature of the world; from this developed the *epos,* or symbolical narrative, and finally the *logos,* the word as rational explanation. The three stages correspond to the development of language, from literal concreteness through metaphor to abstraction, and **[4/5]** finally correspond to the history of thought and knowledge.[1] Today, literature, philosophy, religion, and even science are still mythologies in that they are alike founded on some imaginative scheme, and ultimately speak in metaphor. None gives us the whole truth and nothing but the truth; all are selections from experience, versions of the supreme metaphor Reality. If we believe that some one version contains the essential truth, then all the others are still more plainly mythologies; but in any event all serve the same purpose of organizing experience. Likewise society itself is founded on myths, and could not exist without them. They survive not only as old superstitions but as tradition; they are the common meanings, faiths, purposes that hold a group together and constitute its "way of life."

In literature, more particularly, we may trace the development from myth to heroic legend, to romance, to realistic story. Yet all great literature still tends to resemble or become myth. This is most apparent in consciously allegorical or symbolical work, such as *The Divine Comedy, The Faery Queen, Paradise Lost, Prometheus Unbound* and *Faust.* It is no less true of *Hamlet* and *The Misanthrope,* of *War and Peace, Vanity Fair, The Brothers Karamazov* and *The Return of the Native.* As Thomas Mann remarks, the mythical is

the typical; it is the pri- **[5/6]** meval norm of life, "the pious formula into which life flows when it reproduces its traits out of the unconscious." At the same time, we may distinguish the conscious use of mythical material, the deliberate recreation of the myth. In modern literature, the supreme example is Mann's Joseph story.

Such purposes are also conscious in Thomas Wolfe, however; and here is the lead to the main import of his work. From the outset he felt that he "belonged with the Mythmakers," and conceived his task in terms of the myth. "O lost!" runs the refrain of *Look Homeward, Angel,* a "Story of the Buried Life." "Remembering speechlessly we seek the great forgotten language, the lost lane-end into heaven, a stone, a leaf, an unfound door." The central theme of Wolfe's entire work was the search for a father and a home, for "the image of a strength and wisdom external to his need and superior to his hunger, to which the belief and power of his own life could be united." His specific theme, in other words, is the central problem of all writers today, in a "realistic" age that prides itself upon facing the facts but is swamped by them. Our vast store of knowledge is too often a jumble of undigested or indigestible facts, our experience too often a violent succession of facts without philosophical meaning or immediately with all too shocking meaning. We still live by myths, for the most part unconsciously; we too seldom have a clear, steady image, a coherent mythology. And the key to Wolfe's achievement is the gradual widening and deepening of the implications of his theme, the transformation of a private legend into a public myth —a modern *Pilgrim's Progress.* **[6/7]**

In his quest Wolfe was as terribly confused as terribly sincere; no other impor-

[1] Plato is the clearest example of this development, even apart from the myths he introduced into his dialogues. Although it is conventional to distinguish his poetry from his philosophy, his philosophy is as plainly a development from myth. His Ideas are not purely logical concepts but images, divine symbols; he is personifying the world of reason as the early myths personified the world of nature. And no less mythical, in this sense, are such concepts as Schopenhauer's Will.

tant modern writer has appeared so often naïve, extravagant, maudlin, ludicrous. He began like most young writers, only more so: writing the story of his own life in capital letters, underlining and italicizing it, adding exclamation points. Specifically, the main trouble was that his myth was the religion of genius, his controlling image the romantic image of the God-like artist as one possessed, set apart from his fellowmen, privileged to demand of them not merely a living but an immortal life. Tumult is the insignia of this artist, the proof of his depth and sincerity; he seethes with imperishable thoughts, and then seethes still more because his fellows seem willing to let these thoughts perish. For Wolfe this image was further intensified and distorted by typically American experience. He was a young writer in the small town, whose relatives and neighbors regarded him as queer; he was a country boy dazzled by the big city, and then lost in it; he was a yokel at once awed and infuriated by the wealthy, the cultured, the sophisticated; he was a proud Southerner who had rebelled against his own people, yet was resentful and suspicious of the Yankee; he was a proud American who knew that Europe was effete, but had to go there to find real culture. He was also a child of the reckless 'twenties, homeless among all the boys who were making good, bitterly aware that they were not making for good, yet infected by the gross popular myths he despised. For his image of the privileged artist, above all ordinary social obligations, was a variant of the popular image of the rugged individual, another symbol of an age of special privilege without social responsibility. [7/8]

Nevertheless Wolfe kept his head better than most of his contemporaries. Despite his intense concern with himself and with the Artist he had created in his own image, he was always close to the oldest, deepest simplicities: the good earth, the life of common men, the common destiny of mortality, the flow of time and the river. In particular, he was close to native traditions, which in the 'twenties and 'thirties

were suspect among intellectuals on both the Right and the Left. Like many other writers, he often felt profoundly alienated from America, but he was still more profoundly drawn to it; the very violence of his revulsions indicated the strength of its hold on him; and all his flights to Europe, or into angry rhetoric, were transient and unavailing. From the beginning, the greatness of America had been one of his main themes, if only because he needed a great subject to prove the greatness he so passionately and naively aspired to. In time he came, with increasing clarity and sobriety, to identify the legend of his hunger as an American legend, and to seek his image in the history and the destiny of the nation.

What brought Wolfe to his social senses was the great depression that ended the 'twenties. In his constant prowlings about New York he saw everywhere the human wreckage of the social collapse, the appalling incongruity of the few rotten in their wealth and the many helpless in their wretched poverty. He came to define the root evil as "single selfishness and compulsive greed." He recognized it as an ancient evil but also as the special vice of American life, in its strident individualism and blatant materialism. At the same time, however, Wolfe was deeply impressed by the fortitude of the people. He came to feel a solidarity [8/9] with them in their suffering and their ability to survive. He came to realize that he was not actually singular, that his prized individuality was not the sum of his differences from others, and that even the qualities that distinguished him were valuable chiefly because of all that united him with his fellows. At this time he drew up, in *The Story of a Novel,* a complete statement of his task as a Mythmaker[.] [9/10]
. . . .
This is a noteworthy statement of an epic intention. It points to Wolfe's most conspicuous achievement: no other American novelist has given so vivid, exhilarating a sense, in such rich, precise detail, of "the enormous space and energy of Amer-

ican life." But if the statement is admirably sober for Wolfe, it still needs some qualification, and not merely to make room for other, more modest intentions. Characteristically, he magnifies the "physical task," the necessity of comprehending a "billion forms." The great American novel need not contain all of America, and in this respect is not clearly harder to write than a great Russian or English novel; Wolfe's own narrative, like his firsthand knowledge at the time, was largely confined to a few states in the East and South, yet it was adequate for his large purposes. Likewise he exaggerates the intellectual task of the American artist, who cannot draw on European culture, who must "make a new tradition for himself." Modern America is not so entirely new and unique, the American mythmaker is not clearly obliged to discover and create for himself an entire universe—and indeed had better not try to. The great myths of the past were not such conscious creations; they drew on deep, unconscious sentiment, emotion and desire, the common heritage that is indeed a commonwealth. Today such materials have to be discounted, supplemented, complicated, adapted—but they are still available. Wolfe himself had been drawing heavily on them. And as he finally began to make out the image he sought, the "strength and wisdom external to his need," it turned out to be an ancient image. He came out of his confusion precisely by becoming conscious of his heritage, of a "body of tradition" character- [10/11] istically American but also rooted in an ancient European tradition.

"O lost!" he had exclaimed at the beginning, in lyrical anguish. At the end he declared, in sober prose, "I believe that we are lost here in America"; but he added, "I believe we shall be found." He summed up all he had learned in a symbolic refrain: "You can't go home again." He couldn't go back to his hometown, to art for glory's sake, to youthful dreams of fame, romantic love, or escape in foreign lands. Neither could any American artist go back to the ivory tower, to dreams of the charming past, to bohemian Europe, or to a snug Connecticut farmhouse (with modern improvements). Neither could America go back to normalcy, to the good old days of blind and brutal grab, to a complacent faith in Progress as defined by industrialists and ballyhooed by salesmen—to any easy, comfortable solution, any mere appeasement of the enemies without or within. Nevertheless in the deepest sense Wolfe had gone home again. His image is the great national myth, the American Dream.

This is the image of America as in fact a New World, where man can at last realize his hope of creating a great and good society, an everlasting New Deal with freedom and justice for all. It is an ancient type of tribal myth, in its concept of a unique origin and a unique destiny, but it was inspired more immediately by the natural potentialities of a vast continent, by the pioneering spirit of the frontiersmen, by the democratic ideals of the eighteenth century Enlightenment, by the modern myth of progress. It appears as the background of many folk legends and tall tales; as a political creed, embodied in the life and [11/12] work of Franklin, Jefferson, Jackson and Lincoln; as a poetic and religious image in the work of Whitman, Emerson and the Transcendentalists; as a philosophical faith in William James and John Dewey. It has also taken many crude forms, of naive optimism, noisy chauvinism, brawling individualism, vulgar materialism. It remains a living tradition because it has always had to fight for its life, especially against the mythology of big business. If the constant struggle for the realization of the dream is not, as Vernon Parrington conceived it, the central theme of American history (and Wolfe's conception is often close to Parrington's), it is at least a major theme. . . .

6. WOLFE AND THE TRADITION

. . . .

As a whole man, Wolfe was not "just an American"; or we might say that he approached the best in Americanism, which is cosmopolitanism, the ideal of a universal humanity. But he was first and last an American, and as such must be considered in the first and last analysis. A convenient approach to his position in our letters, accordingly, is through Alexis de Tocqueville's *Democracy in America*. Although written more than a hundred years ago, it remains perhaps the shrewdist, most objective analysis of the native tradition, in particular of the old America in which Wolfe had his roots.

The practical-minded American, Tocqueville remarked, is not really inspired by ideas of the supernatural, of Nature, of anything external to man. On the other hand, his daily concerns are not dignified by the manners, rituals, or pieties of an ancient culture: "Nothing conceivable is so petty, so insipid, so crowded with paltry interests—in one word, so anti-poetic—as the life of a man in the United States." But the American is inspired by the image of the whole nation—marching across the wilds, "turning the course of rivers, peopling solitudes, and subduing nature." Such an image of the vast democracy naturally leads to an idea of a still vaster drama, the vicissitudes of the whole human race. And with this exalted idea the individual can return to himself and gaze at a soul no longer puny: "I need [166/167] not traverse earth and sky to discover a wondrous object woven of contrasts, of infinite greatness and littleness, of intense gloom and amazing brightness, capable at once of exciting pity, admiration, terror, contempt. I have only to look at myself." In short, the writer in a democracy cannot use the traditional themes of great poetry; the resources of ancient, aristocratic cultures fail him; but Man remains. "The destinies of mankind, man himself . . . with his passions, his doubts, his rare

prosperities and inconceivable wretchedness, will become the chief, if not the sole, theme of poetry among these nations."

The poetic, not the realistic sense of life has indeed dominated our literature, at least until this century; and the sources of poetry defined by Tocqueville were the sources of the American Renaissance. These were the deepest sources of Wolfe's inspiration. He looked at himself and saw Jason, Dedalus, Telemachus, Faustus, Proteus, Antaeus, Prometheus—he saw Man, in his infinite possibilities. He looked around him and saw America, a new and potentially glorious chapter in the history of Man. Man stood in the presence of Nature, possibly of God, but he stood erect in the foreground, and their presence had meaning only because of his presence. Even in his apparent passion for nature, Wolfe was celebrating chiefly the immensity and grandeur of the American continent; he dwelt on the wild, savage, desolate aspects of nature that were an appropriate background for his own stormy passions as God's lonely American; and the majestic hills, which stirred his imagination chiefly as the "hills beyond," were perhaps less haunting than the whistle-wail of a man-made train snaking through the valleys at night. [167/168]

To be sure, Man has always been the study of mankind. Yet this has not always been considered a proper study, or a sufficient one. It has evident limitations and dangers. In Tocqueville's view, these sources of poetry in a democracy are grand, but they are not abundant. "They are soon exhausted; and poets, not finding the elements of the ideal in what is real and true, abandon them entirely and create monsters." Hence he did not believe that literature in a democracy would prove insipid or earthbound; he believed rather that it would often be "surcharged with immense and incoherent imagery, with exaggerated descriptions and strange creations," and would "lose itself in the clouds." Actually, American literature has tended to both extremes. Tocqueville might have anticipated that writers would come to dwell on daily life in a democracy, whether in patriotic pride or in revulsion. But elsewhere he points to a common source of both the earthbound realism and the cloudy romanticism in our literature.

In democratic communities, each citizen is habitually engaged in the contemplation of a very puny object: namely, himself. If he ever raises his looks higher, he perceives only the immense form of society at large or the still more imposing aspect of mankind. His ideas are all either extremely minute and clear or extremely general and vague; what lies between is a void.

It was this void that Wolfe sought to bridge. He was not entirely successful—he might have done better, again, had he been more intellectual. He was more successful, however, than most typically American writers, from Whitman to Sherwood Anderson. And though comparison in these terms will hardly determine his stature as an artist, it does [168/169] help to measure his accomplishment in the task he set himself as an American mythmaker. [169/180]

. . . .

Here, in contemporary America, is our first and last concern; for the immediate world is the only world we have. And here is the final significance of Wolfe for contemporaries: he made himself at home in this world. It was the sensible thing to do, but it is evidently not an easy thing for an American artist.

Early in the century, a common theme in American fiction was the escape—or tragic failure to escape—to the City, the symbol of freedom, culture and the full life. Then came a revulsion, and a common theme was the return to the farm or the hometown, symbols of the wholesome life. Today we hear that there is no place to go. W. P. Southard [180/181] has recently written on behalf of the young writers who "are trying to discover where in this country of degenerate children an adult can live." In cities he can see only a "blatting arrogant debilitated vulgarity"

or an "astonishing confident obscenity"; he would like to find a small, disciplined community that wants to stay small—but he knows "that our community will not support us." Delmore Schwartz, writing from an academic community, is more emphatic: there is no room in our materialistic society for "such a monster as the cultivated man." Even so sober a critic as Isaac Rosenfeld seems to take as a matter of course the impossible position of American artists, remarking offhand that "the serious American writer cannot but be alienated from American society, close though he may be to it, and much though he may wish to belong." Marjorie Brace adds the logical conclusion: the writer "cannot write seriously without alienating himself from the values of his society, and at the same time he cannot function apart from his audience."

Now, I do not believe that our writers are necessarily or actually in such a bad way. Many serious, cultivated men seem to be functioning well enough, possibly because they have some historical perspective. When our traditionalists and classicists look to the past, they see the great writers who embody their pure ideal, but they seldom see the very impure societies in which these writers lived, or the fate of these societies. They forget that many great writers in the past were also more or less alienated from their society. Euripides, Dante, Racine, Swift, Rousseau, Blake, Byron, Flaubert, Arnold and Turgenev are a few examples off-hand; and some of these—notably Dante—have come to [181/182] be regarded as the very symbol of their age. Artists as naturally tend to oppose as to accept the current imperatives of behavior and belief. Nevertheless, few rebels in the past utterly rejected their society or regarded their cause as hopeless; most were pointing to the future because they had faith in the efficacy of their ideals and of their art. And it is such faith that many contemporaries lack. They are inclined to regard our whole civilization as simply an abomination, and to suspect that the future will be still worse.

They may be right. Possibly our world is unworthy of our attachment; possibly we are living in an impossible age. Yet neither piety nor realism will permit us to take this for granted. As Whitehead has said, the present is holy ground: it contains all that there is—the past is summed up in it, the future is implicit in it. And so to return to Wolfe. He went through all this, experiencing alienation as intensely and thoroughly as any American writer; but he finally came out of it.

Thus he began, like so many, by fleeing to the City. When he was disenchanted, however, he did not go home again; he could appreciate Old Catawba and still know that it was no real haven. He labored prodigiously to assimilate the present in all its multitudinous diversity—to get into, not away from it all. He struggled against the very strong temptation to believe that he was too fine, rare, exquisite a spirit for this world, and that all his difficulties arose from its coarse, vulgar apprehensions. His central theme of a pilgrimage, with all its related motifs, comes down to the central problem of the sensitive individual in an untraditional society: the search for unity beneath the [182/183] increasing division of labor and belief, for a community of faith and purpose beneath the specialization of activity, the diversity of interest, and the protestant individualism of industrial, democratic America. At length Wolfe found himself, by finding such a community. He realized the inevitable dependence of any individual on the group; he approached the ideal relation of the artist to his society, as a spokesman of the common faiths and purposes. And if his best work stems from the period of his estrangement, if his search for a father and a home is more memorable than the announcement of his arrival, the terms of his final reconciliation and acceptance are implicit in all his work.

To begin with, they are concrete terms. They embrace the immediate realities of life in an industrial civilization, the immediate causes of the distress of other contemporaries. Wolfe was as sensitive as anyone to the by-products of our industrial triumphs, the dreary monotony, ugliness, vulgarity, brutality and misery. He never reconciled himself to these human costs —as who should? Yet he was also sensitive to the peculiar values of the machine age, the new forms of beauty and truth, the actual and potential contribution to the greatness of America. He was thrilled by the great bridges, buildings, trains and liners; he saw poetry as well as power, high aspiration as well as greed, in all such symbols of man's conquest of nature. From the beginning he knew that this was always the way with man's works: nothing so glorious that it is not touched with vanity, nothing so commonplace that it is not touched with dignity. He was better able to put up with the attendant evils of the modern way because he was close to the actual [183/184] life of the soil and therefore could not, like the Southern agrarians, so easily recommend agriculture as "the best and most sensitive of vocations," "a form of labor that is pursued with intelligence and leisure." Moreover, he always took for granted what most of the agrarians have since come to realize, sadly—that industrialism is an irreversible process, and there is no going back. If our civilization is destroyed and men start all over again, they may stick to a simpler kind of society. Meanwhile we have to make the best of this kind.

Likewise Wolfe accepted the conditions of a democratic society. In a full awareness of the limitations of common men, he still recognized a community of simple values, as well as a common destiny that ultimately makes all men indeed equal. But here he was inevitably involved in philosophical issues. Like most Americans, and especially those who distrust theory or philosophy, he had an excess of philosophy, mostly unconscious; for his testament rests, as the justification of the American tradition must finally rest, on some metaphysical assumptions about the nature of man and the universe. The issue here is forced by W. H. Auden. Wolfe's fiction strikes him as "grandiose rubbish," and he attributes it to a "false conception of human nature." After experimenting with various modern faiths, Auden has returned to the doctrine of Original Sin; he declares that a democratic society must be grounded on the presupposition that "men are equal not in their capacities and virtues but in their natural bias toward evil." He speaks here for a large and growing company. British writers in particular —for example, Aldous Huxley, Evelyn Waugh and Christopher Isherwood—have been heading [184/185] for Rome or India; even the worldly Maugham has toyed with mysticism; and we may expect to hear much more about the essential evil of man, or the essential vanity of all worldly interests, as men feel unable in any other terms to understand or cope with the monstrous folly and evil of our world.

Now I believe that Wolfe's mature conception of human nature was not false. Certainly he was not blind to the ancient evil—his deep consciousness of it was one reason why he was never taken in by the fashionable faiths that seduced Auden. He nevertheless felt, like most of the tragic poets before him, that man's fate is tragic because human sorrows are not the consequence merely of human evil, and because the frailty of man is also the source of his dignity and worth. In this view, the doctrine of original sin is as false to the actual complexities and paradoxes of the good life as is the opposite doctrine of natural goodness. But at least it should be clear that Auden is denying the historic faith of democracy. His premise that man is naturally evil is the premise of political thinkers like Machiavelli and Hobbes, and it is the logical basis of the absolutist, authoritarian state; children of original sin cannot be trusted with freedom. The democratic faith must rest on the assumption that in the mass, in the long run, men are fit to govern themselves, and have enough intelligence and virtue to be deserving of life, liberty and the pursuit of happiness. This faith is accordingly

liable to arrogance and shallow optimism, as the history of America makes plain enough. But Wolfe is not guilty of these excesses.

Similarly with another fundamental (if generally un- [185/186] conscious) premise of historic democracy—the assumption that the active type of man who struggles against evils is more admirable than the passive type who endures them. Activism has been the basic tradition of the Western world since the Middle Ages; it is at the root of science, industrialism and democracy alike; it has found its fullest expression in America. The ultimate in this way of life is the Faustian life of Wolfe. Even after he sobered down he clung to its ruling principle, for the wisdom he learned was not the wisdom of resignation. At the end he had the typically American belief that "something should be done" about the evil he saw— something drastic, even to the complete reconstruction of our society; though just what or how he did not pretend to know. Today, however, the very principle of activism is under attack. Like T. S. Eliot, writers are turning to the quietism of the Christian tradition, or like Aldous Huxley to Hindu philosophy. Their attitude may be described as a "failure of nerve," a flight from reality. It may also be described as a rediscovery of the "perennial philosophy," the wisdom of the East. This way of life has an evident value, it worked for thousands of years in Egypt and India, it is recommended in the commonplaces even of Western moralists; and I can see no grounds for absolutely proving its inferiority to the American way. Nevertheless it is more compatible with a caste system than with a democracy. Democracy has logically encouraged a full, free development of human potentialities, and an effort to control circumstances rather than submit to them.

All this is to say that the democratic faith remains a faith, not a self-evident, universal truth. As a faith and a [186/187] hope Wolfe announced it. But this raises the final question about the adequacy and validity of his American myth. More important than the discovery of America, it has been said, was the invention of America. God was once the guarantor, if not the author, of American democracy. The universal moral law to which the founding fathers appealed was the law of God; the "natural rights" of man that supposedly antedated the state were God-given rights; and throughout their history Americans have taken for granted that their manifest destiny was underwritten by the constitution of the universe. (Even their very worldly activities were undertaken in the name of God, for "God helps those that help themselves"—and was notably beneficient to the pious industrialists and speculators of the last century, who helped themselves to a large share of the country's wealth.) Wolfe's catholicity stops short of God. In his lyrical epilogue he does hear a voice speaking of "a land more kind than home, more large than earth," but throughout his pilgrimage he never listened for such intimations of immortality. His actual theme was the transient life of man on this earth—"loneliness forever and the earth again!" His living faith was that man, with the courage of truth, could make a better life. Wolfe was religious only in the intensity with which he sought the truth.

Here again he is restating the traditional democratic faith in contemporary terms, naturalistic and humanistic. Possibly they are not the best terms; this faith has unquestionably been shaken by the decay of Christian faith. Nevertheless we cannot recover the traditional certitudes by a mere effort of will. The fact is that the only religion [187/188] possible for many men of good will is a religion of humanity, a natural idealism. And at least a robust faith is possible on these terms. Wolfe is in line with such thoroughly characteristic Americans as William James and Oliver Wendell Holmes, Jr. Far from being dismayed by their acknowledgment of ultimate uncertainty, they were the more devoted to the democratic ideal; for they regarded the good life as an adventure in an evolving, unfinished world, an experiment that is more hopeful as well as more dangerous because its conditions are not absolute and unalterable—an experiment that both permits and demands freedom. Whether or not it fails (as so many experiments in civilization have failed), we may say that American democracy, in its ideal conception, and even in its limited realization, is one of the great historic adventures of the human spirit. And because the myth has traditionally been allied with religion, we may add that the terms of Wolfe's myth not only permit an epic grandeur but are not, at bottom, so utterly different from the terms of the ancient epics.

Thus the Olympian gods of Homer have a clear dramatic value, but little ideal or religious value. Their constant meddling in human affairs is due to injured vanity or mere caprice, not to any concern for justice. They have less dignity, in fact, than the human heroes, and are treated with less respect by Homer. His men have their own values and their own honor, and they go gallantly to their deaths in the belief that their destiny is Hades— a darkness more tangible than that which Wolfe saw enveloping the life of man. Likewise the historic adventure of American democracy is at least as impressive and elevated as the Trojan adventure that inspired Homer. In our realism and our [188/189] sophistication, we properly make reservations that Homer did not; we are perforce aware that the whole enterprise is also very gross and noisy, and that its most conspicuous motives are economic, not spiritual; and we are then likely to forget its heroic, epic quality. We are the more likely to disparage it because we seldom complicate the past as we do the present. In the fear that we may be living in the twilight of an age, we forget that Homer did live in such a twilight. He was celebrating a glorious past, not a glorious promise—his Achaean civilization was in fact entering the shadows.

We must then add, of course, that

Wolfe was no Homer. The comparison emphasizes not only all the unheroic, inglorious qualities of his work but its incompleteness. At the end he had an exceptionally full sense of our whole situation, a clear image of our faith and our hope; he had not achieved a complete imaginative organization of our situation, an adequate symbolic expression of our faith and hope. The epical promise of America, in literature as in life, is still unfulfilled. "Probably we are still a folk," wrote Constance Rourke, "—an imperfectly formed folk—rather than a schooled and civilized people." Or perhaps we are an unhappy combination of folk and civilization; as a simple folk we might have had our Homer. Meanwhile we remain impatient for outcomes, as we have always been, and may grow weary of the everlasting promise that is always in the future. But meanwhile, too, I should say that Wolfe was our closest approach to a Homer. Given "the billion forms of America" and "the dense complexity of all its swarming life," his life work was perhaps as close as we can expect to come to an American epic.

Hungry Gulliver: A Critical Study of Thomas Wolfe*

PAMELA HANSFORD JOHNSON. For biographical data see "Thomas Wolfe and the Kicking Season" (p. 60). In this selection from *Hungry Gulliver*, Lady Snow examines Wolfe's views of society.

Wolfe recognised the evils of society and was filled with noble rage and disgust by the inhumanity of man to man; but his essential idealism prevented him from perceiving the causes of social disease or from accepting any positive theory as to a means by which the cure might be sought. In a sense he is a symbol of America herself, reflecting more nearly than any other writer of his time the state of mind of a great country faced suddenly with political and economic crisis—a vast country of tremendous potential for social, industrial and cultural expansion, baffled by problems that appear to be without connecting link. Trends of supreme importance flow strongly, but to no convergence. Great industrial progress keeps pace with great depressions; the highest standard of living in the world glitters above a hard stratum of appalling poverty; the unquestionably great contribution of America to the history of democracy, through the War of Independence and the Civil War, is balanced by a history of repression to which the existing labour laws, the fear-ridden life of the Southern Negro and the memory of the Sacco and Vanzetti case bear witness.

More Englishmen understand England, more [**129/130**] Frenchmen France, more Russians Russia, than Americans their own country: in America patriotism appears to be more mingled with bewilderment than in any other land in the world.

Wolfe loved his country with a peculiar and moving personal force and believed in her superb and golden future; but of her complex social and economic structure he had only the vaguest and most troubled of ideas.

He could never, by his nature, have been a politician; his view of men is too near-sighted for that. He sees a character as if he stood breast to breast with him, their faces almost touching; men are to him so huge, so oppressive in their closeness to himself that he is never able to comprehend the forces which move them and which they themselves move. It is because of this inability to understand anything related to the structure, social and economic, of society that at the end he railed against a world which appeared to be none the better for his brief lifetime of railings[.]

. . . .

If Wolfe has nothing in common with Spengler or [**130/131**] with Miller, neither has he with Koestler or Céline. He is not anarchistic any more than were the Elizabethans, with their prodigious and chaotic curiosity. He does not desire the eternal search; he passionately desires a solution. Not to be lost—to be found. The enormity, the richness, the squalor, the wildness and the locked and costive meanness within America tear him to the heart. He is looking for some sort of equation. He dreads the answer, for the very agony of the questioning holds the sum of wonder

* Pamela Hansford Johnson, from *Hungry Gulliver: A Critical Study of Thomas Wolfe* (New York: Charles Scribner's Sons, 1948), pp. 129-134, 151. Used by permission of Charles Scribner's Sons, Lady Snow, and Curtis Brown Ltd.

and beauty; but he cannot rest until that answer is discovered:

> I believe that we are lost here in America, but I believe that we shall be found . . . I think that the true discovery of America is before us. I think the true fulfilment of our spirit, of our people, of our mighty and immortal land, is yet to come.[*]

All his life he was given to saying nothing nobly; but always in the faith that even an abstract nobility was better than no nobility at all, that it was at least a shout of affirmation on the side of the angels. It was not in his nature to contribute more than this to the eternal cerebral struggle to discover for mankind a good manner of living.

His incapacity for practical political thought gave him a horror of being nudged into any direct political action. "What to do?" he wrote to Mrs. Roberts, on April 6, 1938 . . . [131/132]

> Like you, I have become in the last few years tremendously involved with the state of the world—as my consciousness of life has enlarged, my consciousness of self has dwindled; there are things now that so afflict me in the state of man that I think I would take up arms against them, or give my life to stop them— but what to do?[1]

People urged him, he protested in his tone of angry apology, to sign his name to petitions for this or for that cause— on behalf of the Spanish Republic, the sharecroppers in the South, Tom Mooney, the "Scottsboro boys." What should he do about all this?

> The observation of Voltaire in *Candide* that at the end of all the best thing is for a man to tend his garden used to seem cynically and selfishly callous to me, but I am not so sure now that it does not contain much deep wisdom and much humanity as well. Perhaps the best thing that a man can do is just to do the work he is able to do, and for which he is best fitted, as well as he can. And perhaps his greatest service to other men can be rendered in such a way as this.[2]

Perhaps. Yet underlying this conclusion

is this drag of Wolfe's fear that once he became involved in any political movement, he would be caught by the obligations of political discipline. He was, he continued feverishly, always being badgered by worthy people [132/133] to take sides or make proclamations. Many writers and leagues of writers seemed to be tied up in all this sort of thing, and while he "admired their energy," and did not question their sincerity, how on earth did they find time to get their own work done? "One does not write books by carrying placards in front of the French Consulate, or having interviews with President Roosevelt."[1]

These explanations to Mrs. Roberts have the dull ring of self-justification in the face of buried doubt. Doubtless he had no time to picket consulates or talk to the President: yet he could surely have found one second in which to append a signature had he wished to do so.

> . . . I think I would take up arms against them, or give my life to stop them . . .[2]

The truth is that by the spring of 1938 Wolfe was in full political retreat even from those vague points reached by implication. He did not admire for their energy the writers engaged in political controversy; he dreaded them. They were a threat to his passionate isolation, an isolation all the more intense and all the more comprehensible because of his unique obsession with the flight of time. He really did have a sense of being engaged with Time in a struggle to the death. A symbolic painting might have shown him desper-[133/134]ately scrawling away down the length of an interminable papyrus while Time, an enormous eagle, ripped with her beak at parchment and pen, and

[* *You Can't Go Home Again* (Harper & Brothers, 1940), p. 741.]
[P. 132] [1] *The Atlantic Monthly* (February, 1947). [See also Elizabeth Nowell, *The Letters of Thomas Wolfe* (Charles Scribner's Sons, 1956), p. 738.]
[P. 132] [2] *Ibid.*
[P. 133] [1] *The Atlantic Monthly* (February, 1947).
[P. 133] [2] *Ibid.*

flapped her wings about his head to blind him. From this struggle he could allow nothing to deflect him, not even the nag of his own social conscience. He was engaged in cultivating, "at the end of all," not a garden, but the desert of an entire continent. . . . [134/151]

. . . .

. . . His is a young man's socialism, based on the generous rage, the infuriated, baffled pity; like the majority of young, middle-class intellectuals, he looked for "the people" in the dosshouse and upon the benches of the midnight parks. Wolfe's hero, the typical man of extremes, the psychopathic rebel, never makes contact with any sort of organised labour; for him, the protagonists of the conflict are, on the one hand Mr. Jack and on the other the half-starved rotting vagrant crouching in the latrine by Brooklyn Bridge.

A Cycle of Fiction*

MAXWELL GEISMAR (1909-   ) is writing a multi-volumed history of the American novel, of which three volumes have appeared, in one of which, *Writers in Crisis*, he gives over fifty pages to Wolfe. Mr. Geismar also edited the *Portable Thomas Wolfe*. The selection reprinted here is a portion of an unsigned chapter on twentieth-century American fiction in *The Literary History of the United States*. It is presented both as a summary statement of Professor Geismar's view of Wolfe and as the treatment of Wolfe in the standard work on American literary history.

While the meaning of the lost generation became plain in the words of Dos Passos, the phrase itself was given a final twist by a new literary figure, who applied it to "those men of advanced middle age who still speak the language that was spoken before 1929, and who know no other. These men indubitably *are* lost. But I am not one of them." But with Thomas Wolfe, of course, we come to still another "younger generation," those who were raised on internal crisis. The impact of the depression years—"the unending repercussions of these scenes of suffering, violence, oppression, hunger, cold, and filth and poverty going on unheeded in a world in which the rich were still rotten with their wealth"—left a scar upon their lives, but a conviction in their souls. Since Wolfe was a primary figure among these new writers, his career may be used to summarize the entire shift of values that occurred in the thirties.

In Faulkner and Wolfe, too, were represented two poles of the modern South. Born in 1900, in Asheville, North Carolina, and descended from hill people, Wolfe was also caught up in the web of Southern emotionalism so pervasive in Faulkner's work. But while Faulkner seems to work steadily backward, Wolfe's movement is continuously forward; while the older writer explored the dissolving reaches of memory, the younger came to face the dimensions of the future. And while Faulkner marked the final full expression of the aesthetic nihilism that evolved out of the American twenties, Wolfe became perhaps the central spokesman for the artistic beliefs of the 1930's.

In a sense Wolfe's four huge novels, reaching well over a million words, may be considered as a single novel (or perhaps the beginning of a novel, since Wolfe rewrote the childhood episodes of the first volume in a later volume, and this, too, he considered still not a true beginning, but merely "something which led up to the true beginning"). *Look Homeward, Angel* (1929) deals with the early life of the Southern protagonist. *Of Time and the River* (1935) deals with his Northern adventures and first contact with the life of wealth and culture and sensibility: that life "so beautiful and right and good" toward which, as the young Wolfe felt, "all the myriads of the earth aspire"—or at least all the myriads of the American

* [Maxwell Geismar], Section 6 of "A Cycle of Fiction" (Chapter 77), *The Literary History of the United States*, ed. Robert E. Spiller, Willard Thorp, Thomas H. Johnson, and Henry Seidel Canby (New York: The Macmillan Company, 1948), II, 1309-1311. Copyright for Revised Edition, 1953 by The Macmillan Company, and used with their permission.

earth. For this was also the vision of a Mark Twain in Boston, and a Henry James in London, of Dreiser in New York, Cather in Nebraska, and Scott Fitzgerald on Long Island: this is the perennial fable in the national letters of the Provincial and the Magic City. And both *The Web and the Rock* (1939) and *You Can't Go Home Again* (1940) deal with the realization of this vision—and its final inadequacy—and with still another and a new beginning. [1309/1310]

Moreover, this huge novel, multiformed and sometimes inchoate as it was, with its alterations always in progress, formed a central document of the period. Just as Dos Passos reinvigorated the naturalistic novel by means of the symbolist techniques, so Wolfe regenerated the whole tradition of native realism through the electric charge of curiosity, of lyricism, of anger and protest, and perhaps even of pure excitement which he put into it. In fact, he probably carried sheer energy to its highest pitch in the national letters, and this energy became matter. The emotional force of *Look Homeward, Angel,* for example, was materialized in its panorama of the general Southern scene, and, for all the obvious adolescent excesses and limitations of Wolfe's first novel, in the notable central portraits of the novel: those of Oliver Gant and Eliza Gant. Characters: that was one of Wolfe's plain contributions to the American novel—characters who, for all their idiosyncrasies, were by no means merely "eccentrics." It is interesting, too, that the weakest point of a national tradition based on "individualism" and the democratic character should be its indifference to individuals who are neither tycoons nor criminal cases—its indifference, in short, to character. Furthermore, the central conflict of the Gants, between Eliza's outrageous lust for property and Oliver's insatiable hunger for experience—a conflict that is not lacking in the American mind itself—became the central theme of the tetralogy.

The "Fame" which is sought by the artist-hero in *Of Time and the River* is nothing more than a barely sublimated form of Eliza's materialism. And the remarkable quality of Wolfe's unending evocations, descriptions, and evaluations of New York in *The Web and the Rock* is that he catches at once the fascination of the "Enfabled Rock" for the provincial mind, and the provincial's realization that this is not enough. Perhaps no other American has done so well with the first enchantments and terrors of the city. Both here and in *You Can't Go Home Again* Wolfe went, as Scott Fitzgerald never quite could go, beyond the whole glamorous pageantry of "that distant Babylon, cloud-capped and rosy-hued there in the smoke of his imagination."

There was never much doubt as to just whom Wolfe was talking about in these patently autobiographical novels; but the change of his hero's name from Eugene Gant to George Webber was more than a mere change of name. The mature Wolfe was no longer primarily concerned with one young man, however gifted, but with all young men; and not merely with his own experiences in society but with society's experience; not with the "superior individual" of Mencken and Fitzgerald but with Sherwood Anderson's "the general." So it was necessary to return and reevaluate his hero's youth and education—in fact to create a new youth and education. And in the world of the mountain grills in *The Web and the Rock,* or in the microcosm of Libya Hill during the boom and the bust of *You Can't Go Home Again,* [1310/1311] Wolfe did just that, while in the archetypal portrait of Judge Rumford Bland (one of his most memorable brief portraits) he seemed to present a local cousin of the Eumenides. Just as Wolfe's hero had been forced to renounce Esther Jack, the great lady of his provincial fantasies, since "love was not enough," he could now understand both the stature and the failure of the contemporary American writer, Lloyd McHarg, since "fame was not enough." And in the history of the Federal Weight and Scales Company, or in the portrait of "Mr. Jack at Morn," he displayed a notable increase in his satirical power. As a matter of fact, Wolfe would have been, and to a degree already was, a major social satirist.

Still, was it now claimed that he had lost his lyrical gift, by some of those who had earlier claimed that his only gift was the lyric? Probably he had done nothing more eloquent in his earlier works than the passages on New York ("Smoke-blue by morning in the chasmed slant, on quickening the tempo of the rapid steps, up to the pinnacles of noon") and on the rustle of the leaves across America:

'Promised, promised, promised, promised, promised,' say the leaves across America. . . . And everywhere, through the immortal dark, something moving in the night, and something stirring in the hearts of men, and something crying in their wild unuttered blood, the wild, unuttered tongues of its huge prophecies—so soon the morning, soon the morning: O America.

Nor had he done anything less rhetorical than the final words to that New York editor whom he had molded into his "Fox": "Man was born to live, to suffer, and to die, and what befalls him is a tragic lot. There is no denying this in the final end. *But we must, dear Fox, deny it all along the way.*" Where were the provincial accents now? Certainly the path that Wolfe took led him through all the heartbreaking detours that mark our literature from Melville to Dreiser. In July, 1938, after having delivered a new manuscript of more than a million words, he became ill with pneumonia. He died that September.

If he was ignorant and superstitious as the hill folks were, and stumbled into many gargantuan pitfalls—some those of his own making too—he had the persistence and cunning as well as the long legs of the hill people, and he walked with the mountain walk.

[Wolfe and the National Neurosis]*

W. M. FROHOCK. For biographical data see "Thomas Wolfe: Of Time and Neurosis" (p. 69). This selection is the beginning portion of that essay.

Tom Wolfe's great poem rises out of our national neurosis, and his characteristic anxiety state is one that most of us have experienced in some measure. Much of America is still rural. Most Americans feel that they have rural origins. Yet our centers of education and culture, through which in the process of our growth we naturally pass, are as a rule urban in spirit and sensitive to the metropolitan influence. Thus in the case history of the educated American there is a record of the emotional adjustment by which the two cultures—urban and rural—were more or less successfully brought to terms. The city is always moving ahead and the country always catching up, so that the young man coming out of the country to the city crosses not only a gap of miles but also a gap of years. We live as if in two centuries at once and belong entirely to neither; and the boy who comes from the back-eddy of Maine and arrives on the campus of a New England university wearing his first "College Cut" suit knows as well, by instinct, what Wolfe is talking about as if he had been born in the hills of North Carolina.

Home is the place where you were once and where you really belonged, even though as you remember it you were not always happy there; a part of you which should have been permanent, a place to which you could return after a long stay somewhere else. But it turns out not to be the place where, as Frost says,

when you return they have to take you in. It is not in their power to take you in. You [47/48] have been away, having gone with the premonition that you could not come back, and when you try to return the place has changed and you have changed (O Lost!) and nothing is as it has been. You are, in many senses, the victim of time.

If you are from the South, the feeling may be so much the stronger because you are more aware of the differences. (To find a southerner who is not conscious of being a southerner is rare, whereas your Yankee, for instance, has to migrate from New England to discover that the whole world is not populated by people like himself!) And Wolfe was from North Carolina. Yet the difference was one of degree and not of kind. The breath-taking titles themselves—*Look Homeward, Angel; Of Time and the River; You Can't Go Home Again*—point to the vast predicament in which a man finds himself trapped and frustrated because everything ebbs, flows, shifts, and refuses to be seen whole; even *The Web and the Rock* juxtaposes an image of permanence with an image of change. And however much his being from the South dramatized this predicament for Wolfe, the predicament is general. It is a paradox that a nation with as short a history as ours should be as obsessed as we are with the flight of time.

Wolfe himself saw the predicament as both general and at the same time ex-

* W. M. Frohock, from "Thomas Wolfe: Of Time and Neurosis," *The Novel of Violence in America 1900-1950* (Dallas: Southern Methodist University Press, 1950), pp. 47-66. Reprinted by permission of Southern Methodist University Press.

tremely personal. The major part of his effort as an artist went into trying to fix the illusory shiftings of memory before they should become lost. Again and again he spoke of his purpose as being to set down, in the time he had, his vision of life. Now, after all the years of controversy since *Look Homeward, Angel* precipitated the sterile debate which centered so often about such questions as whether Wolfe was "magnificently abundant" or "merely garrulous," the scope of his vision remains the central ques- [48/49] tion about him. As he wrote to his old teacher, Mrs. Roberts, he had the Dantesque ambition to create a universe; he did not dodge the question, nor can the serious reader evade it. Every writer of course creates a universe, in the sense, at least, of having to give his characters a world in which to breathe and live. But Wolfe was self-conscious about doing it. He had ready at hand the characters to people his universe. His concern was to give them a habitation, and this habitation is central to his vision.

One might say that he should have written of his ambition to *re*-create a universe. This would have described more accurately the process of recording a vision of the past as viewed through the distorting lens of violent and tortured temperament. "The world I create," he wrote to Mrs. Roberts, ". . . is always inside me." In another connection he wrote that the process of writing a novel was very much as if a great black cloud had gathered inside him and suddenly burst. He never hid—how could he?—the very evident fact that he was writing about himself; the unnecessary little foreword to *Look Homeward, Angel,* in which he defends his method on the somewhat preposterous grounds that there is much of Swift in *Gulliver,* serves only to show how well Wolfe knew what he was doing and how apprehensive he was, as he would always be apprehensive, of what the critics might say. His material was his own experience, as every new fact we learn about him, every new letter published, every anecdote, drives home. Under the name of Eugene

Gant or George Webber, the figure of Tom Wolfe always stands in the center of his vision.

How completely different from Dos Passos, who was writing at about the same time and, to a great extent, about the same America! Dos Passos' great strength in *U.S.A.* is his ability to maintain his own detachment. As the result of [49/50] a discipline which can be traced through his earlier books, Dos Passos can give his reader the feeling that the events which make up his fiction would have taken place just as surely if there had been no novelist at hand to note them down. His ability to establish his perspective—which he finally achieves by the device of presenting his autobiography as a sort of comment on the fiction—has a great deal to do with the success of his great trilogy. Wolfe is the diametrical opposite. The events of his story derive their meaning entirely from their effect upon the central, autobiographical character.

As Dos Passos depends essentially on a discipline which originated in France during the middle years of the nineteenth century, Wolfe seems to go back all the way to the English Romantics. Given the nature of his talent, it is probably just as well that he grew up out of reach of literary modes, that he read more of Virgil than of the little magazines at Asheville, that no one made him give up Melville for Henry James, that he went to the state university and that he reached the literary hotframe of Harvard only after he was a man grown. He seems never to have played the sedulous ape or to have submitted himself to the current literary disciplines or to have acquired the writer's suspicion of himself, of the accuracy of his own senses, or of the validity of his report on them, which marks so much of the literature of our time. He never acquired the constraining awareness of the importance of technique which has conditioned men like Dos Passos. Literary sophistication simply was not his line: who else could have written, with anything like Wolfe's unawareness of the ludicrous side of what he was doing, his endless variations on lines from Shakespeare? One of his major sources of strength was that he was so completely and miraculously out of date. "I began life," he [50/51] wrote, again to Mrs. Roberts, "as a lyric writer." He ended life as nothing else.

Romantic lyric poetry—and we are agreed that Wolfe's poem is romantic in many ways, including the way of revolt— is the poetry of youth. The greatest praise we give to a poet who in mature years writes lyrics of freshness and originality is that he "seems so young." This strikes me as one of the most helpful keys to Wolfe; his vision of life and the world in which he makes his characters live are the vision and the world of a very young man.

.   .   .   .

The American Mind*

HENRY STEELE COMMAGER (1902-   ) is a noted historian and professor of history at Amherst College. In *The American Mind* he was writing a social history and a history of ideas in America since 1880.

. . . .
The depression . . . made everything that was merely plaintive and precious and whimsical seem dated. It tore the novelists away from satire that was often an expression of superciliousness, and disillusionment that was often too personal, and brought them back to the main current of protest and reform. The situations that had titillated, the crises that had agitated, even the hothouse tragedies that had stirred the readers of *Babbitt* and *The Beautiful and the Damned* seemed brittle and exotic at a time when hunger stalked the land. And as F. D. Roosevelt was closer to Bryan than to Coolidge, or even to Wilson, so the novelists of the thirties had more in common with Garland and Sinclair than with Lardner or Fitzgerald. At least they were no longer embarrassed, as Hemingway confessed himself embarrassed, "by the words sacred, glorious, sacrifice, and the expression in vain . . . There were many words that you could not stand to hear and finally only the names of places had dignity."

Hemingway, Dos Passos, and Wolfe had all emerged in the twenties as Fitzgerald's Sad Young Men, as self-conscious members of the lost generation. Hemingway had, indeed, all but copyrighted the lineaments of that generation in *The Sun Also Rises;* Dos Passos had elegized it in *Three Soldiers* and *Streets of the Night;* Wolfe, a late-comer to the Babylonian scene, had discovered it independently of Paris and Gertrude Stein, as it were, and thus given it a flavor of homespun authenticity. In the thirties, when they reached maturity, they changed in varying degrees the focus of their interest, addressed themselves not so much to the tragedy of their own lost souls but to the tragedy of man's inhumanity to man: Hemingway who at last found a theme worthy of his talent, Dos Passos who discovered that the script of a symphony blown in the wind would never ravish the soul, Wolfe who at the close of his life struggled toward a recognition of something larger than himself. And they were joined by two newcomers: John Steinbeck who worked his way from Sir Henry Morgan's quest for gold to the Joads' search for security, and James Farrell who was sired, as it were, by Dreiser and whose whole attitude toward his own day was expressed in the bitter title of one of his novels—*A World I Never Made.*

Of them all, Thomas Wolfe's quarrel with his society remained [**267/268**] the most personal and the most nearly artistic; more consistently than any other major novelist, he wrote autobiography. *Look Homeward, Angel, Of Time and the River,* and *The Web and the Rock* all indict the society in which Wolfe was so conscientiously and so articulately uncomfortable, yet it is difficult to escape the feeling that what was chiefly wrong with that society was that it was hard on a young man from North Carolina in search of his soul. . . . [**268/275**]

* Henry Steele Commager, from *The American Mind* (New Haven: Yale University Press, 1950), pp. 267-268, 275-276. Reprinted by permission of Yale University Press.

. . . .
What then is the explanation of the minority report which imaginative writers filed on the American economy? It explains nothing to say that they were out of touch with reality: they had taken out a patent on realism. Perhaps it was that American economy had developed so rapidly and so spasmodically that it left little room for the amenities and the artist was more sensitive than others to ugliness. Perhaps it was that the transformation of a rural to an urban economy had been too abrupt and the artist, whose roots in the past were intellectual as well as personal, had failed to make the readjustment. Perhaps it was that the novelists were, almost by nature, protestants: those who were content rarely bothered to write novels to advertise their felicity. Perhaps it was that the novelists, after all, were idealists, that they took seriously the promise of American life, expected to realize the American dream. They were not put off by the shibboleth of free enterprise, for they knew that the great tradition was the tradition of free men. "We must strike once more for freedom," wrote the [275/276] youthful Dos Passos, "for the sake of the dignity of man." And that was what concerned most of those who addressed themselves to social and economic issues—not, perhaps, Faulkner or Caldwell or Lardner but the major figures from Howells to Steinbeck —freedom and the dignity of man. Thomas Wolfe spoke for them all in almost the last thing that he wrote:

I believe that we are lost here in America, but I believe we shall be found. . . . I think the true discovery of America is before us. I think the true fulfillment of our spirit, of our people, of our mighty and immortal land, is yet to come. I think the true discovery of our own democracy is still before us. And I think that all these things are certain as the morning, as inevitable as noon. I think I speak for most men living when I say that our America is Here, is Now, and beckons on before us, and that this glorious assurance is not only our living hope, but our dream to be accomplished. (*You Can't Go Home Again*)

Thomas Wolfe and the Middle-Class Tradition*

WALTER FULLER TAYLOR (1900-   ) is professor of English and dean of Blue Mountain College. He is the author of the standard study *The Economic Novel in America* and of *A History of American Letters.*

During the past quarter century, criticism in the United States has been curiously hesitant about dealing with the persistent middle-classness of much American literature. The impact of the middle classes on formula fiction has, to be sure, recently drawn comment from so acute an observer as Howard Mumford Jones; the appearance of that comment is, in itself, no occasion for surprise. What is surprising is that so long a time should have passed before that kind of observation could be received in an atmosphere free of hostility. Twenty years ago Marxist and other highly articulate critical factions would have attacked vigorously any estimate except a pejorative one of the middle-class tradition in our literature.

Had the criticism of the 1930's and 1940's owned a friendlier knowledge of Main Street, it might have come to grips better with the meaning and the main drift of the novels of Thomas Wolfe, and Wolfe himself might have been less moved to describe the greeting accorded native genius as a kick in the teeth, followed by a kick in the pants. For Wolfe, notwithstanding his occasional role as romantic rebel, was really of, by, and for the social Center. Even in his rhetorical accounts of his personal *Sturm und Drang* he is often enough the sensitive young bourgeois, and his bourgeois provenance grows the more evident as his view turns away from himself and outward upon the perennial human comedy. Large areas of his fiction are in the truest sense *social;* in these areas, especially, his middle-class *Weltanschauung* affords, in one of his own metaphors, a door that opens on an understanding of much that might be carelessly judged anomalous or just rhetorically turgid. [543/544]

With a completeness so entire as to be faintly comic, the life of the young Thomas Wolfe was nurtured, enclosed, and saturated by a middle-class civilization. His father, as a stonecutter, was not only an artisan but a successful small businessman; his mother was owner of a boardinghouse and a dealer in real estate. Their joint possessions, suggesting the family's typical upper-bourgeois position, were probably close to the $100,000 which, in *Look Homeward, Angel*, Wolfe attributes to the Gants in 1912. Their state, North Carolina, was by long tradition predominantly middle-class; the folk of their mountain region impressed Wolfe as "good small people, . . . common, plain, and homely." Like other growing boys of his class, Wolfe could take for granted good shelter, clothing, and food, and could enjoy a score of pleasant small luxuries: iced tea for the Carolina summer or watermelons hauled to town bedded in sweet hay. Like the others, he read such things as the Frank Merriwell series and the success stories of Horatio Alger. He attended a not-too-expensive private school, a practice common enough a generation ago, and he went on from that school to the state

* Walter Fuller Taylor, "Thomas Wolfe and the Middle-Class Tradition," *South Atlantic Quarterly*, LII (October, 1953), 543-554. Reprinted with the permission of the *South Atlantic Quarterly.*

university. The story of his boyhood and youth is in its events and tangible surroundings a typical middle-class biography of a young man whose own talents and energies were not typical at all.

But the unique flavor of Wolfe's environment came not from his social class alone, but from that class as it lived, quite without class consciousness, in a particular place and time—the interior South of the early years of this century. Southern culture dwelt then (to speak of it out of friendly recollection) in a not unpleasing post-Victorian stability, an Indian-summer afterglow from the vanishing nineteenth century. Its habitual ways of perception and feeling arose from a linguistic, a rhetorical, sometimes a classical way of education. Education, whether in an "academy" or a university, still implied first of all learning in the humanities or at most in the liberal arts. Far better than the more formalized and technical training of the present, that literary and humane learning was suited to Wolfe's craving for experience. Still in his early teens, he was nevertheless ready for the awakening to literature he received from the daemonically effective teacher he called Margaret Leonard—"The singing tongues of all the world were wakened into life again under the incantation of her voice." Later, on going to Chapel Hill, [544/545] he was naturally interested both in the pioneer work of the Carolina Playmakers and in the study of formal philosophy. He was, in short, quite at home in a university long possessed of a distinguished humanistic tradition.

In its blending of moral idealism with a recognizable "way" of literary imagining, Southern culture was then at one with and in part the child of the work of the great Victorian poets, whether English or American. If the South had once been Walter Scott-land, it had become Alfred Tennyson-land. For it was Tennyson or Longfellow or more rarely Browning whom the growing youth read on his way up through school, with whom he felt intuitively at home, and from whom he

learned a refined romantic idealism. When Wolfe speaks of the belief of his *alter ego* Eugene in "brave heroic lives . . . the fine flowers of tenderness and gentleness . . . beauty and . . . order, and . . . the goodness and glory of a woman," he is not indulging in mere rhetoric or describing a trait especially unusual. He is, rather, just recording accurately the idealism that Southern post-Victorian youth had from their Victorian predecessors.

Wolfe's own closest imaginative affinity is with the great Victorians, although, curiously, he speaks of these writers less often than of others. His furious restlessness, his Faustian searching, recalls repeatedly the tempestuous soul-history of Carlyle; his bluff humor and violent caricature are almost as Dickensian as Dickens himself. In speaking of the artist as "the language of man's buried heart" he echoes the feeling and almost the phrasing of Matthew Arnold. Through what are presumably his latest utterances—"a wind is rising, and the rivers flow"—he felt, thought, and spoke in the kind of image and symbol which the nineteenth-century poets had made the common possession of men liberally read in the English language. Such similarities are not, of course, accidental, but are the effect, the characteristic shore-shape and scenery, of one continuing stream of culture.

The novelist in his function as an observer of society cannot of course see men and manners in the absolute, *sub specie aeternitatis*. He can use only, whether for worse or better, the particular angles of vision afforded by his own personality, his time, his place, his experience. He observes or overlooks; he observes with this or that emotional coloring according to his own previously established per- [545/546] sonal values, according to the habitual patterns, the creative "matrix" of his thinking. For Wolfe those values, that matrix, were supplied by the life of the middle classes in the interior South before the First World War, by a culture that had adopted as its own the idealism and the imagery of the nineteenth-century poets. Against the essentials of that culture Wolfe, for all his violence of feeling, never rebelled; he remembered it nostalgically and drew from it his deepest strength. That post-Victorian world remained for him the spiritual home to which he felt he could not go again, but which nevertheless he carried with him wherever he went.

From the particular vantage ground of that broad social *via media* Wolfe observed the people on both sides of the economic scale, the very wealthy and the proletariat. He observed with sympathy and friendliness, often enough, but never with any genuine sharing in either social extreme. Never identified with either laborer or plutocrat, he remained always the onlooker, the observer, the outsider. He is the outsider in that delicately shaded scene, in *Of Time and the River,* in which he paints the predawn life of a nameless Hudson River town, with its anonymous train and station workmen, its taxi drivers, its whorehouses and their casual patrons. For all these things are seen not by a participant but as if in a magically quieting and softening light, through a Pullman window from a berth, by a wakeful youth whose real belonging was to another world. However often Wolfe's Eugene might return to the town, plunge into it, submerge himself in it, he remained, like his creator, the visitor from outside, the youth behind the Pullman window.

Often enough Wolfe was attracted to and pleased by the workaday proletariat; he could enjoy the tough adequacy of the city-nurtured truck drivers he knew in Brooklyn. But deep poverty, the poverty of shiftlessness and bestial lethargy, stirred in him chiefly disgust and violent revulsion. George Webber's furious, blind hatred of the slums and slum dwellers in Libya Hill is a hatred belonging to Wolfe himself. Always prone to hyperbole, he outdoes his own superlatives in heaping avalanches of invective on the very poor: on their meanness, vileness, brutishness, and reptilian proliferation. His rage at their "murderous nonchalance," at their "bestial passivity" which "made man less than dung," is unmixed with pity or rational understanding. It is emotion only, the indigna- [546/547] tion of a well-born young man who expected more than that of human beings and of life.

Toward the very wealthy, Wolfe's feelings are more divided, but they arrive at last at a reluctant rejection, a rejection not so much of the people themselves as of the society created by them. If he invests the life of the Hudson River aristocracy with graciousness and a genuine warmth of affection, he conveys, increasingly, a certain emptiness and unreality in it all and turns away from it at last as from so much "Circean make-believe." If, in speaking of the Jacks' wealthy, sophisticated group in New York City, he respects Mrs. Jack's craftsmanship and Mr. Jack's competence in finance, he conveys nevertheless the feel of some intangible corruption permeating that brilliant circle. His antagonism is the sharper, of course, because of his identification with George Webber's embarrassment as a protégé of the wealthy; he resents with George the possessiveness and condescension which could pigeonhole a play with the label "a rather good O'Neill." Here, as with the Hudson River aristocracy, the feeling conveyed finally by Wolfe is one of rejection. How much of that rejection is Wolfe's own and how much that of George Webber or Eugene Gant does not matter greatly. What matters is that it is this attitude, rejection, that the narrative leaves as a precipitate in the reader's experience.

These antagonisms of Wolfe's, which have been dubbed "provincial," are in actuality national and American—historically, traditionally so. In his aversion from either extreme—great wealth or deep poverty—Wolfe is at one with the cosmopolitan William Dean Howells; and, as with Howells, his at-homeness, his central core of concern, is with the people of the middle-income groups. His middle-class characterizations, however, far exceed those of Howells in vividness of realization, in adventurousness, and above all in variety. For it was from these classes—indeed, from his own family—that he drew the painters' models for his various portraits of the Gants: W. O., with his self-pity and his wonderful flights of rhetoric; Eliza, with her massive possessiveness; Ben, with his winsome affection for Eugene; Luke, with his blasts of stuttering buffoonery. From the same middle class he drew into his fiction people as diverse as the remarkable teacher Margaret Leonard, the incalculable girl-woman Laura James, the liquor-headed Robert [547/548] Weaver, the exquisite Francis Starwyck, the elderly, emaciated, and startlingly comical Bascom Pentland, and the very Semitic Abe Jones and his fellows at their metropolitan university. From the same fertile source—to turn to the George Webber series—came the fine Indian baseball player and farmer, Nebraska Crane, the polite and tragic Negro Dick Prosser, the Olympian football hero Jim Randolph, the priestly collegian Gerald Alsop; the Horatio Alger-like Jarvis Riggs; and the inimitably cynical Judge Rumford Bland, who, riding in Pullman car K-19 with the leading citizens of Libya Hill, proclaims them overloudly to be "as eminent a set of sons-of-bitches as were ever gathered together in the narrow confines of a single Pullman car." These people, and more in abundance, make up a populous human comedy so various as to be quite literally bewildering.

In this variety of characterization Wolfe can hardly have aimed deliberately at any social criticism, but the criticism is nevertheless there. Unspoken, implicit, it resides in the variousness and the sharp individuality of Wolfe's people, in their colorfulness and abounding energy, in the conviction and the brilliant completeness with which the author brings them off. The Wolfe gallery of portraits is the entire though uncalculated reply to the charges of dulness and standardization with which Lewis, Mencken, and others were fond of belaboring the American bourgeoisie. Even the more sympathetic

Howells had resigned himself to finding the face of everyday America somewhat drably featured—quiet, workworn, careworn, and homely. But Wolfe, by finding it always lively, often crude and violent, colorful, and above all infinitely various, arrived, without explicit statement, at one of the few really fundamental criticisms of what we glibly call our way of life.

Occasional passages excepted, such criticism remains only implicit in *Look Homeward, Angel, Of Time and the River,* and *The Web and the Rock;* but in *You Can't Go Home Again* Wolfe's observation of society becomes more self-conscious, more apparently calculated. His story deals not just with people as individuals, but with people as their lives are interwoven in some complex social pattern; and sometimes, surprisingly enough, the moral of the story is stated as patly as in an old McGuffey reader. Yet he never became a system-maker, for he doubted the wholeness of the "truths" [548/549] that could be pinned down to logical statement. Learning, to him, was not a formulation of doctrine, but a "finding out something for oneself with pain, with joy, with exultancy, with labor, and with all the little ticking, breathing moments of our lives"; knowledge was "a potent and subtle distillation of experience." Accordingly, in *You Can't Go Home Again,* the experience Wolfe imagines for George Webber is more than that of just grasping an idea; it is that of living himself into a full, many-sided realization of some broad segment of society.

One social area, so realized and lived into, is that of the people at a New York apartment house at the time of Mrs. Esther Jack's party. Near the beginning of the story—in the chapters "Jack at Morn" and "Mrs. Jack Awake"—there are few hints of its direction; nor are there many more in the passages on the apartment-house staff and servants, John and Henry and Herbert and Nora. Gradually, the web of imagined life is expanded; other people are introduced—the charmingly "lost" Amy Carleton, the distressingly perfect Lawrence Hirsch, the entertainer Piggy Logan with his puppet circus. The unscheduled climax, the fire, which acts as the catalyst of the story, intensifies, enlarges, even magnifies it, drawing into it the behavior of the evacuees, the huge activity of the fire department, and the flooding of the subterranean railway tracks so that stalled trains are "backed up to Albany." Now it is commonplace to speak of the complexity, the interdependence of life in a twentieth-century metropolis. But it is something beyond the commonplace to live imaginatively into and through one set of these complexities, to realize with Wolfe's people the "tremendous web in which they felt they had become enmeshed—a web whose ramifications were so vast and complicated that they had not the faintest notion where it began or what the pattern was."

Even more explicitly moralized is Wolfe's sequence on the speculative boom of the twenties and its catastrophic collapse into the Great Depression. It is a twofold story: that of the man Randy Shepperton, and that of the small city Libya Hill. Shepperton, pleasant, euphoric, naturally gifted, a person wholly different from the victim-of-society stereotype, is caught in the intolerable sales pressures exerted by his firm, the Federal Weight, Scales, and Computing Company —or, rather, between those pressures on the one [**549/550**] hand and the depression on the other. Dismissed when he falls short of his sales quota, unable to find other work, he dissipates his moderate resources and finally goes on relief. Libya Hill, caught under the crash of the speculative pyramid built up by the Citizens Trust Company, undergoes panic, a series of suicides, and something close to financial ruin.

The ruin has in Wolfe's account little enough to do with the techniques of production and finance. Instead, it is accounted for on straightforwardly stated ethical grounds. Not merely Libya Hill, but the United States, had gone off the track as long ago as the Civil War. Our common life had developed into "something ugly—and vicious—and corroded at the heart of its power with easy wealth and graft and special privilege." With the individual, deeper than the ruin of possessions lay often the "ruin of the human conscience," the ruin of men "who found out, as soon as these symbols of their outward success had been destroyed, that they had nothing left—no inner equivalent from which they might draw new strength." But these abstractions are not stressed; they are tossed in almost casually. Wolfe's first concern is with his people, with their concrete, objective story, and with the task of imaginatively realizing both people and story in all their intricate relationships.

In both series of episodes—those of the apartment house and of the depression— people, story, and meaning are all seen from Wolfe's habitual viewpoint, mid-American, ethical, and middle-class. From the same viewpoint he saw and reported, though less thoroughly, the mood of the Third Reich in 1936. Long fascinated by the German language and by German culture, Wolfe as George Webber was aware of the sense of power expressed by Hitler's Germany, of the lavishness of the German handling of the Olympic games, of the many evidences of German organizing genius. But he was sensitive also, in time, to a wariness in personal associations among Germans, to an aloofness, to a hostility toward one another in even the most casual meetings, to an insidious psychology of fear that was permeating the entire folk of the police state. He felt that he was witnessing the tragedy of "a great people who had been physically wounded and were now desperately ill with some dread malady of the soul." He felt also that the malady was a tragically unnecessary one. In the apologue extending through "Five Passengers for Paris" and [**550/551**] "The Family of Earth," the dramatic interest may lie in the story of the little Jewish *Rechtsanwalt* attempting to flee the Reich. But the meaning—a moral pointed up with an almost Victorian definiteness—

lies surely in the picture of the friendliness, kindliness, and good will among the five diverse passengers, a friendliness in which all men might meet naturally "if only it weren't for these God-damned politicians."

The art that "carries" observations so wide-ranging as these, so cunningly woven into narrative, and so carefully pointed up each toward a single spire of meaning, does not come by mere chance. It is calculated, and the calculation rests on, or rather grows organically out of, an underlying social philosophy. Such a philosophy, organically rooted in his middle-class inheritance, Wolfe did own and express, although, being himself, he would not express it with the system and clarity of a Jefferson or Franklin.

The clearly patterned answer, the merely rational solution, were in fact always suspect to Wolfe, and he was led by both temperament and conviction to avoid them. Acute observer that he was, he remained also very much the romantic man of feeling, of intuitive perception, convinced that "there are sometimes reasons of which the reason knows nothing." He saw the experience of man not as a simple fixed order but as complexity and ceaseless change. "The essence of reality is questioning; the essence of time is Flow, not Fix." Therefore his views of society do not appear in any geometrically precise pattern, but only in broad and somewhat fluid outline. Nor do those views consist of ideas only, for their deepest roots are emotional; he felt his thoughts before he thought them.

Wolfe was profoundly affected always by a persistent home-feeling, a sense of belonging, an instinctive identification with the greatness of the American land itself and with the abundant energies of its people. No one save possibly Whitman has shown such feeling for "the wild, sweet, casual, savage, and incredibly lovely earth of America," or has so blended with that various magnificence of landscape a sense of the greatness of our destiny. No other novelist has caught so well the force,

the incalculable power of twentieth-century America, the dynamism with which the land and its myriad people, continuously interacting, create the thing "still fierce with life, still savage with its hunger, . . . indestructible and everlasting, [551/ 552] . . . America." Therefore, knowing the vastness and the energy of his nation, Wolfe could acknowledge wihout fear or loss of hope those things within it that he judged evil and thus as enfeebling and destructive. Chief among those evils were the selfishness and greed that had flourished since the Civil War, a selfishness and greed that were creating, on the one hand, the unbearable tensions of high-pressure salesmanship and, on the other, a mood of fear in which men dared not look straight at the truth. People committed to these false values were, in Wolfe's peculiar sense of the word, lost; these forms were dying and must die. Believing so, Wolfe could look on the Great Depression, for all its tragedy, as a liberation of the nation's enduring power from this destructive course, as an escape from a dead chrysalis. Though we were lost in America, we should be found; "the true fulfillment of our spirit, of our people, of our mighty and immortal land, is yet to come."

Such optimism may be emotional, even instinctive; but it is not emotional and instinctive only. With Wolfe it rested on a solid groundwork of philosophy and ethics and finally on his view of the nature of man. It was here—in his answer to the fundamental question: What is man?— that Wolfe broke most sharply away from the prevailing naturalism of the twenties and thirties, with its assumption that man is only an automaton in a mechanistic universe, and its affinity for frustration and despair. Always repellent in its belittling and simplifying of human nature, the naturalistic view of mankind grew menacing when it spawned a spurious primitivism devoted to the glorifying of violence and the enjoyment of cruelty. Hostility toward this naturalistic world-picture, felt as a powerful undercurrent in Wolfe's earlier novels, boils up to the surface in *You Can't Go Home Again,* in his rejection of the atavism that had found its deadliest expression in Hitlerian Germany. When George Webber realized that Hitlerism was only a recrudescence of an old barbarism,

he began to look for atavistic yearnings in himself. He found plenty of them. Any man can find them if he is honest enough to look for them. The whole year that followed his return from Germany, George occupied himself with this effort of self-appraisal. And at the end of it he knew, and with the knowledge came the definite sense of new direction toward which he had long been groping, that the dark ancestral cave, the womb **[552/553]** from which mankind emerged into the light, forever pulls one back—but that you can't go home again.

While so decisively rejecting modern naturalism, Wolfe drew for his own view of the nature of man on other and older springs, on nineteenth-century liberalism, on the classics, and on the Bible. If he did not, like the psalmist, regard man as only a little lower than the angels, he would at least cherish "every proud illusion of the priceless value, dignity, and sanctity of his individual life." And, like others to whom the individual human being is important, he thought habitually in terms of moral choice, in terms of moral good and evil. His were not always the conventional virtues, to be sure; he was not greatly concerned with sobriety and not at all concerned with Victorian refinement. Yet in his pages the moral basis of judgment appears and reappears continuously and expresses itself often in a surprising rigidity of principle. It was because of this rigid integrity that he was so careful to cast his opposition to Nazism in other molds than the half-truths of conventional anti-Nazi propaganda. In confronting so serious an evil there could be no compromise, no trimming the truth to the winds of expediency: "You could not be wrong about wrong." Nor could you afford to escape the conflict with wrong by seeking the passivity of fatalism. You might not be able to deny the tragic doom of man "in the end," but you must "deny

it all along the way." You must actively oppose evil, must work toward conquering and destroying man's greatest enemies —"fear, hatred, slavery, cruelty, poverty, and need."

Wolfe's social *credo* grew naturally, all but inevitably, into another American version of the idea of progress. No other end product could have come from the blending of his passionate faith in America with his sense of the greatness of man, his habit of moral judgment, and his conviction of the need for overcoming embattled evil. The essence of religion, he came to think, is the belief that "man's life can be, and will be, better." And the "better" life is to be created not by collective action, but by the freest possible exercise of the energy and talent of each individual. "So, then, to every man his chance—to every man, regardless of his birth, his shining, golden opportunity— to every man the right to live, to work, to be himself, and to become whatever thing his manhood and his vision can combine to make him—this, seeker, is the promise of America." **[553/554]**

These ideas are, of course, anything but new. Their significance lies in the very fact that they are so entirely traditional. In Wolfe's premises of the greatness and the moral nature of man and of the obligation laid on man to contend with evil, most of the great Victorians, on whichever side of the Atlantic, could have found an acceptable core of belief. Upon that common ground could have met men as different otherwise as Carlyle and Howells, Tennyson and the later Whitman, Arnold and Henry James. For Wolfe's expectation of a progress wrought by the freeing of each man's ability to dream and to do, there is almost embarrassingly rich American precedent from the time of Crèvecoeur and Paine through that of the great antislavery leaders and into that of the Utopian-minded Edward Bellamy and Henry George. These were the common assumptions, these the values that, grown almost into native folkways, permeated Wolfe's middle-class environment during what Van Wyck Brooks has called "the confident years before the first World War." With that environment, notwithstanding his occasional feuds with his family and fellow townsmen, Wolfe remained essentially at one. Its values remained his values; and from that older time he carried over into the tension-ridden 1930's a tonic, nativist social philosophy of activism, of moral integrity, and of hope.

Economic Ideas in Contemporary Literature—The Novels of Thomas Wolfe*

WILLIAM F. KENNEDY (1911-   ) is professor of economics at the University of California at Santa Barbara. The selection reprinted here is the conclusion to Professor Kennedy's evaluation of Wolfe's economic ideas. In the early portion of the essay he concludes that Wolfe grew up in the upper five per cent of his society economically.

▶ • • • • • • • • • • • •

SOCIAL RESPONSIBILITY OF WOLFE

The modern novel can have important impacts on public policy, and society is justified in imposing some responsibilities upon the novelist. Social responsibility differs from social awareness or social consciousness, the latter terms referring to the recognition by the author of the relationships between his characters and society, while responsibility involves the relationships between the product of the novelist and his readers. Primarily, the novelist has the responsibility of giving society fair and honest treatment of its problems. This permits criticism of society but it does not permit reckless, unsubstantiated, and malicious attacks upon society.

In some respects the novelist can be held to the same standards of responsibility as the social scientist. When the novelist purports to be reporting on the social scene he should be required to see the facts as they are, to report them honestly, and not to tamper with the evidence. But this will cover only a small part of the work of the novelist. He is primarily interested in values and is concerned with the social scene only to the extent that it affects values. When the novelist makes a judg-

ment on the effect of some aspect of the social system on values, the social scientist might offer helpful criticism. For example, if a novelist developed the idea that the free enterprise system was faulty in that it blocked the growth of affection in the family because it provided only a low standard of living, the economist could offer data showing the comparatively high living standards attained under such a system.

The novel is a work of art which is something more than a bundle of judgments [47/48] that are verifiable by scientific method. As a work of art, it cannot be criticized as if it were a list of scientific propositions presented in accordance with the methodology of the social sciences. This work of art may communicate something to its readers about the social system, and the nature of this communication is a matter of social responsibility of the novelist. He is responsible for the over-all effects of his art. Is his effect upon the minds of his readers an entirely negative one? Does he create a destructive or completely cynical frame of mind toward the solution of economic and social problems? It is such criteria that Professor Clark has in mind when he appraises a large part of current literature:

Toward the economic system, current literature seems starkly and dangerously negative,

* William F. Kennedy, from "Economic Ideas in Contemporary Literature — The Novels of Thomas Wolfe," *Southern Economic Journal*, XX (July, 1953), 35-50. Reprinted by permission of *The Southern Economic Journal*.

presenting it as an arid waste of sordidly selfish and otherwise purposeless striving. Unsparing criticism is essential to a free system, but this somehow lacks sufficient two-sided understanding to be constructive in effect, and instead impresses one as the kind of criticism that is either impotent, or likely to throw the baby out with the bath. . . . I am not indicting it as a whole, merely registering what seems a widespread and dangerous tendency in its representation of things economic.[31]

The question of how well Wolfe met his social responsibilities as a novelist will be determined by an application of these criteria to his economic ideas. Is he negative, and if so, to what degree? The term, negative, may be used in several senses. In one sense it can be used to mean a failure to provide a positive program, and in this sense it should not form the basis for a charge that the novelist has failed to meet his social responsibilities, for a good novel does not purport to present a positive program and a practicable blueprint for social action.

In another sense negative may mean impotent, that is, lacking in intellectual or moral power or vigor. Professor Clark's statement carries this connotation. In this sense, literature that is esoteric, precious, and limited to the highly personal would be classified as negative. Wolfe does not fit into this category. He has a high degree of social consciousness; he is observant of social and economic matters and does not disdain the humble, every-day work of his fellowmen. In addition, Wolfe explicitly condemns this school of literature. With considerable bitterness, Wolfe attacks some of the "Intellectuals" he knew—Haythorpe, the aesthete, and Collingswood and Spurgeon, intellectuals who ended up as Communists. He also criticizes the fugitives and "futilitarians," giving an excellent portrait of Rickenbach Reade, one such literary fugitive, in his rural retreat.[32]

Are Wolfe's economic ideas negative in the sense that they imbue the reader with despair of social reforms? Or are they negative in the milder degree of having

no application to his times? In neither sense can his economic ideas be classified as negative. Wolfe had his first book published in 1929 and wrote until his death in 1938. This period coincided with the Great Depression, during which there was a great ferment of economic ideas, notions, and panaceas. The underlying attitude of this period was critical of pre-depression institutions and ideas. Readers [48/49] who were influenced by Wolfe's ideas would find nothing in them that would tend to block acceptance of the many changes then occurring in thought and institutions. On the contrary, Wolfe's influence probably aided popular acceptance of many novel enactments under the New Deal.

Wolfe's denunciation of speculative excesses and the unsound financial structure built by the leaders of finance in the Twenties encouraged and supported a public attitude that demanded the economic reforms embraced in the Securities Act of 1933, the Banking Acts of 1933 and 1935, the Securities and Exchange Act of 1934, and the Public Utility Holding Company Act of 1935.

The majority of the voting public that came to feel during the depression that our individualistic political philosophy had been pushed too far and that the times called for social legislation, such as the Social Security Act of 1935, could find support in Wolfe's thesis that the enemy was "single selfishness and compulsive greed." Wolfe's compassion for the sufferings of the poor in the depression was a persuasion on the side of those who advocated an active role by the government in relief of the unemployed.

Wolfe's work can be described as negative in two senses. In the first sense his writing is negative or inadequate on what Wolfe would call the spiritual rather than the economic side. The chief fault he found with the social system was that it

[31] John Maurice Clark, "Economic Means—To What Ends?", *American Economic Review*, Part 2, Supplement, December 1950, p. 49.
[32] *You Can't Go Home Again*, Chap. 36.

gave primacy to economic rather than spiritual fulfillment, but he fails to convey his meaning of spiritual fulfillment.

Wolfe does not submit the matter of spiritual fulfillment to a profound intellectual examination. He seems content to leave it in terms of a nineteenth century statement of the Law of Progress.

And the essence of all faith, it seems to me, for such a man as I, the essence of religion of people of my belief, is that man's life can be, and will be, better; that man's greatest enemies, in the forms in which they now exist—the forms we see on every hand of fear, hatred, slavery, cruelty, poverty, and need—can be conquered and destroyed.[33]

He excuses his failure to think through the problems of spiritual fulfillment because his nature is opposed to the finality of formulation, but the result is that he ends up in sentimentality. At the end of the last book he speaks of a premonition of death and a voice telling him:

To lose the earth you know, for greater knowing; to lose the life you have, for greater life; to leave the friends you loved, for greater loving; to find a land more kind than home, more large than earth. . . .[34]

Whether one reads this as a premonition of physical or spiritual death, it is sentimental and pietistic because it is unrelated to the life and thought which he has built into his novels. It is tacked on to the finished work and does not flow from the materials he used.

Wolfe fails not only to think through the matter of spiritual fulfillment but also to portray a life in his characters that carries spiritual conviction. His protagonists largely feed gross appetites and pursue materialistic goals. Although [49/50] none rises to any great spiritual level, there is an evident spiritual growth that perhaps was cut short by the death of the author at the relatively young age of thirty seven. At times the struggle with the Ego seems strongly motivated by unworthy interests of writing more novels and gaining more fame in order to revenge himself upon his critics.

The spiritual faults of protagonists and author affect the economic observations and ideas of the novels. To discharge his social responsibilities, the novelist must be an honest reporter of the social scene. Wolfe achieves a high degree of freedom from the bias of his social class and economic interests in reporting the facts of the social scene of his time, but toward some of the persons involved there is evident a quality of resentment or even malice. This is directed toward persons of superior intellectual or economic position and sometimes toward classes of people, such as the wealthier Jews or urban Irishmen, who had been conditioned by an environment that was strange to the author. In many respects Wolfe failed to outgrow the backwoods culture of the western Carolinas of his youth.[35]

Finally Wolfe is negative in the sense of the school of modern criticism that holds that the modern artist lives in protest against his society. This school finds Western society dominated by a concern with the exterior life manifested by a striving for things and by a neglect of the interior life with which the artist deals. Malraux holds that true art cannot flourish in our present society because its members are not dedicated to values for which they would suffer poverty, derision, and death.[36] In this view the mass of society goes one way and the artist, another.

Wolfe reflects this viewpoint. He describes the spiritual emptiness of the American people in the midst of their great material progress, and from this he

[33] *Ibid.*, p. 738.
[34] *Ibid.*, p. 743.
[35] After this paragraph was written, Mr. Edward C. Aswell, Wolfe's editor, told me details of Wolfe's life which show that he came to recognize that he had a prejudice against Jews and that he made strenuous and successful efforts to uproot it. Fairness to Wolfe requires a recognition of this personal reformation which would have been reflected in his subsequent work if he had lived.
[36] Andre Malraux, "Art, Popular Art, and the Illusion of the Folk," *Partisan Review*, September-October 1951, p. 495. Lewis Mumford is concerned with this problem and much of his writing is devoted to the attempt to solve the conflict between art and society. See Lewis Mumford, *The Conduct of Life* (New York: Harcourt, Brace, 1951).

argues for fundamental reform of society that would go far beyond the kind of reform effectuated by the New Deal. This fundamental reform would develop a society dedicated to values to which the artist could give complete devotion. The artist would be at "home" in this society, a yearning suggested by Wolfe in the two titles, *Look Homeward, Angel* and *You Can't Go Home Again.*

The City as Symbol*

BLANCHE HOUSMAN GELFANT teaches English at the New York State University Medical Center at Syracuse. She has worked on modern American literature and particularly on John Dos Passos. The following selection is from her study of the representation of the city in recent American fiction.

In defending himself against the charge that he was merely an autobiographer, Thomas Wolfe was led to consider the relationship between the actuality of life and the reality of art—that is, between literal fact and its literary recreation. No matter how literally true to life the novelist may try to be, Wolfe pointed out, his reality must be different from actuality, for "everything in a work of art is changed and transfigured by the personality of the artist."[30] Perhaps the most striking example of how Wolfe's own unique personality changed and transfigured his material can be seen in his literary treatment of New York. New York overwhelmed Wolfe with its multifarious forms, changing scenes, and strange dark polyglot people. But while it held this intrinsic interest for him as a place, it never functioned in his novels merely as physical setting or atmosphere. For Wolfe found in its various and changing scenes the objective correlative to his own volatile emotions as well as to what he held to be timeless and impersonal truths. As he re-created the city, he imposed upon it his personal meanings, so that he moved always from literal transcription to symbolic statement. Consequently, the city that emerges in his novels is a unique imaginative conception, [119/120] for it is a city "changed and transfigured" by the creative processes of art.

As a symbol, the city has an organic place in the pattern of quest that underlies Wolfe's life and work. "Man's search to find a father," Wolfe said, was "the deepest search in life . . . central to all living."[31] The quest for a father, for certitude and wisdom, led Wolfe, as it led his heroes, to wandering; and their first destination was a great city of the North. The city—New York in particular, but also the city as generic—came to be equated with every object of youth's quest; and in time it was equated also with all that youth achieved and with all that frustrated him. Youth's journey to the city is, of course, a traditional theme. In America, it had particular historical relevance to the period of industrialization and rapid urban growth. It is also a timeless theme, for youth is ever in quest. And for each person who undertakes the journey, the theme has personal implications. All city writers reveal in their art the personal meanings that the city holds for them, but some (like Dreiser, for example) try to achieve a typicality which is, in effect, an emphasis upon historical truth. Wolfe emphasized the timeless and the personal elements of youth's quest—indeed he equated the two. Eugene Gant is the modern Telemachus in search of a father. Wolfe attempted to give the quest epic proportions, and the city enters the epic as Proteus, god of ever-changing

[30] *The Story of a Novel*, 22.
[31] *Ibid.*, 39.

* Blanche Housman Gelfant, from *The American City Novel* (Norman: University of Oklahoma Press, 1954), pp. 119-132. Reprinted by permission of the University of Oklahoma Press.

forms. For as Wolfe's violent moods changed, as his insights deepened, and his attitudes took mature definition, the meaning of the city also evolved and changed. . . . [120/127]

. . . .

. . . As Webber–Wolfe thus "lived, felt, and experienced the full weight of that horrible calamity,"[45] the depression, he became at last fully aware of a world outside of, and separate from, himself. All along, he had seen the city as the projection of his inner image. But now, at last, the city imposed upon his mind its own reality. It was a thing in itself, and not merely the protean counterpart of his thoughts and moods. And because it became an objective reality, the city symbol reflects Wolfe's orientation towards a more objective view of life. The jungle image of the city, which expresses George Webber's sobered view at the end of You Can't Go Home Again (as well as Wolfe's own in The Story of a Novel) is far removed from the golden vision of the dreaming young Southern boy. The hopes of a magic city are brought face to face with the horrible reality of half-human men prowling the streets of Brooklyn and sleeping in filthy latrines. This is the image of a desperate reality. One's response to it, George Webber says in You Can't Go Home Again, must not be, however, resignation or despair, but courage. Wolfe himself took courage from the fact of man's endurance, which helped him survive even this "horrible calamity." He affirmed, directly and through his protagonist, his faith in the common people. But this faith was expressed only as an explicit affirmation, for its dramatic potentialities for his art remained unrealized as death cut short his career.

This pattern of social awakening is particularly characteristic of the literature of the thirties, understandably so, since that was the decade of the depression. But there were other expressions of disillusionment with the city that bore the [127/128] more unique stamp of Wolfe's personality. What Wolfe had to say about the awful

desolation of city life was not individual, but his impassioned denunciations, his rantings, and his often brilliant and essential impressions of city people were in his own definitive idiom. He saw the desolation of city life concretized in the "emptiness of city youth" and in the "new look" of the subway riders. The city youth, "poor, sallow, dark, swarthy creatures . . . with rasping tongues, loose mouths and ugly jeering eyes," became Wolfe's representation of a modern kind of "death-in-life."[46] His objection to the appearance of these polyglot people reflects his own prejudices and snobbishness; but also it reveals his feeling that the city deprived youth of the "grand dreams and the music of the fleeting and impossible reveries— all that makes youth lovely and desirable, and keeps man's faith."[47] Passages in Of Time and the River, recapitulated in You Can't Go Home Again, summarize the sociological thesis that Farrell dramatizes in at least eight novels—that a spiritual poverty in the city deprives youth of its grand potentialities. Wolfe saw also in the defenseless, weary faces of the city's subway-riders the same "new look" of desolation, a "horrible, indefinable, and abominably desolate and anonymous look"[48] of men separated from nature and submitted to the violence of subterranean machines.

Wolfe's prowlings in Brooklyn and his observations of the beaten faces of the common people of the city seemed to him to verify his belief that modern man was dislocated and homeless. The city became again his key symbol for expressing his central theme of man's homelessness, aloneness, and alienation; and in expressing this, it became also symbolic of the ironies of time. The pathetic attempts of people to establish a home in the "great No Home of the earth" are revealed to [128/129] Eugene Gant when he visits a young couple in their small rented apart

45 Wolfe, The Story of a Novel, 59.
46 Of Time and the River, 498.
47 Ibid.
48 Ibid., 594.

ment. The transience of city life and the essential homelessness of man are also epitomized by the Leopold Hotel: here the pretence at making a home and taking roots is pathetic as well as ironic. The real condition of man, suggested in the refrain in *Of Time and the River,* is that of the homeless and isolated wanderer in the city: ". . . we walk the streets, we walk the streets forever, we walk the streets of life alone."[49]

This homeless wandering represented also the condition of alienation of the American artist. His quest for a certitude and a spiritual fatherland was doomed to failure in a city that was "the most homeless home in the world." In *The Web and the Rock,* Wolfe stated the futility of the search for a stone, a leaf, a door: "the city the place where men are constantly seeking to find their door and where they are doomed to wandering forever."[50] The defeat of the quest for certitude, which left the artist alone and homeless, was on one level related to the sociological conditions of life in the city, to instability, anonymity, rootlessness, and impermanence. But it was also related to the inexorableness of time itself. Time defeated the artist in his quest as much as particular social and spiritual conditions. And once again, the city became a symbol of Wolfe's frustrations over the brevity of man's time and his recognition of a separate immutable time. The city stands as the rock of immutability: time flows past it, just as the Hudson River flows past Manhattan. Man is caught and carried away in its flowing stream. Though he makes his gestures and thinks he has achieved his ends, he discovers, when his brief time is past, that he has left no mark upon the immutable rock; there is no permanence to his identity.

Wolfe's contest with time was represented in part by his [129/130] obsession with "Amount and Number," his desire to devour all knowledge, to remember all facts, to experience all places and forms of life. This was what he saw as the legendary hunger of youth, and again the city

became the counterpart to his compulsive desire. The city was big enough and varied enough both to stir and to feed this hunger. The metaphor of eating the city expresses this: Youth comes "to eat you [Wolfe writes in *Of Time and the River*], branch and root and tree; to devour you . . . to consume you to your sources, river and spire and rock, down to your iron roots; to entomb within our flesh forever the huge substance of your billion-footed pavements, the intolerable web and memory of dark million-visaged time."[51]

The desire to incorporate the city, also a desire to become part of permanence and immutable time, is, Wolfe believed, doomed to frustration. To youth and to the artist, the city "promises all" but "offers nothing." Actually, however, both Wolfe and his heroes found in the city certain objects of their quest, but they rejected all of them except artistic fulfillment as empty and futile. George Webber, for example, found that love, as he experienced it most intensely with Esther Jack, was "not enough." Fame, as personified by Lloyd McHarg (Sinclair Lewis) was depleting and as barren as the empty pleasures of the rich. Ties with one's spiritual father—Foxhall Edwards (Maxwell Perkins)—were constricting and had finally to be denied. What remained, then, of one's youthful dreams? What was accomplished by man's frenzied activities? What lasted of his turbulent passions? While on the one hand, Wolfe's thought moved in the direction of certain social affirmations, and he pronounced his belief both in his own creative work and in the democratic ideals of America, on the other hand, he saw the frustration of all hopes as time caught man in its stream. This frustration is overtly declared in Wolfe's [130/131] outburst against the immutable city upon which youth, for all his heartbreaking efforts, cannot make any lasting impression: "What have we taken from you, protean and phantasmal shape

[49] *Ibid.,* 155.
[50] *The Web and the Rock,* 229.
[51] *Of Time and the River,* 508.

of time? What have we remembered of your million images, of your billion weavings out of accident and number, of the mindless fury of your dateless days, the brutal stupefaction of your thousand streets and pavements? What have we seen and known that is ours forever? Gigantic city, we have taken nothing—not even a handful of your trampled dust—we have made no image on your iron breast and left not even the print of a heel upon your stony-hearted pavements."[52]

Thus, in creating a modern and personal version of the legend of youth's quest and frustrations, Wolfe used the city as his key symbol. As Proteus, the city underwent constant change. It was the correlative to both dream and reality, to hope and realization, and to every disturbed and turbulent emotion, every awakening idea, every obsession and affirmation that was part of Wolfe's inner life. It was his knowledge and his language, always "changed and transfigured" by his personality. Yet despite the many literary uses Wolfe made of the city, there were certain things he did not do, and to some extent these measure his deficiencies as an artist. He could not bring order to his use of this symbol, just as he could not give order to all the materials of his art. His response to the city was emotionally dictated, so that his symbolic use of it depended upon vacillating moods and irrational changing emotions. He contradicted himself, mainly because he lacked control enough to direct his materials. He moved always in a world of extremes: New York was a "golden legend" or else a brutal, violent jungle thick with stunned and

stupefied man-swarms. He could summarize sociological truths about the everyday life of the city-dweller and his hurt- [131/132] lings through subterranean pathways; but he seldom gave a concrete dramatization of urban manners. He tried to epitomize the city in a single City-Voice or in one inclusive image; but he often did little more than give a gross travesty of Brooklyn speech or create an image which was distorted by his own intemperate way of viewing life. He remained for all his prowlings and his intimate knowledge of the jungle qualities of the city, a giant stranger and somewhat of a snob, proud, in this world of polyglot peoples, of his pure American background. Only in the end, when the objective fact of low urban life overwhelmed him, did the external reality impose itself upon his mind more strongly than his subjective emotions imposed themselves upon the scene. For "Faustian" as was his mood and his hunger, the city was yet more immense than he, and finally it impressed upon him its own truths concerning sociological and spiritual situation in modern America. Wolfe's recognition of man's homelessness and frustrations in the city and of the social injustices implicated in the gross inequalities of wealth places him in the main tradition of twentieth-century city fiction. But his unique distinction as a city novelist lies in his personalization of the city as he "changed and transfigured" it and made it his central, protean symbol.

[52] *Ibid.*, 509.

The Time of Thomas Wolfe*

LOUIS D. RUBIN, JR. (1923-   ) is chairman of the Department of English at Hollins College and a former executive secretary of the American Studies Association. A co-editor of *Southern Renascence* and *South*, both collections of criticism of twentieth-century Southern writing, Rubin has himself studied most of the major figures of the "Southern Renaissance." He recently published a novel, *The Golden Weather*, dealing with childhood in Charleston.

If the novels of Thomas Wolfe show an autobiographical protagonist contending with life in town and city, the battle is waged on a field which, for all its particularities of place, is far from being fixed and permanent. Everything in the Wolfe novels is changing: the narrator himself, his friends, the life going on around him, the towns and cities in which that life takes place. The theme of all the novels, stories, and plays, whether taken as a whole or piece by piece, is man caught up in time, and more particularly, the manifestation of time in the world, which is change.

From the beginning, Wolfe was preoccupied with change. In *Look Homeward, Angel* the members of the Gant family are shown in contrast with time, fighting against it. We see them as they are born, as they live, and as they die, and their finite careers and time-circumscribed consciousness are contrasted with the earth around them, with the history of man, and with the eternity of time-space.

From at least his twelfth year onward, the Eugene Gant of *Look Homeward, Angel* is acutely conscious of change. And in both Eugene and his creator Thomas Wolfe, this takes the form of an intense awareness of and preoccupation with time. Time—its various facets, its apparent con-

tradictions, its limitations, its dimensions —is the central motif of the Wolfe novels. Not only is it implicit in Eugene Gant's and George Webber's life; it is also on frequent occasions an explicit concern of the author. Wolfe discusses it in *The Story of a Novel*, where he finds a contrast between present and past time, which exist chronologically and progress one into the other, and a kind of "time [28/29] immutable," which does not change and which exists in a wry commentary on the changeability of mortal, chronological duration.

The extent to which thoughts of time and change dominated Wolfe's thinking may be seen in certain passages from the four completed novels. At crucial moments in the histories of Eugene Gant and George Webber, the thoughts of time and change appear inevitably, serving to add another dimension to the problem. Before we begin the work of analyzing what time and change meant to Thomas Wolfe, and in what terms he conceived of them, let us examine some of the ways in which thoughts of time crop up in the four novels and in the autobiographical statement of purpose, *The Story of a Novel*.

In this work, Wolfe declares that "dreams of guilt and time" tormented his sleeping hours as well as dominated his

* Louis D. Rubin, Jr., from "The Time of Thomas Wolfe" (Chapter 2), *Thomas Wolfe: The Weather of His Youth* (Baton Rouge: Louisiana State University Press, 1955), pp. 28-35, 43-46, 50-51, 169-170. Reprinted by permission of the Louisiana State University Press.

waking days. He tells of one such dream in which the sum total of all his experience—"my daily conflict with Amount and Number, the huge accumulations of my years of struggle with the forms of life"—would present itself before him:

And the fruit of that enormous triumph, the calm and instant passivity of that inhuman and demented immortality, was somehow sadder and more bitter than the most galling bitterness of defeat in my contention with the multitudes of life had ever been.

For above that universe of dreams there shone forever a tranquil, muted, and unchanging light of time. And through the traffic of those thronging crowds—whose faces, whose whole united and divided life was now instantly and without an effort of the will, my *own*—there rose forever the sad, unceasing murmurs of the body of this life, the vast recessive fadings of the shadow of man's death that breathes forever with its dirgelike sigh around the huge shores of the world.[1]

The passage shows clearly how Wolfe thought of chronological time as existing in ironic contrast to a much greater kind of duration, which did not change and seemed to mock all of mortal existence, limited as that existence was by change and death. Why should the spirit of mortal be proud? he seemed to be asking, and failing to find a satisfactory answer.

In *Look Homeward, Angel* Wolfe speaks of Old Gant as [29/30] having "a tragic consciousness of time—he saw the passionate fulness of his life upon the wane, and he cast about him like a senseless and infuriate beast."[2] And again, "he knew that the century had gone in which the best part of his life had passed; he felt, more than ever, the strangeness and loneliness of our little adventure on earth: he thought of his childhood on the Dutch farm, the Baltimore days, the aimless drift down the continent, the appalling fixation of his whole life upon a series of accidents."[3] Here we find at least three theses about time. First, the past is irrevocable. Second, mortal man lives in loneliness and solitude. And third, what purpose there is in life comes about through chance alone, and man is at the mercy of chance.

The motif appears in all the other novels and collections of short stories. In *Of Time and the River,* as he waits for the train that will take him home to his father's death-bed, Eugene Gant hears the noise of time in the railroad station at Boston, "that sound remote and everlasting, distilled out of all the movement, frenzy, and unceasing fury of our unresting lives, and yet itself detached, as calm and imperturbable as the still sad music of humanity, and which, made up out of our million passing lives, is in itself as fixed and everlasting as eternity."[4] In *The Web and the Rock,* George Webber, looking back on his first three decades, hears a clock strike as he lies in a hospital bed in Munich: "The news it bore to him was that another hour for all men living had gone by, and that all men living now were just that one hour closer to their death; and whether it was the silent presence of the ancient and eternal earth that lay around him—that ancient earth that lay here in the darkness like a beast now drinking steadily, relentlessly, unweariedly into its depth the rain that fell upon it—he did not know, but suddenly it seemed to him that all man's life was like one small tongue of earth that juts into the waters of time, and that incessantly, steadily, in the darkness, in the night, this tongue of earth was crumbling in the tide, was melting evenly in dark waters."[5]

In *You Can't Go Home Again* George Webber discusses with his friend Randy Shepperton his failure thus far to begin [30/31] his second novel: " 'No, I haven't started my new book yet! . . . Thousands of words—' he whacked the battered ledgers with a flattened palm—'hundreds of ideas, dozens of scenes, of scraps, of fragments—but no book! . . . And—' the worried lines about his eyes now deepened— 'time goes by! It has almost been five

[P. 169] [1] *The Story of a Novel*, 62-64.
[P. 169] [2] *Look Homeward, Angel*, 20.
[P. 169] [3] *Ibid.*, 22.
[P. 169] [4] *Of Time and the River*, 245.
[P. 169] [5] *The Web and the Rock*, 674.

months since the other book was published, and now—' he threw his arms out toward the huge stale chaos of that room with a gesture of exasperated fury—'here I am! Time gets away from me before I know that it has gone! Time!' he cried, and smote his fist into his palm and stared before him with a blazing and abstracted eye as though he saw a ghost—'Time!' "[6]

The sketch entitled "The Men of Old Catawba," in the volume of short pieces entitled *From Death To Morning,* states the theme explicitly:

The real history of Old Catawba is a history of solitude, of the wilderness, and of the eternal earth, it is the history of millions of men living and dying alone in the wilderness, it is the history of the billion unrecorded and forgotten acts and moments of their lives; it is a history of the sun and the moon and the earth, of the sea that feathers eternally against the desolate coasts, and of great trees that smash down in lone solitudes of the wilderness.

The history of Old Catawba is the history of millions of men living alone in the wilderness, it is the history of millions of men who have lived their brief lives in silence upon the everlasting earth, who have listened to the earth and known her million tongues, whose lives were given to the earth, whose bones and flesh are recompacted with the earth, the immense and terrible earth that makes no answer.[7]

In the last analysis it is time and nature that provide the permanence in Thomas Wolfe's world, whereas the men who live in it are the victims of impermanence. The Old Catawban living and dying in the wilderness is made and unmade briefly and quickly. He dwells with the wilderness and in it, and the sun and moon and earth and sea and wilderness—"the immense and terrible earth that makes no answer"—all contrast their timelessness to his brevity of flesh and spirit. Even in his twelfth year, Eugene Gant had sensed this in *Look Homeward,* [31/32] *Angel,* when he perceived that the mountains that ringed his home city of Altamont "were the cup of reality, beyond growth, beyond struggle and death. They were his absolute unity in the midst of eternal change."[8] Also in that novel there is an

interesting passage in which Old Gant sells the stone angel, which has for so long stood outside his shop, to the keeper of the town brothel, Queen Elizabeth. He had always wanted to carve an angel like this one, but he never learned to do it. Now he has sold the angel to adorn the grave of a prostitute. As he walks out the shop with Elizabeth,

all life seemed frozen in a picture: . . . And in that second the slow pulse of the fountain was suspended, life was held, like an arrested gesture, and Gant felt himself alone move deathward in a world of seemings as, in 1910, a man might find himself again in a picture taken on the grounds of the Chicago Fair, when he was thirty and his moustache black, and, noting the bustled ladies and the derbied men fixed in the second's pullulation, remember the dead instant, seek beyond the borders for what was there (he knew); or as a veteran who finds himself upon his elbow near Ulysses Grant, before the march, in pictures of the Civil War, and sees a dead man on a horse; or I should say, like some completed Don, who finds himself again before a tent in Scotland in his youth, and notes a cricket-bat long lost and long forgotten, the face of a poet who has died, and young men and the tutor as they looked that Long Vacation when they read nine hours a day for "Greats."

Where now? Where after? Where then?[9]

Here in a moment of cognition Gant has suddenly been made aware of the relentless progression of time, and of how much of him has receded into the unredeemable past. Similarly, in the last pages of *Look Homeward, Angel,* the fountain on the square freezes into an instant's immobility, and Eugene and his dead brother Ben see all time walk along the square before their eyes:

[P. 169] [6] *You Can't Go Home Again,* 387.
[P. 169] [7] Thomas Wolfe, *From Death to Morning* (New York, 1935), 204.
[P. 169] [8] *Look Homeward, Angel,* 191.
[P. 169] [9] *Ibid.,* 268-269. There recently appeared in one of the Asheville newspapers a letter in which the writer reminisced about old times in Asheville and spoke of how kind so many of the old residents had been to him, mentioning some by name. It was not until after the edition [169/170] had been placed on sale that someone realized that some persons named in the letter had been employees of Queen Elizabeth's establishment.

He saw the billion living of the earth, the thousand billion dead; seas were withered, deserts flooded, mountains drowned; and gods and demons came out of the South, and ruled above the little rocket-flare of centuries, and sank—came to their Northern Lights of death, the muttering death-flared dusk of the completed gods. [32/33]

But, amid the fumbling march of races to extinction, the giant rhythms of the earth remained. The seasons passed in their majestic processionals, and germinal Spring returned forever on the land—new crops, new men, new harvests, and new gods.[10]

Once again the earth is triumphant—over all of human history. Races come and go, and the seasons of the earth outlast them all. "Where now? Where after? Where then?" It is the change that is so startling to Wolfe. The sudden look backward involves the momentary rediscovery of elapsed time, and thus a momentary respite from the inexorable wearing away process that is time. In a very real sense, then, Wolfe's fiction constitutes a search for lost time, very much as did the work of Marcel Proust. But while Proust worked out a detailed theory of the time experience, and wrote his great novel according to the theory, consciously structured by it, Wolfe more or less stumbled into the time experience, and never worked out his ideas very precisely.

Wolfe's concept of time is given in *The Story of a Novel.* During the writing of *Of Time and the River,* he declares, he was "baffled by a certain time element in the book, by a time relation which could not be escaped, and for which I was now desperately seeking some structural channel." He envisioned three kinds of time, he tells us. The first was the actual present, in which the narrative advanced and which showed the characters and the events in the act of living and moving forward to an immediate future. The second was the past, "which represented these same characters as acting and being acted upon by all the accumulated impact of man's experience so that each moment of their lives was conditioned not only by what they had experienced in that mo-

ment, but by all that they had experienced up to that moment." In addition, Wolfe described a third kind of time

which I conceived as being time immutable, the time of rivers, mountains, oceans, and the earth; a kind of eternal and unchanging universe of time against which would be projected the transience of man's life, the bitter briefness of his day.[11] [33/34]

It will be noticed that Wolfe's "time immutable," which paradoxically flows unceasingly, provides the backdrop against which the human and historical actions are projected, and against which their feebleness is rendered so obvious. Wolfe's novels, reflecting as they do this comparison, thus assume the form which Edwin Muir calls the "chronicle novel." In that oddly neglected and brilliant study entitled *The Structure of the Novel,* Muir divides the novel form into three main types: the dramatic novel in which the action is most important and in which the time structure is important only as it relates to the action; the novel of character in which the development is in terms of space rather than time and which achieves its progression through the cumulative revelation of character and situation; and the chronicle novel. In the chronicle novel time is not relative but absolute, and the characters and events are presented against a background of steadily elapsing time. Using *War and Peace* as an example of this kind of novel, Muir declares that the speed of time is not determined by the intensity of the action, but rather has a deadly regularity which is external to and unaffected by the characters and situations. The emphasis is on the aging of the characters, "on the fact that they are twenty now, that they will be thirty, then forty, then fifty, and that in essential respects they will then be like anybody else at twenty, thirty, forty, and fifty." Change in *War and Peace,* Muir continues, is inevitable and general, "it is regular, arith-

[P. 170] [10] *Ibid.,* 623.
[P. 170] [11] *The Story of a Novel,* 51-52.

metical, and in a sense inhuman and featureless":

. . . everything may happen; and everything does happen. The action on the human plane does not unfold inevitably; we do not see a drama contained within itself and building itself up on its own consequences; we see life in all its variety of accidents and inventions, marked off here and there by certain very important milestones, inscribed with different figures which designate the march of an external and universal process. . . .[12]

The novels of Thomas Wolfe, like *War and Peace,* are constructed in accordance with this scheme. Eugene and the other Gants change. The earth does go on unheeding. The difference, however, apart from questions of technique, seems to be that [34/35] Tolstoy's characters are seldom very much perturbed by the externality and deadly regularity of the time process. They proceed onward, as the present becomes the past, and the future becomes the present and then in its own turn part of the past, too. Tolstoy's characters exist inside the process, and they view time from within it, whereas Wolfe's novels center around Eugene Gant and George Webber, who are not only aware of time but frequently stand outside of time and are horrified by their plight in it. . . . [35/43]

. . . .
. . . Wolfe was recapturing the past. He describes the process in *The Web and the Rock.* We recall how the coming of spring to New York seemed to make him so bitterly conscious of the contrast between mortal life and the time of the seasons, to touch off all his feelings of futility and failure. He also tells us something else of that time:

The first green of the year, and particularly the first green in the city, had a power not only of drawing all the swarming chaos and confusion of the city into one great lyrical harmony of life, it had also such a magical power over all his memories that the life that moved and passed around him became an instant part of all the [43/44] moments of his life. So, too, the past became as real as the present, and he

lived in the events of twenty years ago with as much intensity and as great a sense of actuality as if they had just occurred. He felt that there was no temporal past or present, no *now* more living than any reality of *then;* the fiction of temporal continuity was destroyed, and his whole life became one piece with the indestructible unity of time and destiny.[30]

Now this supplanting of the present by the past, and the resulting erasure of the bounds of chronology, occurred at a time when George Webber was feeling thoroughly depressed and miserable, and we read on to find that George's woes increased rather than decreased. Relief, then, seemed to come only when this process of remembering the events of the past was taking place. To escape from the harsh and painful contemplation of the nature of present time and of his own impotence in it, George Webber summoned up remembrance of twenty years ago, when he was a child in Libya Hill. "The quality of my memory is characterized, I believe," Wolfe wrote in *The Story of a Novel,* "in a more than ordinary degree by the intensity of its sense impressions, its power to evoke and bring back the odors, sounds, colors, shapes, and feel of things with concrete vividness."[31] The power of "total recall" of the past seems to permit Wolfe to subvert, momentarily at least, the swift flowing passage of time, and to overcome mortal change. We remember the image of the completed Don, in *Look Homeward, Angel,* who sees himself in a photograph taken long ago. For a moment time is erased and the past is recaptured. That this was the method of inspiration for *Look Homeward, Angel* is shown by Wolfe's depiction in *Of Time and the River* of Eugene Gant's activities in France at the time the first novel was begun. He tells of Eugene's stay in the town of Tours:

In a cold, little room in one of the buildings facing on the court, he now settled down, and there began for him one of the most extraordi-

[P. 170] [12] Edwin Muir, *The Structure of the Novel* (London, 1928), 98-100.
[P. 170] [30] *The Web and the Rock,* 541.
[P. 170] [31] *The Story of a Novel,* 31.

nary and phantasmal time-experiences of his life. Day passed into night, night merged into day again like the unbroken weaving of a magic web, and he stayed on, week after week, plunged in a strange and legendary spell of time that seemed suspended and de- [44/45] tached from the world of measurable event, fixed in unmoving moment, unsilent silence, changeless change.

Day and night now, from dawn to dark, from sleeping until waking, in that strange spell of time and silence that was neither dream nor sleep nor waking vision, but that like an enchantment was miraculously composed of all, obsessed as a man exiled, banished, or condemned by fate to live upon a desert island without possibility of escape or return—he thought of home.

For the first time, Wolfe continues, he began to write, and he produced thousands of words, at breakneck speed and at terrible effort. "And in those words was packed the whole image of his bitter homelessness, his intolerable desire, his maddened longing for return."[32]

The result was the material from which *Look Homeward, Angel* was constructed. "Like Mr. Joyce," Wolfe declared in *The Story of a Novel,* "I wrote about things that I had known, the immediate life and experience that had been familiar to me in my childhood. Unlike Mr. Joyce, I had no literary experience. I had never had anything published before. My feeling towards writers, publishers, books, that whole fabulous far-away world, was almost as romantically unreal as when I was a child. And yet my book, the characters with which I had peopled it, the color and the weather of the universe which I had created, had possessed me. . . ."[33] Wolfe was in his middle and late twenties when he wrote and completed the book, and in if [it] he was dealing with Eugene Gant as a child and a youth. Only toward the very end does Eugene grow near toward manhood, and it so happens that these are the weaker chapters of a novel that is generally of a piece, and without any really poor writing. The scenes in *Look Homeward, Angel* are in truth distinguished for "the color and the weather of the universe" in which they exist, and one recalls a remark made by Eugene Gant much

later on, in the story "The Return of the Prodigal" (*The Hills Beyond*), written near the very end of Wolfe's life. Wolfe had finally revisited Asheville after seven years of absence, and to describe the occasion he abandoned George Webber to return to his earlier hero, Eugene Gant. In depicting [45/46] Eugene's return to the mountain country, Wolfe wrote that "suddenly Eugene was back in space and color and in time, the weather of his youth was round him, he was home again."[34] Space and color and time are what are so conspicuously lacking in the later novels about Eugene Gant and George Webber in New York and Europe, and so abundantly present in the stories of Altamont and Libya Hill. It is when Wolfe wrote about the long-ago past that his work took on those dimensions. . . . [46/50]

.   .   .   .

. . . Thus he could get back into a time when, as with the Eugene Gant of *Look Homeward, Angel* in his sixth year, it would be possible to say that "his sensory equipment was so complete that at the moment of perception of a single thing, the whole background of color, warmth, odor, sound, taste established itself, so that later, the breath of hot dandelion brought back the grass-warm banks of Spring, a day, a place, the rustling of young leaves, or the page of a book, the thin exotic smell of tangerine, the wintry bite of great apples. . . ."[41] He would regain momentarily the knowledge, which the child of four had possessed, of "the lone integrity of 'I.'" Proust has outlined his theory as follows, in "The Past Recaptured": [50/51]

. . . let a sound already heard or an odour caught in bygone years be sensed anew, simultaneously in the present and the past, real without being of the present moment, ideal but not abstract, and immediately the permanent essence of things, usually concealed, is set free and our true self, which had long seemed dead

[P. 170] [32] *Of Time and the River,* 856-59.
[P. 170] [33] *The Story of a Novel,* 8-9.
[P. 170] [34] Thomas Wolfe, *The Hills Beyond* (New York, 1941), 121.
[P. 170] [41] *Look Homeward, Angel,* 81.

but was not dead in other ways, awakes, takes on fresh life as it receives the celestial nourishment brought to it.[42]

The remembrance of a minute "released from the chronological order of time" recreates for Proust the human being similarly released to enjoy the minute. For such a person, Proust declares, the word death would have no meaning: "situated outside the scope of time, what could he fear from the future?"[43]

Eugene Gant sensed that if he were to seat himself on the staircase in the dark hall of the house in St. Louis he would be able momentarily to flee the time-world of appearance into the realm of essence: "my core, my kernel—here am 'I'!" Likewise, Marcel Proust felt that through the recurrence of a physical sensation, such as tasting again a *madeleine* or standing on uneven cobblestones that recalled the feel of similar cobblestones in Venice, he would be able to step outside the realm of time for the moment and into the contemplation of eternity.

The sense of recapture, however, is soon lost. "This illusion, which brought close to me a moment from the past, incompatible with the present, never lasted any length of time," Proust wrote. Wolfe spoke too of the moment of awareness going, "going like faces in a dream—coming, going, coming, possessed and held but never captured, like lost voices in the mountains long ago." Elsewhere, however, we have noted that the sense of the long ago past displacing the present, becoming one with it, would last imaginatively for long periods, and it seems to have been during these periods that Thomas Wolfe wrote much of *Look Homeward, Angel.*

. . . .

[P. 170] [42] Marcel Proust, *The Remembrance of Things Past*, trans. C. K. Scott Moncrieff and Frederick A. Blossom (New York, 1932), II, 996.

Whether Wolfe was familiar with Proust's time theories is questionable. At one point in *Of Time and the River* he mentions Proust, but the chances are that if he had really understood what Proust was about, it would have occasioned much excitement on Eugene Gant's part. Nor does Wolfe so much as mention Proust in *The Story of a Novel.*

[P. 170] [43] *Ibid.*

Full Circle*

ROBERT E. SPILLER (1896-   ) is professor of English at the University of Pennsylvania. He is the author of *Fenimore Cooper, Critic of His Times*, and co-editor of the standard *Literary History of the United States*. The following selection is from his book-length study of the pattern of American writing, *The Cycle of American Literature*.

Dos Passos sought to resolve the central conflict of modern living in terms of society as a whole. Thomas Wolfe (1900-1938) confronted the same conflict within a single human soul—himself. Wolfe was even more free of dogma or doctrine than was Dos Passos, but he depended, as did his fellow naturalist, upon the most modern knowledge in his field of interest: for him, psychology. Whereas Dos Passos looked outward to the panorama of moving and changing life that passed before him, Wolfe looked inward and tried to capture, through observation and memory, the essence of its meaning for the artist within him. A realist in his approach to his material, he was a master symbolist in its expression. The sensory impression received through a voracious sensibility had to be paralleled, detail for detail, by subjective reaction and consequent meaning. Substituting the modern view of man and nature for the idealism of the transcendentalists, he revived their organic theory of art and developed a symbolism which bears a close relationship to that of Emerson, Melville, and Whitman. His confusions were those of the naturalistic view of the universe dictated by modern science; his illuminations were those of American aesthetic experience at its best.

It is impossible to separate Thomas Wolfe the writer [263/264] from Eugene Gant and George Webber, the two protagonists of his fiction. The life of his major character is always entangled in the life of its creator and it always derives its power directly from the imagination as the events of experience are reviewed within the creator's mind. Wolfe seems constantly to have tortured himself in his efforts to get his art outside his personality and to find in aesthetic objectivity the meaning of his experience, but it is perhaps fortunate that he did not succeed. His was not the way of a deliberate artist like Faulkner or Eliot. Once wholly outside himself, Wolfe would probably have lost his vision; he could no longer have commanded its unfolding. In the novels in which he thought he had succeeded, he achieved only a philosophical objectivity—only a command of ideas, not of sensation—and these novels are correspondingly weaker than the earlier ones. His art was one with his genius, organic and spontaneous rather than calculated and controlled.

The tendency of all naturalists to write long and detailed autobiographies has given us a remarkably full knowledge of just who Wolfe was, of the events and experiences of his life, and of what he was trying to make of it. In addition to his self-revealing novels, he has left many letters to his mother and others and a long essay, *The Story of a Novel* (1936). The

* Robert E. Spiller, Section 4 of "Full Circle" (Chapter 11), *The Cycle of American Literature: An Essay in Historical Criticism* (New York: The Macmillan Company, 1955), pp. 263-269. Copyright 1955 by The Macmillan Company and used with their permission.

parallel of fact and fiction begins with the birth of Gant-Webber-Wolfe in the hill-entombed town of Altamont, Old Catawba (Asheville, North Carolina), the son of a tempestuous giant of a stonecutter from the North and a repressed but equally violent Southern mother. It proceeds to his schooling, his early loves and hesitant friendships, his stormy family relationships and his romantic dreams, his further education in the University at Pulpit Hill (Chapel Hill), and his final [264/265] revolt and departure from his mountain prison, first in spirit and then in fact, for the North and a writer's career.

The theme of this epic is that of escape, its failure, and the effort to return "home." The cycle of one man's life is therefore the symbol of the basic human cycle from womb to tomb, and the quest for freedom from this earthbound fate is the struggle for identification with the father rather than with the mother. Borrowing freely from the system of symbols offered by psychoanalysis, but putting them to his own use, Wolfe proceeds then to describe his rise and fall in alternate hope and despair.

Eugene Gant is the protagonist of two novels: *Look Homeward, Angel* (1929) and *Of Time and the River* (1935). The first tells the story from birth to the moment of departure for Harvard to learn the art of playwriting at Baker's 47 Workshop, which Wolfe attended in 1920-1922; the second carries him through this experience and on to the wander year in France. As a detailed study of childhood and adolescence, it suggests the romantic *Weltschmerz* of Carlyle, Rousseau, and Goethe. Eugene suffers his own *Sturm und Drang,* his own everlasting nay and yea. His lack of control of these feelings is reflected in the torrent of words that pours from his creative pen, sometimes startling and deeply moving, sometimes revolting in their meaningless rhetoric. It is reported that when Thomas Wolfe once submitted a manuscript to Maxwell Perkins, the editor at Scribner's, he brought it to the publisher's office in a truck; when

Perkins had finished the task of cutting and editing he returned it to his rooms in a taxi. Of such tall tales is the legend of the gargantuan Wolfe made. Anecdote heaps upon anecdote as though he were a Paul Bunyan of the pen. [265/266]

Whatever the cause—Perkins, Wolfe, or the inherent form of the material itself—his first novel has a much tighter internal unity than has any of its three and a half successors. The mother-father complex is understood and constantly present in a series of symbols: the encircling hills and the angel of death, the river and the train, and the recurring trio of a stone, a leaf, a door. "Which of us is not forever a stranger and alone?" asks Wolfe, and Eugene answers with the wailing cry, "O lost, and by the wind grieved, ghost, come back again!" In the death of his brother Ben, his longing to lose himself in another living human being was once and forever thrown back, unanswered, upon him: you can't go home again. "It had grown dark. The withered leaves were shaking." This was his realization of dawning maturity, and the novel was done.

Young people in general read this story with avid interest because the experience of adolescence is here so fully and accurately realized, and then they read on into its successors, only to discover that what seemed like the unity of life revealed through art is lost again. *Of Time and the River* opens with the account of the train trip north, an episode which might well have served as an introduction and background for subsequent events but which runs on to the length of a short novel in itself. Success had freed Wolfe from some of the authority of his editor, with a resulting disproportion of material and feeling. To those who like their Wolfe straight, this is an advantage; but the novel also lacks a compelling central theme. Neither the friendship with Starwick, the love of Ann—"strong, grand, and tender"—nor the recapture of his childhood memories was sufficient theme to hold his spiritual wanderings to their course. [266/267]

. . . .

In the opening of *The Web and the Rock,* a renamed Eugene Gant, now less gangling and more compact in appearance but still huge and awkward, steps off the boat from Europe in the person of George Webber and takes up the life of a writer and teacher in New York and Brooklyn. His job **[267/268]** as instructor in English composition at the fictionalized Washington Square College helps him to tide over the period until the publication of his first novel (about his own youth in North Carolina). His emotional life is soon centered on Esther Jack, the wife of a successful and indulgent businessman, and herself a scene designer in the new theater movement. The novel follows the course of this stormy love almost to the final parting. For Wolfe it is more than the courting of an attractive woman—it is first his absorption and then his rejection of the city as a place of refuge—for Esther is the voice of his needed but unwanted maturity. The events once more are but symbols of his inner quest, even though they are recounted with such detailed and literal truth that the mystic quality which carried the earlier novels is here lost for long pages. Wolfe's newly discovered objectivity which he prized so highly had merely robbed him of some of his emotional and rhetorical power, but when he allows the story to seize him and write itself in the old manner his power returns. The green sorcery of that "final, fatal and

ruinous April" when he parts from Esther conquers him with hate as well as love. After the storm, he finds that again he can utter his "wild goat-cry of pain and joy and ecstasy." With that he remembers through his pain the hills that he had left.

You Can't Go Home Again is Webber's —and Wolfe's—final renunciation of the North Carolina part of his past also. A less unified novel than its predecessor, it contains more of the old Wolfe because, in his friendships with Sinclair Lewis and Maxwell Perkins, he gives of himself with his recaptured egocentric abandon. In the end it is America itself that he turns to as the foreboding of early death seizes him: "To find a land more kind than home, more large than earth—"

Wolfe never quite grew up in the ordinary sense because **[268/269]** he rejected all that Esther Jack and Maxwell Perkins and the city had to offer him. In short, he successfully fought off his own completed maturity; but his loss was also a gain. By holding on to youth to the end, he realized the unquenchable hunger and thirst of life, and his faith in the power of words to resolve the conflicts of mind and heart made it imperative for him to reveal all of himself—and with himself, humankind— more fully than has any other modern American novelist. He was by his inescapable nature the spontaneous, organic artist of America that Whitman had struggled to become.

Thomas Wolfe*

MALCOLM COWLEY (1898-   ) was for many years literary editor of *The New Republic* and is now literary adviser to The Viking Press. His *Exile's Return* is an excellent account of the expatriate movement in American writing in the 1920s, and *The Literary Situation* is a collection of essays studying the problems of the contemporary American writer.

During his early days in New York, Wolfe used to write in bound ledgers opened on top of the icebox, so that he stood at his work like a factory hand. Later he wrote at a table, using ordinary sheets of manuscript paper, but more of them than anyone else with good eyesight, for ninety of his penciled words filled a sheet. He wrote at top speed, never hesitating for a word, as though he were taking dictation. The moment a sheet was finished, he would push it aside without stopping to read it over or even to number it. In the course of filling thousands of sheets with millions of words, he developed a wart on the middle finger of his right hand "almost as large and hard," he said in a letter, "but not as valuable, as a gambler's diamond."

He was not so much an author of books as a member of that much less familiar species, the writing man, *homo scribens*. His life was spent in conjugating a single verb in various tenses—*scribam, scripsi, scriptum est*—with the result that his working habits and problems are even more interesting to study than the works themselves. Indeed, they reveal the works in a rather unexpected light and help to explain why their real virtues were achieved at an inevitable cost to the writing man and his readers.

The first of his problems was how to maintain a steady flow of words from the vast reservoir of his conscious memories to the moving tip of his pencil. Before the flow could be established he would go through weeks or months of self-torture, walking the streets of Brooklyn at night, fleeing to Europe, staying drunk for days on end. Once the flow started, it might continue for months, during which his pencil sprayed out words like water from a hose. "You forget to eat, to shave, to put on a clean shirt when you have one," says Wolfe's autobiographical hero George Webber in *You Can't Go Home Again*. "You almost forget to sleep, and when you do try to you can't—because the avalanche has started and it keeps going night and day. . . . You can't stop yourself—and even if you could you'd be afraid to because there'd be all that hell to go through getting started up again."

Revision formed part of his system too, but not the usual sort of revision that consists in making interlinear changes, then having the draft retyped. "When he was dissatisfied with a scene or character," says his friend Edward C. Aswell, who had watched him working, ". . . he would put it aside, and rewrite it some different way from start to finish." In other words, he had to start the flow over again and continue until he had reached the end of an episode. He would remember new details and incidents the second time, so that his rewritten manuscripts were longer—often several times longer—than the first drafts.

* Malcolm Cowley, "Thomas Wolfe," *Atlantic Monthly*, CC (November, 1957), 202, 204, 206, 208, 210, 212. Copyright 1957 by Malcolm Cowley, and reprinted with his permission.

After being copied by a typist, they were tied in a bundle and put away in the big pine packing box that stood in the middle of his parlor. Then, in the same frenzy of production, he might go to work on another episode, often one remembered from a different period of his life.

His friends wondered how it was that he could reach into the packing box and, after a little fumbling, produce the desired episode, even if it had been written months or years before. I think the answer must be that he had his own filing system, chronological by subject matter. If the episode belonged to his boyhood, it would go below the episodes relating to his studies at Harvard, which in turn went below his years of teaching at Washington Square College and his love affair with Aileen Bernstein, which went below his struggles to write a second novel. All were parts of "the book" into which he planned to transcribe [202/204] all his life, his world and time, in a continuous flow of memories. His ambition, announced by George Webber, was "To use myself to the top of my bent. To use everything I have. To milk the udder dry, squeeze out the last drop, until there is nothing left."

Unfortunately the book of his life was too big to be published or even to be written. His memories would have to be divided into separate books, or novels, and each of these would have to be something more than a chronological series of events; it would also have to possess its own structure and controlling theme. That was the problem of changing flow into form, which always puzzled him and for which he found a solution only in his first novel, as if without trying.

Look Homeward, Angel had a natural unity because, as Wolfe said in a letter to Mrs. Margaret Roberts, his English teacher in Asheville, it was "the story of a powerful creative element"—that is, Eugene Gant, or the author as a boy—"trying to work its way toward an essential isolation; a creative solitude; a secret life—its fierce struggles to wall this part of its life away from birth, first against the public and

savage glare of an unbalanced, nervous, brawling family group, later against school, society, all the barbarous invasions of the world." As always it was a book of memories, but they were shaped and controlled by a theme close to the author's heart, the familiar theme of the young artist in a hostile environment. It had a natural beginning, which was the artist's birth, and a natural end, which was his escape from the environment.

But what could he do after writing *Look Homeward, Angel?* "I've got too much material," George Webber tells his friend Randy Shepperton. "It keeps backing up on me . . . until sometimes I wonder what in the name of God I'm going to do with it—how I'm going to find a frame for it, a channel, a way to make it flow. . . . Sometimes it actually occurs to me that a man may be able to write no more because he gets drowned in his own secretions." Then after a pause George says, "I'm looking for a way. I think it may be something like what people vaguely mean when they speak of fiction. A kind of legend, perhaps."

In 1930, the year after the publication of *Look Homeward, Angel,* Wolfe was looking for a legend into which he could fit everything he had felt and seen after leaving Asheville. Since he was in Europe at the time, and since his strongest emotion, outside of the passionate desire to write another book, was longing for the home he had lost—irretrievably, so he thought, for Asheville people had threatened to lynch him if he came back—he fixed upon the Antaeus legend of the giant born from the marriage of earth and water. He gave the legend a special turn, however, to fit his circumstances. In a letter to Maxwell Perkins, his editor at Scribner's, he explained that the argument of the new book would be:

. . . of the Lybyan giant, the brother of Polyphemus, the one-eyed, and the son of Gaea and Poseidon, whom he hath never seen, and through his father, the grandson of Cronos and Rhea, whom he remembereth. He contendeth with all who seek to pass him by, he searcheth alway for his father, he crieth out: "Art thou my father? Is it thou?" and he wrestleth with that man, and he riseth up from each fall with strength redoubled, for his strength cometh up out of the earth, which is his mother. Then cometh against him Heracles, who contendeth with him, who discovereth the secret of his strength, who lifteth him from the earth whence his might ariseth, and subdueth him. But from afar now, in his agony, he heareth the sound of his father's foot: he will be saved for his father cometh!

Of course the giant born of earth was Eugene Gant again, or Wolfe in person. His brother Polyphemus was intended to stand for the sterility that hates life; probably he was to be represented by Francis Starwick, the homosexual dramatist who appears in *Of Time and the River.* Gaea or Earth was to be introduced in the same novel as Mrs. Esther Jack, but the manuscript chapters about her were omitted from the published book and filed away; later they would figure in *The Web and the Rock.* Heracles the antagonist was to be the city of New York. As for the father, Wolfe's plan was that he should never be seen. But in a final chapter called "Pacific End"—later Wolfe thought of it as a final complete book, though he never got round to writing it—Antaeus was to hear "the thunder of horses on a beach (Poseidon and his horses) ; the moon dives out of clouds; he sees a print of a foot that can belong only to his father, since it is like his own; the sea surges across the beach and erases the print; he cries out 'Father' and from the sea far out, and faint upon the wind, a great voice answers 'My Son!' "

It was a magnificent conception, if slightly overblown; the trouble was that Wolfe was psychologically unable to carry it through. Like Eugene Gant he was gripped by an obsessive desire to say everything, with the result that "all ordered plans, designs, coherent projects for the work he had set out to do . . . were burned up in a quenchless passion, like a handful of dry straw." Soon the Antaeus legend got mixed with others, and the

hero—without ceasing to be Wolfe—was called upon to play cessive parts of Orestes, Faustus the student, Telemachus, [204/206] Jason, and Faustus in love. The more he worked on the book, the farther he seemed from its "Pacific End." By the beginning of the fourth year after the publication of *Look Homeward, Angel,* he had written a million new words, on his own estimate, and the great conception was not so much burned up as buried like Herculaneum under a flow of lava. It was Perkins who saved him, by suggesting how he might make a novel out of one segment of the material, saving the rest for other books. Even then almost half the segment had to be pared away before *Of Time and the River* was published in 912 pages.

The plan he evolved for a third novel was less Wagnerian. As he described the book in a letter to Aswell, who had become his editor after Wolfe left Scribner's, "It is about one man's discovery of life and the world, and in this sense it is a book of apprenticeship." The hero's name would be changed from Eugene Gant to George Webber, and his height would shrink from six feet five to five feet nine; Wolfe was looking for a protagonist whose angle of vision didn't quite duplicate the author's, so that his world could be treated more objectively. Webber would be the eternal innocent on his painful way to knowledge—another Candide or Wilhelm Meister—and the lessons he learned in a succession of adventures would be summed up in the title, *You Can't Go Home Again.*

It was a conception better suited to Wolfe's writing habits than that of his second novel had been, for it was loose enough so that one episode after another could be fitted into the scheme. But already, as he worked on it, the episodes had proliferated and some of them had grown almost to the length of separate books. His immense store of memories was imposing its pattern on the narrative, or its lack of pattern. The bandylegged figure of George Webber was being presented less and less objectively until it became indistinguishable from the author's figure; George seemed to grow taller as one looked at him. By the spring of 1938 Wolfe had once again written more than a million words, which he turned over to Aswell before leaving for the West. Most of the words—too many of them—were published in three volumes after his death. No one can say how Wolfe himself would have finished the novel, or group of novels, or in how much time, or how and whether, if he had lived, he could have brought himself to relinquish all that private wealth of words.

But although he was incapable of solving the larger problem of form, he did solve a lesser problem in a way that is often overlooked. Wolfe's unit of construction was the episode, not the scene or chapter or novel. He always had trouble connecting the episodes, many of which were complete and strikingly effective in themselves. Two of the best are "The Web of Earth" and "A Portrait of Bascom Hawke," both of which were printed in *Scribner's Magazine,* although the "Portrait" was afterward taken apart and fitted into *Of Time and the River.* Other fine episodes are the long passage about the death of Old Gant, written for inclusion in the same novel while Wolfe and Perkins were revising it; the account of the students in Professor Hatcher's (or Baker's) famous course in the drama; the disintegration of Francis Starwick; the story of Nebraska Crane (partly in *The Web and the Rock* and partly in *You Can't Go Home Again*) ; and the visit to Nazi Germany called "I Have a Thing to Tell You." If these had been published separately, from the text of the original manuscripts—as *The Story of a Novel* was published—Wolfe might have gained a different reputation, not as an epic poet in prose, but as the author of short novels and portraits, little masterpieces of sympathy and penetration. But with his mania for bigness, one can't be sure that he would have enjoyed that other kind of fame.

Most of Wolfe's faults as a writer were closely and fraternally connected with his virtues; both resulted from his method of composition. Take for example the fault most frequently and justifiably urged against him: that he was unable to criticize his own work, that he couldn't distinguish what was good in it from what was absurd or pretentious, and that he wouldn't take criticism from others. Wolfe acknowledged the fault even when he was a very young man; at twenty-two he said in a letter to George Pierce Baker, "I admit the virtue of being able to stand criticism. Unfortunately it is a virtue I do not happen to possess." It wasn't that he was lacking either in humility or in critical talent. One couldn't talk with him about books for ten minutes without finding that he was perceptive and discriminating about other people's work, if he had read it. He didn't apply that sort of discrimination to his own work not through inability to do so, as he sometimes said, but chiefly as a matter of policy.

In a sense he chose to be only half of an author. The usual author is two persons or personalities working in partnership. One of them says the words to himself, then writes them down; the other listens to the words, or reads them, and then silently exclaims, "This is good, this is what you wanted to say, but *this!* Can't you say it again and say it better?" A result of the dialogue between the writer and the reader within is that the usual manuscript moves ahead spasmodically—a sentence or two, a pause while another sentence **[206/208]** is phrased and rejected and rephrased, then a rapidly written paragraph, then another pause while reader and writer argue silently (or even aloud) about what has been said, then the sound of a page crumpled and dropped into the wastebasket, then a day's interval, perhaps, then another page that goes better. . . . [Mr. Cowley's ellipsis]

With time always pressing him, Wolfe couldn't afford to stumble ahead by a process of inner dialectic. There had to be that uninterrupted flow of memories from mind to paper; if he once questioned the value of the memories or changed the words that came to him, the flow halted for the day or night or perhaps for weeks. The solution he found instinctively, but later supported with arguments, was to suppress the critical side of his nature, or at least to keep it silent until an episode was finished; then if the inner critic objected to what he had written, he would do it over from the beginning, again without allowing the critic to interrupt. It was an effective system for producing words— very often accurate and truly inspired words—but it involved a great deal of wasted effort for the writer and wasted time for the reader of his published work.

Another fault urged against him is his use of formulas, including stock phrases, paired nouns or verbs where only one is needed ("grief and anguish," "sneered at and derided"), as well as the inevitable and therefore useless epithet. Here again the fault results from his system of writing and is closely connected with virtues that it helped him to achieve. Wolfe composed his novels, or rather the episodes that went into his novels, much as ancient bards, standing before a company of warriors, composed their epic poems. Like them, if for different reasons, he had to maintain an unbroken flow of words, with the result that there had to be moments when his pencil moved automatically while his mind was preparing the next powerful effect.

I couldn't help thinking of Wolfe when reading a passage in Moses Finley's illuminating book, *The World of Odysseus:*

The repeated formula [Finley says] is indispensable in heroic poetry. The bard composes directly before his audience; he does not recite memorized lines. In 1934, at the request of Professor Milman Parry, a sixty-year-old Serbian bard who could neither read nor write recited for him a poem of the length of the *Odyssey*, making it up as he went along, yet retaining meter and form and building a complicated narrative. The performance took two weeks, with a week in between, the bard chanting for two hours each morning and two more in the afternoon.

Such a feat makes enormous demands in concentration on both the bard and his audience.

That it can be done at all is attributable to the fact that the poet, a professional with long years of apprenticeship behind him, has at his disposal the necessary raw materials: masses of incidents and masses of formulas, the accumulation of generations of minstrels who came before him.

Wolfe was perhaps the only American author of this century who could have duplicated the feat of the Serbian bard. That was because he had the same sort of equipment: partly an enormous store of characters and incidents (drawn from his own experience, not from the traditions of the race), and partly a supply of epithets, metaphors, and synonyms (remembered from his early reading) that could be applied to any human situation. His writing was a sort of chant, like the declamation of a Homeric bard.

Poetry of a traditional sort can be written faster than prose, and Wolfe kept falling into traditional poetry. His books, especially *Of Time and the River,* are full of lines in Elizabethan blank verse:

Were not their howls far broken by the wind?

huge limbs that stiffly creak in the remote
demented howlings of the burly wind,

and something creaking in the wind at night.

Page after page falls into an iambic pattern, usually a mixture of pentameters and hexameters. Other passages—in fact there is a whole book of them called *A Stone, A Leaf, A Door,* selected from Wolfe's writing by John S. Barnes—are a rather simple kind of cadenced verse:

Naked and alone we came into exile.
In her dark womb
We did not know our mother's face.

Often there are internal rhymes and half-rhymes: "October is the season for *returning*: the bowels of youth are *yearning* with lost love. Their mouths are *dry* and bitter with *desire*: their hearts are *torn* with the *thorns* of spring." Again there are phrases almost meaningless in themselves, but used as musical themes that are stated and restated with variations, sometimes through a whole novel. "A stone, a leaf, a door" is one of the phrases; others are "O lost" and "naked and alone," in *Look Homeward, Angel,* and "of wandering forever and the earth again," repeated perhaps a hundred times in *Of Time and the River.* All these patterns or devices—cadence, meter, rhyme, assonance, refrains—are those into which the language naturally falls when one is trying to speak or write it passionately and torrentially. They are not the marks of good prose—on the contrary—and yet in Wolfe's case, as in that of **[208/210]** a few other natural writers, they are the means of achieving some admirable effects, including an epic movement with its surge and thunder. They also help Wolfe to strike and maintain a *tone,* one that gives his work a unity lacking in its structure, a declamatory tone that he needs for his effort to dignify a new race of heroes and demigods, to suffuse a new countryside with legend, and to bring new subjects into the charmed circle of those considered worthy to be treated in epic poems.

His persistent immaturity—still another fault that is often urged against him—was not so much a weakness of character as it was a feature of his literary policy. He had to play the part of an innocent in the great world. He had to have illusions, then lose them painfully, then replace them with others, because that repeated process was the story he wanted to tell. He had to be naïve about his emotions in order to feel them more intensely and in order to convey the impression—as he does in his best work—that something as commonplace as boarding a train or writing a book is being experienced not only for the first time in the author's life but for the first time in history. If he had learned from the experience of others, he would have destroyed that sense of uniqueness. If he had said to himself with the wisdom of middle age,

"There must be a catch somewhere," in his exultation, or, "You'll feel better about it tomorrow," in his bottomless despair, he would have blunted the edge of both feelings and made them less usable as memories.

God said in the proverb, "Take what you want and pay for it." That might have been the motto and moral of Wolfe's collected works and of his private life as well. Determined as he was to find words for every experience, he denied himself many of the richest experiences because they might have interfered with his writing, or simply because he had no time for them. He never had a real home after he was seven years old; he never owned so much as a square foot of the earth he loved (even his grave is in a family plot) ; he never planted a tree or a garden, never married, never fathered a child. Much as he loved good company, he spent most of his time alone in dingy lodgings or roaming the streets at night. He played no games, took part in no sports, displayed no social accomplishments. Indeed, he had few amusements: eating and drinking were the first two, and afterward came travel, making love, and conversation, in about that order of importance. He didn't enjoy music, or much enjoy art (except the paintings of Breughel and Cranach) ; he stopped going to the theatre after his quarrel with Mrs. Bernstein; and though he liked to talk about books, I suspect that he did comparatively little reading after he left Harvard. His real avocation was the physical act of writing; his one preoccupation was preparing for the act. He said in a letter to Mrs. Roberts, written a few months before his death:

. . . there is no rest, once the worm gets in and begins to feed upon the heart — there can never after that be rest, forgetfulness, or quiet sleep again. . . . After this happens, a man becomes a prisoner; there are times when he almost breaks free, but there is one link in the chain that always holds; there are times when he almost forgets, when he is with his friends, when he is reading a great book or poem, when he is at the theatre, or on a ship, or with a girl — but there is one tiny cell that still keeps working; even when he is asleep, one lamp that will not go out. . . .

As far as I am concerned, there is no life without work — at least, looking back over my own, everything I can remember of any value is somehow tied up with work.

The price Wolfe paid in his life was not the price of his debauches, which were intense while they lasted, like all his other activities—once he landed in jail and another time in a German hospital with a broken head, richly deserved—but which were occasional or intermittent. He paid more for his one great virtue than for all his vices. He paid for his hours of steady writing, for his sleepless nights, for his efforts to remember and interpret everything that happened, to find a key to it all, to give form to his memories. The price was partly in terms of health, for he was drawing sight drafts against his constitution without stopping to ask whether there was still a credit balance.

But there was also a price in mental health that most of his critics have been too considerate to mention, even long after his death. His alternating moods of exuberance and despair became more extreme; especially the periods of despair were longer and deeper. Many physicians would say that in his last years he was a victim of manic-depressive psychosis.

He also developed paranoid symptoms, as manic-depressives often do. There were ideas of reference and delusions of persecution and grandeur. At times he thought the whole literary world was leagued in a conspiracy to keep him from working. "As for that powerful and magnificent talent I had two years ago," he wrote to Perkins in January, 1937, "—in the name of God is that to be lost entirely, destroyed under the repeated assaults and criminalities of this blackmail society under which we live? *Now* I know what happens to the artist in America." His farewell letter to Perkins was a magnificent **[210/212]** piece of sustained eloquence—130 of his manuscript pages—but in places it was a crazy man's letter. One fine sentence is often quoted: "And I shall wreak out my vision

of this life, this way, this world and this America, to the top of my bent, to the height of my ability, but with an unswerving devotion, integrity and purity of purpose that shall not be menaced, altered or weakened by any one." But the following sentences, which reveal his state of mind, are usually slurred over:

I will go to jail because of this book if I have to. I will lose my friends because of it, if I will have to. I will be libeled, slandered, blackmailed, threatened, menaced, sneered at, derided and assailed by every parasite, every ape, every blackmailer, every scandalmonger, every little Saturday Reviewer of the venomous and corrupt respectabilities. I will be exiled from my country because of it, if I have to. . . . But no matter what happens I am going to write this book.

That is impressive as eloquence, but not as a statement of the facts. Wolfe was planning to write a book that might have hurt a few persons, notably Mrs. Bernstein and some of the staff at Scribner's, but not so much as some of his neighbors in Asheville had been hurt by *Look Homeward, Angel*. Nobody was trying to keep him from writing it. For the author it would involve absolutely no danger of prison, blackmail, ostracism, or exile. "I am a righteous man," he said in the letter, with an undertone of menace, "and few people know it because there are few righteous people in the world." There are many with delusions of righteousness, which they use as an excuse for being unjust to others. Wolfe was becoming one of them, as he must have realized in part of his mind—the Dr. Jekyll part, as he sometimes called it. At this point, as at some others, he was losing touch with reality.

It had better be made clear that his fits of despair were not the "down" phase of a manic-depressive cycle. There was no loss of appetite or vigor, no moping in silence; on the contrary there were quarrels, broken furniture, and a torrent of spoken and written words. The fits did not recur at regular intervals and they were not induced by mere pretexts; on the contrary they had understandable causes, usually connected with his work. As Wolfe said to Alfred S. Dashiell of *Scribner's Magazine* in one of his many letters of apology:

The effort of writing or creating something seems to start up a strange and bewildering conflict in the man who does it, and this conflict at times almost takes on physical proportions so that he feels he is struggling not only with his own work but also with the whole world around him, and he is so beset with demons, nightmares, delusions and bewilderments that he lashes out at everyone and everything, not only people he dislikes and mistrusts, but sorrowfully enough, even against the people that he knows in his heart are his friends.

I cannot tell you how completely and deeply conscious I have been of this thing and how much bloody anguish I have sweat and suffered when I have exorcised these monstrous phantoms and seen clearly into what kind of folly and madness they have led me.

It had all started so boyishly and admirably with his gift for feeling joys and sorrows more deeply than others. He chose to cultivate the gift because it helped him in his writing, and gradually it had transformed his character. At first he was proud, if in a rather sheepish fashion, of sometimes losing control of himself. He wrote to his sister Mabel in May, 1929, "Don't be afraid of going crazy—I've been there several times and it's not at all bad." It was indeed an almost normal state for a romantic artist forcing himself, provoking himself, beyond the natural limit of his emotions. Soon he began to feel the sort of dismay he expressed in the letter to Dashiell, but it was becoming too late to change his professional habits. There were always occasions in the literary life for those fits of manic exultation and, increasingly, of despair—the sense of loss on publishing a book, the insults of a few reviewers (notably Bernard DeVoto), the strain of getting started again, the fatigue that followed months of steady writing, the disappointment when Perkins felt that his latest work wasn't quite his best, the injustice of a suit against him for libel— and all these hurts became more painful as he brooded over them in solitude or drank to forget them, until at last he couldn't help interpreting them as signs that his talent was threatened by a vast conspiracy. His psychosis, if we call it that, was not organic or toxic, nor was it functional in the usual sense of being an illness due to unsolved emotional conflicts. Like the oversized wart on the middle finger of his right hand, it was a scar he had earned in combat, a professional deformation.

Thomas Wolfe*

C. HUGH HOLMAN. For biographical data see "The Loneliness at the Core" (p. 57). The following selection on Wolfe's theories of time and language is from a pamphlet designed to introduce serious readers to the nature of Wolfe's work.

. . . .
The most obvious of Wolfe's strengths is his ability with language. The word has for him unique powers; he was fascinated by language, enchanted with rhythms and cadences, enamored of rhetorical devices. Language was the key he sought to unlock mys- [29/30] teries and to unloose vast forces; he approached it almost in the spirit of primitive magic. This aspect of language he expressed in the paragraph printed as a prologue to *The Web and the Rock*: "Could I make tongue say more than tongue could utter! Could I make brain grasp more than brain could think! Could I weave into immortal denseness some small brede of words, pluck out of sunken depths the roots of living, some hundred thousand magic words that were as great as all my hunger, and hurl the sum of all my living out upon three hundred pages—then death could take my life, for I had lived it ere he took it: I had slain hunger, beaten death!"

Another aspect of his effective use of language is his accurate and vivid dialogue. Wolfe had a remarkable ear for folk speech, and his people speak personal dialects set down with great verisimilitude. His characters sometimes seem to talk forever, but their speech is always marked by distinctiveness in diction, syntax, and cadence. Accuracy, however, is a less obvious quality of their speech than gusto and vigor are. There is a feeling of great energy in the speech of most of them.

The clearest example of Wolfe's mastery of the spoken language is to be seen in *The Web of Earth* but it is apparent in almost everything that he wrote.

He sought, he declared, a language, an articulation: "I believe with all my heart, also, that each man for himself and in his own way, each man who ever hopes to make a living thing out of the substances of his one life, must find that way, that language, and that door—must find it for himself." He sought this language, this tool of communication, not only in the rolling periods of rhetoric but also in the sensuous image drawn from the "world's body," which is a distinctive aspect of the language of lyric and dramatic writing. And here, in the concrete and particularized representation of the sensory world, he was triumphantly the master. It is Wolfe's ability to evoke the world's body which is respon- [30/31] sible for the sense of total reality which his work produces in the young and impressionable, and it is this seeming immersion in the sensuous which makes him sometimes appear to be more the poet of the senses than of sense.

This concern with language, one so great that he might have said of his total work, as Whitman did of *Leaves of Grass,* that it was "only a language experiment," is the logical expression of one of Wolfe's major themes, the loneliness at the core of all human experience. He saw each individual in the world as living in a compartment in isolation from his fellows and

* C. Hugh Holman, from *Thomas Wolfe* (University of Minnesota Pamphlets on American Writers, No. 6; Minneapolis: University of Minnesota Press, 1960), pp. 29-37. Copyright 1960 by the University of Minnesota.

unable to communicate adequately with them. It is this tragedy of loneliness that is at the heart of Eugene Gant's experience and makes *Look Homeward, Angel* a book which can appropriately bear the subtitle "A Story of the Buried Life." The desire to break down the walls keeping him from communion with others is at least a part of "man's hunger in his youth," in *Of Time and the River.* The need Wolfe's characters have for a language with which to breach the isolating walls is very great. In a scene in *Of Time and the River,* Helen, Eugene Gant's sister, is lying awake in the darkness: "And suddenly, with a feeling of terrible revelation, she saw the strangeness and mystery of man's life; she felt about her in the darkness the presence of ten thousand people, each lying in his bed, naked and alone, united at the heart of night and darkness, and listening, as she, to the sounds of silence and of sleep. ... And it seemed to her that if men would only listen in the darkness, and send the language of their naked lonely spirits across the silence of the night, all of the error, falseness and confusion of their lives would vanish, they would no longer be strangers, and each would find the life he sought and never yet had found." There are few lonelier people in fiction than W. O. and Eliza Gant. Each is lost in an envelope of private experience and each tries vainly to express himself—W. O. through rhetoric, [31/32] invective, alcohol, and lust; Eliza through garrulity, money, and real estate. The terrible incompatibility in which they live reaches its almost shocking climax when, in the last moments of Gant's life, they finally speak across the void to each other, and Gant's expression of kindness dissolves Eliza into tears.

Wolfe described the controlling theme of all his books as "the search for a father" —the theme he said he consciously made central in *Of Time and the River* at Perkins's suggestion. But he defined that search as a search for certainty, an "image of strength and wisdom external to his [man's] need and superior to his hunger." In one sense, this search is the seeking for an individual with whom communication can be established and maintained. The search grows out of Eugene's loneliness in his childhood and the sense of isolation which he has in his world. It is intensified by his inability to communicate his love to his brother Ben. In his later life, whether for Gant or for George Webber, it finds expression in the relations established and broken with Francis Starwick, Esther Jack, and Foxhall Edwards, to name only the major figures. About all these relationships there is a recurrent pattern: the new person is approached with eagerness; an intense relationship is established; then a failure of communication and understanding occurs; and Gant-Webber rejects the friendship. The affair with Esther Jack is, perhaps, the clearest example of this pattern. It is debatable whether the idea of the search for the father, with its suggestion of myth and of fable, defines as well as does the representation of loneliness the fundamental theme of Thomas Wolfe, whether that loneliness be described as the search for "a stone, a leaf, an unfound door," as the urge to wandering and the counter tug of home (so well articulated in *The Web of Earth* and parts of *Of Time and the River*), or as the desire vicariously to be one with and to understand "ten thousand men" in the cities, the towns, and the hamlets of America. [32/33]

Here Wolfe's concern with oppositions takes on its tragic overtone. The essentially contradictory aspect of life creates barriers of race, of place, of heritage, of language, and each of us can say with Wolfe at the end of the Gant-Webber chronicle, as he says at its beginning: "Naked and alone we came into exile. In her dark womb we did not know our mother's face: from the prison of her flesh have we come into the unspeakable and incommunicable prison of this earth." Thus, as Wolfe sees it, all human experience seeks the "great forgotten language, the lost lane-end into heaven." Certainly, as several critics have pointed out, there are Wordsworthian suggestions here. Out of some transcendent glory of childhood, we gradually are hemmed in by the growing prison house of the world, the luster and glory of life are gradually tarnished, and we are forced further away from communion. But there are also suggestions of a book which Wolfe knew and praised and whose formlessness he defended, Laurence Sterne's *Tristram Shandy*. Sterne's novel is concerned with the education of the young through the impact of the world outside upon the young mind. It is told through the memories in maturity of Tristram, and it is the associational pattern of those memories which determines the form of the book. At the core of *Tristram Shandy* is the tragedy of isolation. W. O. Gant has in one sense a recognizable ancestor in "My Father" Walter Shandy, who sought in vain for a word to communicate with wife and brother. Loneliness, memory, and time are intertwined in the sad comedy of the Shandean world. And so they are in Wolfe's.

For while the Wolfean character cannot find a language through which to speak, cannot break through "the incommunicable prison of this earth," he is the victim of more than silence and the lack of a language—he is also the victim of time. And the entity time is for Wolfe the great factor in life and in his books, and the only really serious philosophical concept which he uses in his [33/34] fiction. One of the structural problems with which he grappled seriously through his novelistic career was finding a means of representing adequately his views of time, which he saw as threefold.

The first and most obvious element of time, he believed, is that of simple chronology, the element that carries a narrative forward; this may be called "clock time." The second element is past time, the "accumulated impact of man's experience so that each moment of their lives was conditioned not only by what they experienced in that moment, but by all that they had experienced up to that moment." This past time exists in the present principally through the action of the memory, being triggered by a concrete sensory impression which in some way recalls the past. However, as Margaret Church has pointed out, memory in Wolfe merely recalls this past; it does not re-create it or actually assert its continued existence, as Bergson's and Proust's theories of time tend to do. All this action—the present and the recollections of the past in the present—takes place against what Wolfe calls "time immutable, the time of rivers, mountains, oceans, and the earth; a kind of eternal and unchanging universe of time against which would be projected the transience of man's life, the bitter briefness of his day." It is this inexorable forward flow of time, pictured as a river or more often as a train, which constantly carries man away from his golden youth, which is "lost and far" and can exist again only in memory.

Wolfe's problem was the picturing of scenes so that an awareness of these three elements of time was created. In a given situation a man caught in his particular instant in time has it enriched and rendered more meaningful as the past impinges upon him through memory, and he gets thereby a sense of the absolute time within which his days are painfully brief. Wolfe gives this concept fictional expression in his four-part story "The Lost Boy." In the first part, a boy, Grover, passes an initiation [34/35] point in life, as his father intercedes for him with a candy store keeper. " 'This is Time,' thought Grover. 'Here is the Square, here is my father's shop, and here am I.' " The second part is the mother's reminiscence years later about Grover on a train trip to the St. Louis fair. Her monologue ends, "It was so long ago, but when I think of it, it all comes back . . . I can still see Grover just the way he was, the way he looked that morning when we went down through Indiana, by the river, to the Fair." The third part is a monologue by the sister, recounting Grover's death. It ends, "It all comes back as if it happened yesterday. And then it goes away again, and seems farther off and stranger than if it happened in a dream." In the fourth part, the brother, who was a very small boy when Grover died, goes to the house in St.

Louis where it happened and tries by the use of memory to bring back the "lost boy." This section ends: "And out of the enchanted wood, that thicket of man's memory, Eugene knew that the dark eye and the quiet face of his friend and brother—poor child, life's stranger, and life's exile, lost like all of us, a cipher in blind mazes, long ago—the lost boy was gone forever, and would not return." The ultimate meaning of the statement "You can't go home again," which Wolfe used over and over in the last year of his life, is to be found here. "Home" is a symbol of the past, of what has been lost; for the holder of a romantic view of childhood, it is a peculiarly effective and revealing symbol. None of us, it says, can return to the lost childhood, the lost community, the fading glory; for time carries us inexorably away. We can't go home again.

In Wolfe's work this vision of time is always associated with the sense of being alone, of being isolated. In *Of Time and the River* he tries to enumerate the concrete memories which taken together make up the remembered past for America, and then he says: "But this was the reason why these things could never be forgotten —because we are so lost, so naked and so lonely in America. [**35/36**] Immense and cruel skies bend over us, and all of us are driven on forever and we have no home. Therefore, it is not the slow, the punctual sanded drip of the unnumbered days that we remember best, the ash of time; nor is it the huge monotone of the lost years, the unswerving schedules of the lost life and the well-known faces, that we remember best. It is a face seen once and lost forever in a crowd, an eye that looked, a face that smiled and vanished on a passing train." And a little later, he describes the way in which the past almost forcefully entered the present for him: ". . . always when that lost world would come back, it came at once, like a sword thrust through the entrails, in all its panoply of past time, living, whole, and magic as it had always been." It is like a sword

because it cuts sharply and deeply and hurts very much. Perhaps the one emotion which Wolfe describes most effectively is this pain from which comes the sudden hunger for a lost and almost forgotten aspect of life, for "the apple tree, the singing, and the gold." Wolfe succeeds in giving us this sense of the onward rush of time and the death of the morning's gold, an awareness of the price that is paid before the "years of philosophic calm" can come. Since this feeling is very much a part of youth and its pain and *weltschmerz*, its inarticulate melancholy, he speaks with peculiar authority to the very young and to those older chiefly through their memories of having been very young.

Wolfe did not theorize about these concepts of time, or, except in passing, discuss them. He probably did not know the works of Proust at all well, despite the degree to which the sense impressions in the present restored the lost past for both of them. Karin Pfister has suggested that Wolfe's time theories may owe something to those of Bergson, to whom Proust was also a debtor. As a novelist Wolfe seemingly was fascinated by the mystery rather than the metaphysics of time. In *The Web and the Rock* he wrote: "Time is a fable and a mystery . . . It broods over all [**36/37**] the images of earth . . . Time is collected in great clocks and hung in towers . . . and each man has his own, a different time."

The river and the ocean he used as large symbols for "time immutable," yet his clearest figure for the ceaseless motion and the inexorable passage of time is the train. No American in the past fifty years has been more the poet of trains. Their rushing across the face of the earth, the glimpses of life to be seen flashing past their speeding windows, the nostalgic and lonely wail of their whistles in the night, even their sounds echoing in depots, which in *Of Time and the River* he imagines to be the very sounds of time itself—all these characteristics Wolfe associates with loneliness and movement and the sad passage of time.

Literature and Western Man*

J . B . P R I E S T L E Y (1894-   ) is a prolific and popular British novelist and critic, his work best known in America being *Good Companions*. The selection reprinted here is the conclusion to his study of literature in the Western world.

.   .   .   .

The last of these four [The other three are Fitzgerald, Hemingway, and Faulkner.]—and the youngest: he was born in 1900 and died in 1938—is Thomas Wolfe. He was a gigantic young man, who wrote —and indeed did everything—gigantically, and his weaknesses, faults, deficiencies, are to scale. He is all too easy to criticise adversely, and this probably explains why he has had rather more than his share of such criticism. He never learnt how to construct a novel, nor indeed even how to keep a narrative going, for he runs to vast length not so much because he goes on and on and on as because he tends to hold a scene and go in and in and in. He is monstrously rhetorical and oratorical, as if a dozen old-fashioned Southern politicians and a dozen jugs of corn whisky were at work in him. Like a bewildered but raging adolescent, trying to grasp the whole world, he seizes hold of everything and bangs about, crying in effect—like the old *Punch* parody of Marie Corelli—"I'm sure there is a Something Somewhere if we could only find it." There was so much thinly-disguised autobiography in his vast chronicles, and he was himself so demanding, over-sized and demonic, that he seemed for ever in trouble, living in a permanent storm centre. He was never at home anywhere, always discovering something alien and sinister in the environment, whether it was Asheville or Harvard, London or New York, Paris or Brooklyn, always hurrying away from some evil he could not define towards some ultimate good he could never reach. As if he belonged to some giant race that lived two hundred years and did not come of age until sixty-five, he remained to the end hopefully, despairingly, furiously young. Yet not without acquiring a little wisdom on the way, rather more [438/ 439] perhaps than his fellow novelists, as we may discover from his last letter to 'Fox' in *You Can't Go Home Again;* this in its denial of pessimistic and fatalistic conservatism says something infinitely worth saying, once and for all: "Man was born to live, to suffer, and to die, and what befalls him is a tragic lot. There is no denying this in the final end. *But we must, dear Fox, deny it all along the way.*"

The truth is that, once his limitations are accepted, Wolfe is one of the most satisfying and rewarding of all these American novelists. It is not only that his scene is big, as indeed it is, but that he explores the scene with a wonderful eye and ear, with astonishing thoroughness, often taking us to a great depth. Because he invented so little, shaped and cut so little, drove himself so hard while he was writing, he was able to give life, down to the last flicker or whisper, to an amazing range of scenes. We may always feel his own presence in them, always be aware of a romantic-fantastic element in their presentation, but this is more than compensated for by the sheer vitality, the

* J. B. Priestley, from *Literature and Western Man* (New York: Harper and Brothers, 1960), pp. 438-440. Copyright © 1960 by J. B. Priestley. Reprinted by permission of Harper and Brothers and William Heinemann Ltd.

abundance and richness of life, the poetic truth he attains. He may seem wilder, more grotesque, when he is among the literary and theatrical groups on the 'Enfabled Rock' of New York than when he is among his own mountain folk; but behind his shout of defiance and derision, his huge slashing caricatures of New York personalities, there is still a kind of poetic truth that compels us to remember his New York when we have long forgotten other men's. He is always surprising us, for he might seem to be the last man to go lumbering among the delicate expatriates, following Fitzgerald, yet is there anybody and anything in Fitzgerald as solidly created, as subtly observed, as Starwick and the scenes that contain him in *Of Time and the River?* And he has episode after episode, like that week-end in the mansion above the Hudson, that carry their vitality so deep into the memory that they seem like our own experiences. American intellectuals, suspicious of his exuberance and underlying romanticism, should never sneer at this writer, for, to us who are not Americans but know the place and the people, Wolfe is one of the small and invaluable company of essentially American creators, one of its huge, wild, shaggy poets whose creations, which have nothing of Europe in them, release in us the wonder, fear and affection we have felt so often as visitors to the American scene. And Wolfe's [**439/440**] faults can be forgiven him, if only because they are mostly the result of a frenzied feeling of time hurrying by. A man's unconscious often knows the secrets of his body, is at least dimly aware of its span of life; and if Wolfe wrote too much too fast, cried to us too often out of bewilderment, confusion, despair, perhaps he too, with unconscious

awareness arriving as premonition, recognised that he had to do so much in so little time: he died at the age of thirty-eight. He at least did not refuse the chance to mature; he never really had the chance; he remains one of the few major *young* writers of this age, a giant of the morning; and everything about him, faulty and over-youthful, candid and vital and endearing, belongs essentially to an America that is itself still a giant of the morning. And indeed any America that shrugs him away, forgetting what he did and tried to do, will be smaller, older, closer to death, even though it may never have lived—as its major novelists, accepting their maturity, might have taught it to live—in the glowing serenity of the afternoon.

So Tom Wolfe, whom we remember so towering and awkward, so eager and alive, and who vanished so soon, is the last writer in this long procession. He is not a bad final choice. He nearly tore himself to pieces trying, as a good writer must, to get everything down on paper, all the sights and the sounds and the smells and the moods and the people, hundreds of them, in the land that now has most power, most wealth, most influence. And there was his wise last word: *But we must, dear Fox, deny it all along the way.* No matter how piercing and appalling his insights, the desolation creeping over his outer world, the lurid lights and shadows of his inner world, the writer must live with hope, work in faith. What literature, which is still concerned with Man himself, with persons and not with statistical units, must deny, if necessary against all evidence and reason, is the ultimate despair, the central place of darkness from which the last gleam of nobility and wisdom has gone.

Suggested Topics for Controlled Research

The materials in this anthology consist of selections by Thomas Wolfe and critical statements dealing with some of the issues which he raises in *The Story of a Novel,* the central document of the collection. To *The Story of a Novel* Wolfe's first novel *Look Homeward, Angel* should be added as a central document; were it not for its great length it would have been included in the anthology. The serious student certainly should be familiar with Wolfe's work—all of it, if possible—but at least *Look Homeward, Angel* and *You Can't Go Home Again,* which represent the early and the late works, if no others.

The materials about Wolfe are grouped into four sections: Part Two, on Wolfe's writing methods; Part Three, reviews of *Look Homeward, Angel;* Part Four, on the characteristics of Wolfe's style; and Part Five, consisting of critiques of Wolfe's work, his themes, his artistic objectives, and his sense of form. To a certain extent the classification of materials in Part Two, Part Three, and Part Four has been arbitrary; for discussions of Wolfe's writing methods, of his style, and of *Look Homeward, Angel* appear in a number of the essays included in Part Five, although they are not dominant in these essays as they are in the selections in the earlier Parts.

These materials lend themselves to two quite distinct uses for the purposes of controlled research. One of these uses is as a body of materials for the study of Thomas Wolfe as a writer; the other is for the study of critical methods and assumptions through an examination of their application to Wolfe.

I have attempted in the introduction to the anthology to suggest some fruitful ways of looking at the world or worlds of Thomas Wolfe. *The Story of a Novel* presents Wolfe's own view of his world and his intention and methods in articulating it in works of fiction. The essays take up most of the issues and present a variety of attitudes toward them. One primary objective of this anthology will be served if you are led to explore the issues Wolfe raises, such as the American attitudes toward writers, the writing of *Look Homeward, Angel* and *Of Time and the River,* the problem of being a promising writer, the question of the use of autobiographical material in fiction, the ideal place in which to work, Wolfe's discovery of America, his dreams of Guilt and Time, Perkins's part as editor, the search for an adequate language, the search for an adequate form, the position of the artist in America. Upon these—and similar questions—Wolfe himself gives testimony and the other writers here represented supply additional facts and opinions. The raw data for many essays on Wolfe as a writer are to be found here.

The other use of this material, for the examination of certain critical methods and assumptions, employs Wolfe as a control or standard by which his critics may be judged. The critiques included represent wide variations of opinion on a number of aspects of Wolfe's work. A reading of this body of material should make it clear to the thoughtful student that intelligent men who are trained readers do not always see the same things when they look at the same works of art. The reason is simple. A work of art is a world in microcosm, a created universe, instinct with its own life and obeying its own principles. A critic's comments on that work are restricted and reducing views of limited aspects of its complex totality. The critic points out certain things that he sees, but by the very act of pointing them out excludes other things in order that we may see more clearly. He imposes on the work what Allen Tate once called "provisional frames of reference" (*The Forlorn Demon* [Chicago, 1953], p. 162). It is obvious that Maurice Natanson, in his essay on

Wolfe's rhetoric, is employing a "provisional frame of reference" which he calls "the New Rhetoric" as a means of getting at the essence of Wolfe's style; Pamela Johnson uses a different "frame of reference" to get at the same style; yet we can be confident that both critics are talking about the same writer. Thus, too, William Kennedy uses a frame of economic ideas, Edgar Johnson a frame of satire, Bella Kussy a frame of philosophical thought, Herbert Muller a frame of myth. One way to see this aspect of criticism is to attempt to determine just what "provisional frames of reference" the critics are employing. An essay analyzing and classifying these "frames" would be useful and instructive.

A study of Wolfe's writing methods and the reactions of differing critics to them would make a good essay. *The Story of a Novel* would be basic, of course, with the comments of Maxwell Perkins and Edward Aswell and the essays by DeVoto, Cowley, Bishop, and others supplying additional information and opinion.

The question of Wolfe's relation to the social issues of his age is a much debated one, and several differing opinions are given in these selections. The comments of writers like Commager, Taylor, Pamela Johnson, Edgar Johnson, Burgum, Muller, and Kussy would be among those to be examined on this issue.

In *Sartor Resartus* (Book II, Chapter IX), Thomas Carlyle wrote: "'America is here or nowhere' . . . Yes here, in this poor, miserable, hampered, despicable Actual, wherein thou even now standest, here or nowhere is thy Ideal." For Wolfe America seems to have had something of this symbolic value. How effectively does he realize it? What America is it that he represents? Is it Taylor's middle-class America? Burgum's normal, average American boy's America? Or is his the young man's uninformed socialism that Pamela

Johnson sees him as having? And how do the critics' own social views seem to affect their estimates of Wolfe? How disinterested do Burgum, Kennedy, Geismar, Priestley, and the others seem to be?

One of the principal means by which the critic attempts to express qualities and aspects of a work of art is by analogy to other works which he assumes the reader to be familiar with. The critics here represented have pointed to a number of writers and works that are in certain ways analogous to Wolfe and his works. Walt Whitman and John Dos Passos have been mentioned more often than any other writers; but Wolfe has also been compared in this anthology to James Joyce, Laurence Sterne, Hart Crane, Theodore Dreiser, Sherwood Anderson, William Wordsworth, Thomas DeQuincey, and Sinclair Lewis. An interesting exercise would be the exploration of the similarities and dissimilarities between Wolfe and one or more of these writers whom you know.

The problem of the use of autobiographical material for fictional purposes was raised by Wolfe's work perhaps more completely than by the work of any other American writer. The question of the validity of Wolfe's use of his own experiences as raw material for his writing could be examined by contrasting several of the points of view on autobiography in these essays. A comparison of the views of DeVoto and Natanson, for example, would be illuminating.

These are but suggestions designed primarily as "pump primers" to get your own questioning and organizing processes to work and to suggest to you that who and what Wolfe and his work were is a fascinating and baffling question, and that criticism approaches it incompletely and imperfectly. Perhaps out of that knowledge you can become yourself a responsible and self-confident critic of Wolfe.

Suggested Topics for Library Research

The materials in this anthology have given you an idea of critical attitudes toward the nature of Wolfe's work, with particular emphasis on his writing methods, editorial problems, his rhetoric and style, his relation to social issues, and the question of form. The essays on these topics may very well lead you to want to know what others have said about them or to explore particular aspects of Wolfe's work and its criticism in greater depth. In that case there are available to you several helpful guides: Elmer D. Johnson's *Of Time and Thomas Wolfe: A Bibliography with A Character Index of His Works* (New York, 1959) is the most detailed listing of materials by and about Wolfe; however, Alexander D. Wainwright's review in *Papers of the Bibliographical Society of America,* LV (July-September, 1961), 258-263, should be consulted for the correction of numerous errors. George R. Preston, Jr., in *Thomas Wolfe: A Bibliography* (New York, 1943), includes, in addition to listings of Wolfe's works, valuable quotations and summaries of reviews. Bernice Kauffman's "Bibliography of Periodical Articles on Thomas Wolfe," *Bulletin of Bibliography,* XVII (May, August, 1942), 162-165, 172-190, lists early periodical comment with concise summaries. C. Hugh Holman's "Thomas Wolfe: A Bibliographical Study," *Texas Studies in Literature and Language,* I (Autumn, 1959), 427-445, summarizes in some detail the present state of Wolfe's scholarship. For current articles and books the annual bibliography in *PMLA* and the quarterly "Articles on American Literature Appearing in Current Periodicals" in *American Literature* should be consulted. A careful scrutiny of the quarterly checklists and the book reviews in *American Literature* will keep the student abreast of contemporary scholarship and criticism about Wolfe or any other significant American writer.

Biographical material has been excluded from the selections in this anthology. However, the exploration of Wolfe's life will prove to be a fruitful topic for library research. The basic materials are *Thomas Wolfe's Letters to His Mother,* edited by John S. Terry (New York, 1943); *The Letters of Thomas Wolfe,* edited by Elizabeth Nowell (New York, 1956); Agatha Boyd Adams, *Thomas Wolfe: Carolina Student* (Chapel Hill, N. C., 1950); *Thomas Wolfe at Washington Square,* edited by Thomas C. Pollock and Oscar Cargill (New York, 1954); his mother's garrulous recollections in *The Marble Man's Wife,* by Hayden Norwood (New York, 1947); his sister's recollections in *Thomas Wolfe and His Family,* by Mabel Wolfe Wheaton and LeGette Blythe (Garden City, N. Y., 1961); the biographical section of *The Enigma of Thomas Wolfe,* a collection of biographical and critical essays, edited by Richard Walser (Cambridge, Mass., 1953); and the standard biography, *Thomas Wolfe,* by Elizabeth Nowell (Garden City, N. Y., 1960). The biographical problems suitable for short research papers are enormous in number; they become obvious on almost every page of these studies.

A number of specialized topics are suggested by the essays in this anthology and could be followed up by library research. The following suggestions are designed merely to point to the kinds of library research that might develop out of a thoughtful scrutiny of these materials:

Edwin B. Burgum said that Wolfe's America is that of the average American boy; Walter F. Taylor said that it is the typical middle-class America. James T. Farrell, in his Introduction to the Modern Library edition of his trilogy of novels, *Studs Lonigan* (New York, 1938), said that its protagonist, Studs, was a normal American boy (p. xi). What accounts for the great variation between the world of

Eugene Gant and that of Studs Lonigan?

Bella Kussy feels that an honest view of the Nazi state converted Wolfe from a self-centered vitalism to a broader social democracy. How well does her and Wolfe's view of the Nazi state (Wolfe's is in *You Can't Go Home Again* and *"I Have a Thing to Tell You"* in *The Short Novels of Thomas Wolfe*) conform to that of historians, such as William L. Shirer, in *The Rise and Fall of the Third Reich* (New York, 1961)?

One of the few painters who appealed at all to Wolfe was Breughel. An interesting study could be made comparing the characteristics of Breughel's art with those of Wolfe's writing. If you undertake this study, you should examine a number of Breughel's pictures as well as read about his methods.

Look Homeward, Angel has been called an "apprenticeship novel." Consult a handbook of literary terms, such as *A Handbook to Literature,* by W. F. Thrall, Addison Hibbard, and C. Hugh Holman (New York, 1960) to find out what this term means. Suzanne Howe's book-length study, *Wilhelm Meister and His English Kinsmen* (New York, 1930), traces the history of the form from Goethe to the twentieth century. How appropriate is the designation for *Look Homeward, Angel?*

Consult Northrup Frye's *Anatomy of Criticism* (Princeton, 1957) on the meaning of critical concepts like *myth* and *epic.* To what extent is Herbert Muller's view of Wolfe as a "mythmaker" and an American "Homer" acceptable in terms of these concepts?

In *The Story of a Novel* Wolfe is scornful of those who have to leave America in order to be artists. A comparison of this attitude with that of the expatriates who were Wolfe's contemporaries would make an interesting study. The best treatment of these writers is Malcolm Cowley's *Exile's Return* (New York, 1951).

Wolfe makes an elaborate use of time ⸳ his fiction. It would be instructive to mpare his theories (as expressed in *The*

Story of a Novel) and his practice (as shown in *Look Homeward, Angel* and *Of Time and the River*) with those of Henri Bergson, in *Time and Free Will* (New York, 1910) and *Matter and Memory* (New York, 1911), and Marcel Proust, in *Remembrance of Things Past* (New York, 1934). If you can read German, you will find Karen Pfister's *Zeit und Wirklichkeit bei Thomas Wolfe* (Heidelberg, 1954) very helpful. If you cannot read German, consult some of the studies of the use of time in fiction, such as Hans Meyerhoff's *Time in Literature* (Berkeley, Calif., 1955) and A. A. Mendilow's *Time and the Novel* (London, 1952).

Mrs. Gelfant sees one of Wolfe's principal themes as being that of the Provincial in the City. A comparison of Wolfe's view of the city and his use of it in fiction with Dreiser's view, as given in his autobiography, *Dawn* (New York, 1931), and his first novel, *Sister Carrie* (New York, 1900), will be illuminating.

In the essays in this volume Wolfe has been called "a realist," "a romanticist," and "a naturalist." Consult a handbook to literature for the general meaning of these terms, and then explore their implications for Wolfe's work. How would you classify him? Why? A deeper comprehension of these terms may be gained from such works as A. O. Lovejoy's *Essays in the History of Ideas* (Baltimore, 1948); Jacques Barzun's *Romanticism and the Modern Ego* (Boston, 1944); Everett Carter's *Howells and the Age of Realism* (Philadelphia, 1950); Robert Falk's essay "The Rise of Realism," in *Transitions in American Literary History,* edited by H. H. Clark (Durham, N. C., 1953); the Summer, 1951, issue of *Comparative Literature* (Volume III); and C. C. Walcutt's *American Literary Naturalism* (Minneapolis, 1956).

If you are a student of psychology, you may find the psychological (and perhaps psychoanalytical) implications of Wolfe's career (as suggested by Malcolm Cowley in his essay in this anthology), Wolfe's phantasies, and his choice of "the search for a father" as his controlling theme to be interesting topics for research.

Wolfe was raised in the South at a time when the "Southern Literary Renascence" was getting underway. In what ways does he reflect its attitudes? What are the bases of his objections to it? (His views are expressed most clearly in *The Web and the Rock* and *The Hills Beyond*.) Compare his views of the South with those of the "Twelve Southerners" in *I'll Take My Stand* (New York, 1930). On this subject, see Maxwell Geismar's *Writers in Crisis* (Boston, 1947); the two collections of critical essays edited by Louis D. Rubin, Jr., and Robert D. Jacobs, *Southern Renascence* (Baltimore, 1953) and *South: Modern Southern Literature in Its Cultural Setting* (Garden City, N. Y., 1961); W. J. Cash's *The Mind of the South* (New York, 1941); C. Vann Woodward's *The Burden of Southern History* (Baton Rouge, 1960); and *The Southerner as American*, edited by Charles G. Sellers, Jr. (Chapel Hill, N. C., 1960).

The principal works of Thomas Wolfe are available in several editions, as follows:

Look Homeward, Angel

First edition: New York: Charles Scribner's Sons, 1929.
Illustrated edition: New York: Charles Scribner's Sons, 1947.
Hardbound text edition: New York: Charles Scribner's Sons, 1952; Modern Standard Authors Series.
Scribner Library Edition: New York: Charles Scribner's Sons, 1960.

Of Time and the River

First edition: New York: Charles Scribner's Sons, 1935.
Hardbound text edition: New York: Charles Scribner's Sons, 1960; Modern Standard Authors Series.

From Death to Morning

First edition: New York: Charles Scribner's Sons, 1935 (re-issued in 1958).

The Story of a Novel

First edition: New York: Charles Scribner's Sons, 1936 (re-issued in 1949).

The Web and the Rock

First edition: New York: Harper & Brothers, 1939.
Hardcover text edition: New York: Harper & Brothers, 1958; Harper's Modern Classics Series.
Paperbound editions: New York: Grosset & Dunlap, Universal Library, No. UL-12, 1957.
New York: Dell Publishing Co., The Laurel Thomas Wolfe, No. LY103, 1960.

You Can't Go Home Again

First edition: New York: Harper & Brothers, 1940.
Hardbound text edition: New York: Harper & Brothers, 1949; Harper's Modern Classics Series.
Paperbound editions: New York: Grosset & Dunlap, Universal Library, No. UL-16, 1957.
New York: Dell Publishing Co., The Laurel Thomas Wolfe, No. LY104, 1960.

The Hills Beyond

First edition: New York: Harper & Brothers, 1943.
Paperbound edition: New York: Pyramid Books, No. R321, 1958 (re-issued in 1961).

The Short Novels of Thomas Wolfe, ed. C. Hugh Holman

First edition: New York: Charles Scribner's Sons, 1961.